GLAM ROCK

Tempo: A Rowman & Littlefield Music Series on Rock, Pop, and Culture

Series Editor: Scott Calhoun

Tempo: A Rowman & Littlefield Music Series on Rock, Pop, and Culture offers titles that explore rock and popular music through the lens of social and cultural history, revealing the dynamic relationship between musicians, music, and their milieu. Like other major art forms, rock and pop music comment on their cultural, political, and even economic situation, reflecting the technological advances, psychological concerns, religious feelings, and artistic trends of their times. Contributions to the **Tempo** series are the ideal introduction to major pop and rock artists and genres.

The American Songbook: Music for the Masses, by Ann van der Merwe
Billy Joel: America's Piano Man, by Joshua S. Duchan
Bob Dylan: American Troubadour, by Donald Brown
Bon Jovi: America's Ultimate Band, by Margaret Olson
British Invasion: The Crosscurrents of Musical Influence, by Simon Philo
Bruce Springsteen: American Poet and Prophet, by Donald L. Deardorff II
The Clash: The Only Band That Mattered, by Sean Egan
Glam Rock: Music in Sound and Vision, by Simon Philo
The Kinks: A Thoroughly English Phenomenon, by Carey Fleiner
Kris Kristofferson: Country Highwayman, by Mary G. Hurd
Patti Smith: America's Punk Rock Rhapsodist, by Eric Wendell
Paul Simon: An American Tune, by Cornel Bonca
Phil Spector: The Sound of the Sixties, by Sean MacLeod
Ska: The Rhythm of Liberation, by Heather Augustyn
Sting and The Police: Walking in Their Footsteps, by Aaron J. West
U2: Rock 'n' Roll to Change the World, by Timothy D. Neufeld
Warren Zevon: Desperado of Los Angeles, by George Plasketes

GLAM ROCK

Music in Sound and Vision

Simon Philo

ROWMAN & LITTLEFIELD
Lanham • Boulder • New York • London

Published by Rowman & Littlefield
An imprint of The Rowman & Littlefield Publishing Group, Inc.
4501 Forbes Boulevard, Suite 200, Lanham, Maryland 20706
www.rowman.com

Unit A, Whitacre Mews, 26-34 Stannary Street, London SE11 4AB

British Library Cataloguing in Publication Information Available

Library of Congress Cataloging-in-Publication Data

Names: Philo, Simon, 1966- author.
Title: Glam rock : music in sound and vision / Simon Philo.
Description: Lanham : Rowman & Littlefield, 2018. | Series: Tempo: a Rowman & Littlefield
    music series on rock, pop, and culture | Includes bibliographical references and index.
Identifiers: LCCN 2018015658 (print) | LCCN 2018016311 (ebook) | ISBN 9781442271487 (elec-
    tronic) | ISBN 9781442271470 (cloth : alk. paper)
Subjects: LCSH: Glam rock—History and criticism.
Classification: LCC ML3534 (ebook) | LCC ML3534.P495 2018 (print) | DDC 781.66—dc23
LC record available at https://lccn.loc.gov/2018015658

Printed in the United States of America

For Linda and Amelie—
"When you rock and roll with me / No one else I'd
rather be."

CONTENTS

FOREWORD

You are holding here in your hands the work of an astrophysicist of popular music. Simon Philo peered into the universe of rock 'n' roll, with finely tuned instruments and his finely attuned knowledge of its history, to map, chart, and better understand glam rock. He traced its origins back to a kind of big bang moment in the 1950s that emitted pulses and particles that formed stars, some of which were named Chuck Berry, Elvis Presley, Jerry Lee Lewis, and Little Richard. As these stars aligned into the constellation rock 'n' roll and then collided with American and British cultures, a show of "northern lights" began. Some say the sky show was harder to see for about a decade as the 1960s burned white hot with earthbound rockers. But as the 1970s began, a Starman appeared on television, visible for the first time to the naked eye, and David Bowie turned our gaze up, out, and beyond. The show was back on again, with rock, roll, and the glamorous splendor of heretofore unearthly sounds and sights.

Consider this book a popular presentation from a scientist who can speak the language of the people and illuminate specifics with the light of bigger contexts. Following his previous writing for this series, *British Invasion: The Crosscurrents of Musical Influence*, Philo develops the story of glam as a socially, politically, musically, and aesthetically vital stage in the evolution of twentieth-century popular culture. He plots its course and the course of the 1970s as a moment of realizing more public, performative statements of personal identity, and notes the confluence of these two culture-shaping streams. While Bowie's radiance commands center stage for a while, Philo's scope is set to wide. Bowie alone does not a star cluster make, and thus Philo explores the compositions and influences of first-generation glam acts such as T. Rex, Roxy Music, Sweet, Slade, and Queen, noting along the way some of their more permanent influences on musical groups since the 1970s.

Glam opened vistas, stimulated the senses, reoriented rock 'n' roll's history, and probably still leaves each person who encounters it somewhere between gobsmacked and wonderstruck. Like watching an eclipse, seeing a shooting star, or holding a meteorite in the palm of your hand, a direct encounter with glam's sounds and visions is an experience you shouldn't pass up anytime the opportunity presents itself. But how nice it is to also have someone help you know more about what it is, where it came from, and how it relates to you, as Simon Philo does here.

Scott Calhoun, Series Editor

TIMELINE

World and Cultural Events	*Glam Events*
	September 26, 1945: Bryan Ferry born in Co. Durham.
	January 8, 1947: David Jones (David Bowie) born in London.
	September 30, 1947: Mark Feld (Marc Bolan) born in London.
April 1948: Marshall Plan secures financial aid for postwar reconstruction; UK receives billions of dollars in loans and grants.	
	December 1955: Bill Haley's "Rock Around the Clock" at no. 1 in the UK, signaling arrival of rock 'n' roll.
	June 1964: King Bees, with David Jones on lead vocals, release "Liza Jane." It fails to chart.

November 1965: Release of Marc Bolan's debut single "The Wizard." It fails to chart.

March 1967: Release of Velvet Underground's debut LP.

April 1967: 14-hour "Technicolor Dream," a happening in London. Pink Floyd perform, Lennon in attendance; John's Children, with Bolan on guitar, release "Desdemona."

June 1, 1967: *Sgt. Pepper* LP released.

June 1967: Release of David Bowie's eponymous debut LP. It fails to chart.

July 1967: Sexual Offences Act decriminalizes homosexual acts in private between consenting men of 21 and over. Only applies to England and Wales.

July 1967: Mick Jagger and Keith Richards, having been initially jailed for drug offenses, are released on appeal; the Beatles perform "All You Need Is Love" to a global TV audience of 400 million.

October 1967: UK reports worst ever monthly trade deficit; "death of hippie" ceremony held in San Francisco's Haight-Ashbury.

June 1968: Stonewall riots in New York mark the beginnings of the gay rights movement.

August 1968: Tyrannosaurus Rex's "One Inch Rock" is released. It will make the UK Top 30.

July 1969: Moon landing.

August 1969: Woodstock Festival.

September 1969: Bowie's "Space Oddity" is released, and

will go on to reach the UK Top Five.

December 1969: Murder of a fan at Rolling Stones' free concert at Altamont Speedway, Northern California.

February 1970: First National Women's Liberation Conference, Oxford, UK.

March 28, 1970: Live debut of Bowie's proto-glam band, Hype.

April 1970: Beatles break up.

June 1970: In the UK, the Conservative Party regains power after six years of Labour Party rule, with a 30-seat majority.

June 1970: Kinks release "Lola."

July 1970: First issue of UK publication the *Ecologist*.

August 1970: 600,000 attend the Isle of Wight Festival to see Jimi Hendrix, the Doors, the Who, Joni Mitchell, Emerson, Lake & Palmer, and Sly Stone.

September 1970: Jimi Hendrix dies.

October 1970: T. Rex releases "Ride a White Swan."

October 1970: Gay Liberation Front founded.

November 1970: US release of Velvet Underground's *Loaded*—last LP with Lou Reed.

January 1, 1971: Slade plays first of the year's 150 gigs at Wolverhampton Civic Hall.

January 1971: First British soldier killed in active service in Northern Ireland in 50 years.

January–February 1971: Bowie makes first visit to the US.

February 1971: Alice Cooper's "Eighteen" in Billboard Top 30.

March–April 1971: T. Rex's "Hot Love" is UK's no. 1 for six weeks. TV appearances confirm the arrival of glam.

September 1971: Bowie in the US to sign with RCA; also meets Lou Reed, Iggy Pop, and Andy Warhol.

September 1971: Release of T. Rex's *Electric Warrior*. Glam's first UK no. 1 LP will be the year's best-seller.

November 1971: National Union of Mineworkers (NUM) begins an overtime ban.

November 1971: Slade's "Coz I Luv You" gives the band the first of its six UK no. 1s; Bowie records the bulk of *Ziggy Stardust* LP in just one week.

December 1971: Release of Bowie's *Hunky Dory*.

January 1972: Miners begin national strike; in what will become known as "Bloody

January 1972: Kubrick's *A Clockwork Orange* on general release in the UK; Bowie "outs"

Sunday," British troops shoot dead 14 unarmed people in Derry, Northern Ireland.

February 1972: Strike ends in victory for the mineworkers, who are awarded a 20% pay raise.

March 1972: UK government takes direct control of Northern Ireland.

June 1972: Watergate break-in.

July 1972: Collapse of secret talks between the British government and the Irish Republican Army (IRA); first issue of second-wave feminist magazine *Spare Rib*.

himself in an interview with Michael Watts in *Melody Maker*.

February 25, 1972: T. Rex plays a disastrous show at NYC's Carnegie Hall.

March 18, 1972: T. Rex plays to 20,000 at London's Empire Pool. It is the height of "Trexstasy." T. Rex will sell an estimated 16 million records in just over a year.

June 1, 1972: Bob Fosse's *Cabaret* goes on general release in the UK with an "X" rating.

June 1972: Release of *The Rise and Fall of Ziggy Stardust and the Spiders from Mars*.

July 1972: Bowie performs "Starman" on *Top of the Pops*; release of Mott the Hoople's version of glam anthem "All the Young Dudes."

July 8, 1972: Bowie headlines at London's Royal Festival Hall with Lou Reed joining him on versions of "Waiting for the Man," "White Light / White Heat," and "Sweet Jane."

August 1972: 60,000 attend the 10-hour Rock 'n' Roll Show at Wembley featuring Chuck Berry, Little Richard, and Bill Haley.

August 1972: Roxy Music performs "Virginia Plain" on *Top of the Pops*; Bowie works with Lou

Reed on the latter's *Transformer* LP.

September 1972: Slade's "Mama Weer All Crazee Now" gives the band its third UK no. 1 in under 12 months; David Bowie kicks off first major North American tour in Cleveland and plays Carnegie Hall at the end of the month.

November 1972: Release of "The Jean Genie."

December 1972: Ringo Starr–directed T. Rex movie *Born to Boogie* goes on general UK release.

December 31, 1972: Estimated 24 million working days "lost" to industrial action in the UK in 1972.

January 1973: UK joins European Economic Community (EEC); Green Party founded as PEOPLE Party; cease-fire in Vietnam.

January 1973: Sweet's "Blockbuster" at UK no. 1 for five weeks; Bowie begins 100-day world tour in NYC on January 25.

March 1973: Last US combat troops out of Vietnam; IRA bombs mainland UK, leaving one dead and 200 injured.

March 1973: Release of Roxy Music's *For Your Pleasure*; Slade's "Cum On Feel the Noize" at no. 1 for four weeks.

April 1973: Pink Floyd's LP *Dark Side of the Moon* at no. 1 in the US; in this year British acts— Floyd, George Harrison, Wings, Led Zeppelin, the Rolling Stones, Jethro Tull, the Moody Blues, and Elton John—hold the no. 1 position on the Billboard album chart for a total of 27 weeks; Suzi Quatro's "Can the Can" is UK's no. 1 single for three weeks.

April 13, 1973: Release of Bowie's *Aladdin Sane* LP, with UK record advance orders.

May 1, 1973: Estimated 1.6 million UK workers take strike action in protest of the government's pay restraint policy and price rises.

May–August 1973: Televised hearings into Watergate break-ins.

July 4, 1973: Bowie "retires" Ziggy at Hammersmith Odeon gig, the last of 61 shows in 53 days.

July 21, 1973: IRA explodes 20 bombs in a single day in Belfast, leaving 11 dead and 100 injured.

August 1973: US publication *Creem* runs "The Androgyny Hall of Fame" as a cover story, featuring Bowie at its center with Bolan, Jagger, Alice Cooper, Iggy Pop, and Elvis orbiting around him.

October 1973: Oil crisis precipitated by Egypt's invasion of Israeli-occupied Sinai; OPEC quadruples the price of oil, effectively ending the affluence that had marked the preceding 10 years.

November 1973: UK miners call another overtime ban; UK government declares a state of emergency.

November 1973: Release of Bowie's *Pin Ups* and Bryan Ferry's *These Foolish Things.*

December 18, 1973: IRA bombs in London injure 60.

December 1973: *Stranded* gives Roxy Music its first UK no. 1 album; Slade's "Merry Xmas Everybody" spends a total of five weeks as the UK's best-selling single. The fastest-selling 45 in UK history, it caps a chart year in which glam singles would hold the top spot for 28 weeks. David Bowie also sets a new record for the number of weeks an act spends on the album chart in a calendar year—182.

January 1974: UK government imposes a "three-day week" to ration power consumption; IRA detonates five bombs in London and two in Birmingham.

January 1974: First Top 10 of the year includes eight glam singles.

February 1974: Miners begin national strike; UK prime minister Edward Heath calls a snap general election and promptly loses; IRA bomb kills 12 on a bus carrying army personnel and their families on the M62.

February 1974: Mud's "Tiger Feet" is the UK's no. 1 for a month and would be the year's best-selling single. It is also the first in a run of three consecutive glam no. 1s—as it is followed by Suzi Quatro's "Devil Gate Drive" and Alvin Stardust's "Jealous Mind."

March 1974: Labour's Harold Wilson becomes prime minister of a minority government; "three-day week" ends.

May 1974: *Diamond Dogs* is released.

June 1974: Bowie is on a six-month tour of North America with the most theatrical (and costly) show ever seen.

July–August 1974: BBC technicians strike keeps glam lifeblood *Top of the Pops* off-air for several weeks.

August 9, 1974: President Nixon resigns.

September 1974: President Ford pardons Nixon.

October 1974: Prime Minister Wilson calls a general election to secure a working majority and wins with a slim majority of three.

October 1974: Rolling Stones release *It's Only Rock and Roll*—their most glam LP; Queen's "Killer Queen" peaks at no. 2 in the UK.

November 1974: IRA murders 21 in Birmingham pub bombings.

December 1974: Mud's "Lonely This Christmas" gives glam consecutive Christmas no. 1s; by the end of '74, glam-pop songwriters/producers Nicky Chinn and Mike Chapman will be responsible for more singles sold in the UK than the Beatles achieved in any calendar year.

January 1975: *Creem* story "Kiss It Goodbye" documents death of glam; *Slade in Flame* movie on general UK release.

February 1975: Margaret Thatcher defeats Edward Heath

February 1975: Steve Harley and Cockney Rebel's "Make Me to become leader of the Conservative Party.

April 1975: Fall of Saigon ends Vietnam War.

May 1975: CBS reports that "Britain is drifting slowly toward a condition of ungovernability."

June 1975: In a UK referendum on EEC membership, 67% vote to remain.

July 1975: UK unemployment is close to 1 million and up nearly 250,000 in just six months.

August 1975: UK inflation hits its peak at almost 27%.

October 1975: Bruce Springsteen declared "future of rock 'n' roll" and features on cover of *Time* and *Newsweek*.

Smile (Come Up and See Me)" spends two weeks at no. 1 on the UK singles chart.

May 1975: Mud's revivalist retread "Oh Boy" is the UK's best-selling single for two weeks.

July 1975: "Fame" gives David Bowie his first Billboard no. 1.

November 1975: Rereleased, "Space Oddity" gives David Bowie his first UK no. 1 single.

November 29, 1975: Queen's "Bohemian Rhapsody" begins a run of nine weeks at no. 1 in the UK.

January 1976: Bowie releases *Station to Station*.

March 1976: Wilson resigns as prime minister.

April 1976: James Callaghan secures the Labour Party leadership and so becomes prime minister.

June 1976: "I Love to Boogie" is
T. Rex's last UK hit single.

August 1976: Start of bitter strike
at Grunwick photo processing
plant over employees' right to
union representation.

September 1976: As the pound
plunges in value against the dollar,
Callaghan tells the Labour Party
conference delegates that "the
cosy world is gone," while his
chancellor, Denis Healey,
confirms the UK will seek a
massive bailout from the
International Monetary Fund
(IMF).

October 1976: The Damned's
"New Rose" is the UK's first punk
single.

November 1976: In London,
IMF demands huge cuts in public
spending as a condition for a loan.
Callaghan and Healey lobby for
smaller cuts; most of the cabinet
simply (and unrealistically) want
no cuts at all.

December 1976: Callaghan and
Healey successful in persuading
both cabinet and IMF to accept
modest spending cuts; UK
receives the loan.

January 1977: Bowie's *Low* LP is
released, featuring "Sound and
Vision." It is the first of his "Berlin
Trilogy."

March 1977: T. Rex on tour with the Damned to promote the release of *Dandy in the Underworld* LP.

April 1977: Studio 54 opens in New York.

June 1977: Violent clashes between strikers and police at Grunwick.

September 1977: Marc Bolan killed in a road accident.

October 1977: Release of Sex Pistols' *Never Mind the Bollocks* LP; rerelease of "Virginia Plain" sees it climb to no. 11 in the UK.

January 1978: UK inflation now under 10%.

July 1978: Grunwick strike over, as strikers concede defeat after almost two years.

November 1978: Transport and General Workers Union strike for more pay; other unions follow suit and so precipitate the so-called Winter of Discontent.

January–February 1979: Nationwide strike action peaks in the coldest winter in years.

February 1979: "Bowie Night" moves to Covent Garden's Blitz Club. New Romantics are on the rise.

March 1979: Re-formed Roxy Music releases *Manifesto*.

April 1979: Bowie releases "Boys Keep Swinging" from *Lodger* LP.

May 1979: Margaret Thatcher elected UK's first woman prime minister.

May 1979: Release of Tubeway Army's "Are 'Friends' Electric?" It will be a UK no. 1 for four weeks.

May 1980: Roxy Music releases *Flesh + Blood*.

August 1980: Bowie's "Ashes to Ashes" is at UK no. 1 for two weeks.

November 1980: Ronald Reagan elected—will firm up the "special relationship" with the UK through the 1980s.

November 1980: Release of Adam and the Ants' *Kings of the Wild Frontier* LP. Its success would mark the beginning of 18 months in which Adam would be Britain's biggest pop star since Marc Bolan.

December 1980: John Lennon murdered outside his New York apartment by psychotic "fan" Mark Chapman.

August 1, 1981: MTV is launched in America.

March 1982: Joan Jett begins a run of seven weeks at no. 1 in the US with a cover of "I Love Rock and Roll."

July 1983: Second "British Invasion"—motored by New Pop and spearheaded by Duran Duran, the Human League, ABC, and Culture Club—peaks with seven UK acts on the US Top 10 singles chart.

July 1985: Live Aid. Queen steals the show.

November 1998: Release of Todd Haynes's *Velvet Goldmine*. Nominated for Best Costume Academy Award . . . appropriately enough.

January 2016: David Bowie dies.

ACKNOWLEDGMENTS

At Rowman & Littlefield, big thanks to Scott. At Derby, for their patient indulgence as I explained for the nth time and at great length why Sweet were much underrated, I would particularly like to thank Doug and Adrian. For being a constant source of joy and pleasure from that day back in February 1974 when I came home with my first purchased 45, I'd also like to thank *the music*. Most important of all, heartfelt and sincere thanks and love go out to Linda and Amelie. Once again, I can only apologize for not being around on the weekend and for making you listen to "Telegram Sam" on repeat when I was.

INTRODUCTION

"Carry the News"

January 2016. The outpouring of grief following David Bowie's death was understandably accompanied by attempts to evaluate his legacy. Given his fifty-year recording career, extensive back catalogue, and shape-shifting tendencies, different Bowies were inevitably summoned. Perhaps to no great surprise, however, it was the early to mid-1970s incarnation—the "glam Bowie"—that was most frequently invoked, as critics, friends, peers, and fans of all ages struggled to come to terms with his passing. It was then—of all the Bowies available—this version that evidently meant the most to the most. So, it is these eulogies that will help us to at least begin to get a measure of glam—to evaluate, assess, and explain the genre as they endeavored to do the same for the man who has, more than any one musician-performer, come to represent it. For the British journalist Suzanne Moore, Bowie was "a guide, an inspiration and a university." "In my youth," she explains, "he showed us the endless possibilities." Moore tells us that she "never grew out of" him (Moore 33); but, at the same time, she is keen to stress that it was with the glam-era Bowie that this lifelong connection was initially forged. In this, she is clearly not alone. Touring the career retrospective *Sound + Vision* album back in 1990, Bowie's fan-made set list was tellingly dominated by material drawn from his glam years.

July 1972. Reportedly written to give Bowie (and, more pressingly, his record label) a hit single, "Starman" would stand out as an un-doomy counterpoint to the ostensibly rather gloomy, often apocalyptic fare to be found on the rest of the *Ziggy Stardust* album to which it had been a last-minute addition. It was euphoric, hopeful, joyful—its message and meaning reinforced by an inclusive, sing-along fade-out reminiscent of "Hey Jude" (1968) or, perhaps more pointedly, T. Rex's still-fresh-in-the-memory glam breakthrough "Hot Love" (1971). The song's powerful connective function was clearly audible. Lyric, in tandem with music, supplying effective unity of purpose. This alien has come to save us, not annihilate nor enslave us. He is even sensitive to our feelings. After all, he is frightened he might "blow our minds." However, the deal was well and truly sealed—the connection dialed in—when a vast army of potential young communicants finally caught sight of Bowie performing "Starman." On July 6, 1972, Bowie and his band, the Spiders from Mars, appeared on the UK's preeminent TV outlet for pop music, *Top of the Pops*. After several years of trying and with numerous false starts along the way, it was this single and *singular* performance that would finally make Bowie a star(man). Yet, typical of the generosity that would help define glam, it was a performance that would also come to mean a great deal for a good proportion of the many millions of young Britons who witnessed it that evening. Here then was a cultural moment akin in impact to the Beatles' first appearance on US TV eight years earlier. Here then was a song every bit as connective as "I Wanna Hold Your Hand" or "She Loves You." In fact, "Starman" sets out the terms of a contract, in which our part, our obligation, is made explicit—"If we can sparkle, he may land tonight."

Glam's inclusivity, its nourishing democracy, was something that its many critics would either miss entirely or deliberately ignore. Even the untypically supportive British rock journalist Charles Shaar Murray concluded that glam "only served to reinforce and emphasise the distinctions between the demi-gods (up there) and the punters." Composing its epitaph in more ascetic punk times, Shaar Murray erroneously charged glam with being "horribly elitist and very destructive" (*Shots*, 226), failing to recognize that taking "the punters" with them was central to the mission of its "demi-gods." Like his "Starman," Bowie is otherworldly yet always within reach. Even though he is dressed like a space-age harlequin with dyed, cropped hair and makeup, he remains human. He may look like an alien, but he is never alienating. Indicatively, his unselfconscious grin never wavers from start to finish, while his outfit/costume—a kind of quilted onesie—is nonthreateningly, even endearingly, homemade. He is warm, humorous, and clearly having fun; not remotely rock-star "cool" as he leads the *Top of the Pops* audience in the almost inevitable hand-clapping the song's extended fade-out seems to demand. Throughout this performance Bowie is always on the lookout for a TV camera and always, it seems, acutely aware of where they are. And as he delivers the line "I had to phone someone so I picked on you," he finds one and looks directly into it, "smiles flirtatiously, points and twirls a beckoning finger at every mesmerised outsider kid in the land." This, according to Stuart Maconie, was the moment when "everyone who'd ever been bullied, overlooked, teased or picked last for games just found a friend" (124), giving us a powerful demonstration of glam's potential to convene a tribe for the nontribal, a true mass cult, a super-subculture. The impact of this single TV performance is encapsulated by future punk Siouxsie Sioux, who recalls that she "was really ill and in a hospital TV room. It was like I was being woken up, like being let out of a chrysalis. Suddenly, I was allowed to just become" because Bowie "gave people the courage to be who they wanted to be, as well as the courage to be who you actually are" (84). "Where I came from, you were pretty much told, 'You're not going anywhere in life.' Seeing Ziggy on *Top of the Pops*, I found that I could escape"—concurs Depeche Mode's Dave Gahan. Bowie "enabled myself and Martin [Gore] and people like us to understand that we weren't alone" (88). Such testimonials serve to confirm Bowie's role as a catalyst, an empowering agent, a liberator, a "cultural politician" (Cagle 11). Showing a generation—in the words of former Smiths guitarist Johnny Marr—"that you could be who you wanted to be" (Marr 87). All this, of course, even before we factor in the impact of those several points in the proceedings when, as the two men harmonize into a shared mic, Bowie casually drapes an arm with nail-polished fingers over guitarist Mick Ronson's shoulder. Bowie's *Top of the Pops* performance of "Starman," via both sound and vision, conspired to serve up much of what the genre—and Bowie himself as one its chief emissaries—could and would bring to the pop table, in providing a perfect illustration of glam as a broad set of ideas and methods for understanding the performance of personal identity. This is important cultural work. Yet glam was—and still is—commonly (mis)understood as marking a retreat from commitment and cause, its challenges downplayed or, worse still, completely ignored, while classic rock's are more often than not overplayed. Perhaps the reason for this is also to be found in Bowie's TV performance on that summer night in 1972. In the unselfconsciously tactile relationship he has with Ronson, for example. According to Van Cagle, glam was "a celebration of sexual difference [that] provided a key to another world, a world that was not often made available to those who were living within the confines of particular localised cultures (for example, small towns)" (98). In the early 1970s, its many supporters either overlooked or, more commonly, celebrated rock's rampant male heterosexuality, machismo, and misogyny; but glam—whether consciously or not—would challenge the heteronormative and in so doing embolden and liberate those who felt they simply could not live by its codes and practices any longer. No matter how painful. "My make-up was smeared with dried blood because I'd been hit over the head on the way to the show for the way I looked," recalled Marc Almond of the price he had to pay for attending a Bowie concert in 1973 (qtd. in Turner, *Glam Rock*, 121).

"Starman," David Bowie, and glam all demonstrate, then, the significance of popular music in people's lives. Not as entertainment—although this is not a function to be dismissed or sneered at or underestimated—but, in making it a part of our identity, as a kind of emotional resource that has it in its gift to help us make sense of who we are and to encourage us to be ourselves. This vital role was confirmed repeatedly in the immediate wake of Bowie's death, as fans of all backgrounds and ages tried to put into words what he meant to them. If there was a common thread, it was that he enabled them to be who they wanted to be rather than who they were supposed to be. Coming "from a small town and what [her] teachers called 'a broken home,'" Suzanne Moore would—in the wake of this first encounter—come to be "guided by Bowie," noting that she and many others like her "could give up trying to be normal now that we entrusted ourselves to him" (33). In the words of sometime producer and longtime friend Tony Visconti, David Bowie "opened the world for people who hid in the shadows who thought they were different, too different to fit into society" (87). This could be achieved via vinyl alone, but—as the testimonials noted and quoted above demonstrate—it was even more likely to occur when (appropriately enough) sound and vision combined. So, July 6, 1972, marks Bowie's emergence as a star. However, now that the "Jean Genie" is finally out of the bottle, we will be granted wishes too. He will take us with him in his role as a transformative agent, via the superinclusive nature of the music. "You're not alone," Ziggy generously and selflessly assures us at the very moment of his own destruction in "Rock 'n' Roll Suicide" (1972). "Give me your hands," he cries. What we learned about Bowie was less important than what he might have revealed to us about ourselves. At its very best, glam could also do this because, in common with the most effective popular music, it connects with us, it includes us. This is something that mainstream rock music had lost sight of in the early 1970s, but which is central to glam praxis. With Bowie, it is sometimes directly embedded in his songs—as when on *Diamond Dogs* (1974) he extends the invitation to "Rock 'n' Roll with Me"—but it could also be demonstrated in the risks he took.

As quintessential glam text, "Starman" can help us build the genre's lexicon. The importance it placed on both the act of looking and being looked at, for example, can be identified as a staple. Glam songs abound with references to visual culture—to image and screen, the world of movies, theater, and art. From Roxy Music's Bogart tribute "2HB" (1972)—in which Bryan Ferry croons that he "was moved by a screen-dream"—to David Bowie's "Drive-In Saturday" (1973), from Cockney Rebel's "Muriel the Actor" (1973) to Sparks' "Looks Looks Looks" (1975). Part of the reason rock critics have tended to view glam with suspicion is that—while by no means always celebratory—these references are more often than not allied to an unapologetic emphasis on, and wholesale commitment to, spectacle and theatricality. Two things that the rock orthodoxy, forged in the late 1960s, simply could not abide—seeing and hearing only artificiality and insincerity. Augmenting the calculated and self-conscious staging of its performance, when Bowie sang, "there's a starman waiting in the sky," he would unashamedly borrow a key melody line from *The Wizard of Oz*'s "Somewhere Over the Rainbow." This did not go unnoticed or unremarked.

In February 1972, as glam was gathering momentum on the back of the success of T. Rex and Slade and the publicity surrounding Bowie's emergence as Ziggy Stardust, a grateful Richard Williams—breaking rank with his sniffy rock journo brethren—wrote that "after a couple of years devoted to worthy but dull earnestness, rock and roll is back where it belongs" (qtd. in Hoskyns 54). That it was "back" was due in large measure to the fact that glam had enthusiastically embraced spectacle, at a time when most rock 'n' roll bands had not and indeed when many flat-out refused to do so. As Roxy Music's Brian Eno confirmed, this embrace was undertaken in full consciousness: "I think all of those bands—us, Bowie and the others—were turning round towards the audience and saying, 'We're doing a show.' In that sense there was a unity, though it wasn't very obvious at the time" (qtd. in Hoskyns 56). For some, Roxy Music and Bowie represented the more esoteric wing of glam, but there was clearly a shared agenda, a common cause—one that was built around this commitment to spectacle, to putting on a show—that would unite all its variant strains. Although happily conceding that the kind of glam he produced "was more contrived than Bowie, without a doubt," acknowledging that "we were very conscious of giving pop back to the kids, and giving them something to smile about and bop to and generally get off on" (qtd. in Hoskyns 44) does not set songwriter-producer Nicky Chinn's charges/clients—which included Sweet, Mud, and Suzi Quatro—all that far apart from the so-called glam sophisticates. For, in whoever's hands, the end product was avowedly "pop" to its shiny core. So glam's love of the spectacular and the theatrical contributed to the frequent charge that it was inauthentic. Just as would the related (and undeniable) charge that so much of it—both in and out of song—was character driven. Of the ten generic signifiers or "signatures" listed by Barney Hoskyns, only the last of these—"self-birth implicit in glam names"—comes anywhere close to being truly genre defining. For much glam is performed by musicians who are not themselves—e.g., Gary Glitter (Paul Gadd), Alvin Stardust (Bernard Jewry), Freddie Mercury (Farrokh Bulsara), Jobriath (Bruce Wayne Campbell), Alice Cooper (Vincent Furnier), Iggy Pop (James Osterberg), Marc Bolan (Mark Feld), and of course David Bowie, who would distance himself even further from David Jones when becoming Ziggy Stardust. All of which supplied yet more ammunition for critics who were constitutionally contemptuous of, and frequently appalled by, what they understood as glam's unnatural contrivances, its guiltless insincerity, and general lack of depth. Glam musicians then—even those who went by their birth names—were all essentially actors playing a part. Something which they would freely admit to in interviews, but which would also be openly acknowledged in song and in performance—as when, for example, dressed as a Pierrot, Cockney Rebel's Steve Harley (Stephen Nice) sang in "Judy Teen" (1974) of a character in a cabaret "swinging on a cane," or when a similarly attired Leo Sayer performed the piano- and banjo-driven "The Show Must Go On" (1973)—a track that, like Cockney Rebel's "Mr. Soft" (1974) quoted Julius Fucik's "Entrance of the Gladiators" (1897).

Glam's near-default tendency to emphasize the performance—to privilege voices, poses, and role-playing—meant that it would run into considerable opposition from a critical orthodoxy for whom "playacting" was anathema. Though often viewed with a mixture of suspicion and disdain, voicing and character-driven songs were of course nothing new in rock music. Paul McCartney, for one, had always demonstrated a propensity for such material in populating his story-songs with a cast of memorable characters—think, "Eleanor Rigby" (1966) or "Penny Lane" (1967) or "Obla-Di, Obla-Da" (1968). This is arguably why most rock critics have tended to favor his more "honest" songwriting partner, John Lennon, who could never be accused of failing to expose his "true" self in his songs—think, "In My Life" (1965) or "Strawberry Fields" (1967) or "Julia" (1968). Post-Beatles, it was perhaps to no one's great surprise, then, that it was McCartney who most enthusiastically embraced the glam modus operandi, when he recorded the hyperventilating James Bond movie theme "Live and Let Die" (1973). Given his track record, McCartney was always a more likely convert than Lennon. As quirky as any Cockney Rebel or Sparks song, his most un-rock-like and most unlikely US number one single "Uncle Albert / Admiral Halsey" (1971)—as its two-songs-for-the-price-of-one title indicated—featured multiple characters inhabiting different stories delivered via a range of voices. With its funny accents and impersonations of trilling telephones, it was reminiscent of a music hall ditty or perhaps a *Goon Show* comedy song. In sharp contrast, Lennon spent the immediate postbreakup years engaged in strenuous attempts to get the sixties out of his system—seen and heard, for example, in the myth-stripping "God" (1971) in which he declared the "dream is over"—resulting in self-flagellating material that was fully committed to sincere self-revelation. "Give Me Some Truth" (1971), he sang, presumably believing that it was out there and within him, while his former songwriting partner was producing archetypal story-songs like "Another Day" (1971)—a track that Lennon himself singled out for very public criticism as the ultimate proof of McCartney's dishonesty in the scabrous "How Do You Sleep?" (1971). Even Lennon's rock 'n' roll covers LP—not released until 1975 but recorded a few years earlier—was construed as an act of personal revelation rather than modish revivalism. It was aided in this by the singer's own liner notes, in which he implied that the songs would help you understand where he came from and so who he is. Spectacularly humorless as he appeared to be in the early 1970s, we can only conclude that Lennon subscribed to the idea that authenticity was absolutely central to rock practice—a credo that would lead most in the world of rock to condemn glam as fake and insincere. In John Lennon's case it would contribute to his rather poisonous in-song attacks on McCartney, who is charged with being a purveyor of "muzak," living with "straights" and having done little more than write the presumably anodyne "Yesterday."

Yet, by 1975, it appeared that even rock's most celebrated ascetic John Lennon had loosened up somewhat, when he belatedly crashed the glam party and collaborated with David Bowie on the American number one "Fame." Possessing a lyric that positioned it closer to Lennon's self-flagellating critiques than anything Bowie had recorded thus far—"Fame puts you there where things are hollow / . . . / What you get is no tomorrow"—it was, however, still a track that was on message for a genre for which the pursuit, pleasures, and pitfalls of stardom held a powerful fascination—"What you like is in the limo." The self-mythologizing that this obsession encouraged is of course nothing new in rock 'n' roll, but glam would take it to a whole new level, without much evidence of guilt and often with lashings of knowingness. This is also part of the reason for humor and irony featuring so prominently—and yet another reason for so many po-faced rock critics taking against it. The genre's acute self-consciousness is evident in the numerous anthems that pepper its discography—from Alice Cooper's "Eighteen" (1971) to Bowie's "All the Young Dudes" (1972) to Marc Bolan's "Teenage Dream" (1974) to Sweet's "The Sixteens" (1975). Although set at different levels, there is a still audible strain of lament, melancholy, and reflection to be found in each of these; but there is always a leavening humor, supplying warmth and generating empathy. It could be pessimistic, but it was never cold or mean spirited. Glam, not glum. The apocalyptic comic-book denouement to Sweet's "Hellraiser" (1973) is exciting rather than terrifying or disturbing; and, even though Bowie's *Diamond Dogs* (1974) was consciously conceived in response to the chaos of the early 1970s and, as such, arguably marked its creator's most direct engagement with that "real world," this did not prevent the title track from showcasing yet another example of glam's humorous chops. After all, its apocalypse-surviving protagonist's first thought on being "pull[ed] . . . out of the oxygen tent" is to "ask for the latest party," with the express intention of making the best of his or her deformities—because, who knows, that "silicon hump" and particularly that "ten-inch stump" might come in handy. So, although it might have been unable to avoid or even ignore all the surrounding disillusionment, glam itself was never disillusioned. Instead, it was humorous and surprisingly self-effacing, cutting through any pretension that might be lurking. Unlike the voguish singer-songwriters of the day or the doomy serio-rock of the likes of Pink Floyd, it was rarely if ever introspective or maudlin. It did not appear to do downbeat. As Bowie and the Sweet demonstrated, even the apocalypse could be a strangely joyous, communal, randy, euphoric affair. More end of pier than end of times. One reason it might have remained essentially good humored and hopeful is because it was so avowedly teen focused and so committed to "pop." A faith evident in its enthusiasm for that most pop of formats, the 45 rpm single. Although musically diverse, glam's debt to—or, more accurately, its kinship with—classic rock 'n' roll is evident in a similarly full-on commitment to instant gratification, thoughtless fun, and hedonism at all costs. Significantly, it is with classic *rock 'n' roll* (1954–1959) and not classic rock (1966–1971), then, that glam shares a direct lineage. For as Mott the Hoople's Ian Hunter gleefully pointed out in "The Golden Age of Rock 'n' Roll" (1974), the former is "good for your body, it's good for your soul." Glam performers could and would publicly identify with classic rock 'n' roll's wholesale embrace of the pleasure principle; but they also admired, and so sought to emulate, the showmanship of "first wavers" like Elvis Presley, Jerry Lee Lewis, Chuck Berry, Gene Vincent, and, most notably, Little Richard. This was a reverence which—appropriately enough—found expression in both sound and vision. Glam channeled classic rock 'n' roll via cover version, pastiche, and even intertextual reference—as when, for instance, both T. Rex in "Get It On" (1971) and Queen in "Now I'm Here" (1975) quote directly from Chuck Berry's "Little Queenie" (1959)—*and* via performances that in costume, props, and moves recalled the sheer unabashed theatricality and spectacle of this "golden age."

In seeking to identify the genre's core ingredients, Barney Hoskyns lists several musically derived "signatures" that would appear to characterize it as the anti-prog—such as an emphasis on the drum and the voice, a constant mid- to fast-tempo rhythm, rather conventional song structures, unadventurous melodies, and relatively short songs marked by brief solos. However, for David Bowie, it was *not* about the musical commonalities. "We were a very odd little genre," he explained. "What became known as glam or glitter rock wasn't a movement at all, musically" (qtd. in Hoskyns 46–47). The diverse glam work of Roxy Music, Slade, Sweet, Cockney Rebel, Sparks, Queen, and Bowie himself makes any attempt at constructing a generic template via musical "signatures" a somewhat reductive, ultimately rather frustrating, exercise. Hoskyns is, however, arguably more persuasive when he turns his attention to what might be termed glam's nonmusical ingredients. Prominent among these, for example, is that unashamed "pop" sensibility that presumably nourished all those songs about cars, girls (and boys), good times, and sex, not to mention that seemingly unquenchable obsession with stardom, fame, and celebrity. Glam can also be defined by the visual dimensions of and in its performance—by costume, staging, appearance, and gesture—and by the visual culture that surrounds it—by single and album cover work, promotional videos, and poster art. "The glam thing was always great fun," recalled Gary Glitter. "We—Marc Bolan, David Bowie, myself, Slade, Sweet—were working in pre-video times, but we'd be thinking visually. When we did *Top of the Pops*, which was our major outlet, we devised some outrageous props. I used to come out on motorbikes, or moons to stand on" (qtd. in Thompson 305). This is not to say that the glam sensibility, its consciousness, could not be transmitted solely through music and lyric. And yet "Starman" was ur-glam, so quintessential, because it functioned so effectively as sound *and* vision—because it reached back in search of more musically direct, even simpler models; because it genuinely reached out to its young audience; because it restored spectacle and theatricality to rock via stagecraft, fashion, and props; because Bowie clearly reveled in the constructed nature of the performance persona; and because, like all glam with its magpie tendency, it treated existing styles and voices as fair game when it came for source material to plunder.

February 1974. For Barney Hoskyns, T. Rex's "Hot Love" (1971) was his "password to the mystery of pop's power and glamour," the song "that seduced [him] and kept [him] coming back for more and more and more" (4). Well, for me, that would be Sweet's "Teenage Rampage," the first single I ever bought. To my mind, "Teenage Rampage" could not have offered a more thrilling introduction to pop music's "power and glamour"—cartoonish but no bubblegum novelty. Fittingly, like many I'm sure, I saw it at the very moment I first heard it. Eighteen months after offering the nation its first sighting of Ziggy, *Top of the Pops* was now liberally and gratefully dosing glam to more than fifteen million viewers every week. On a run of peerless singles that would invariably be backed by memorable on-screen performances, Sweet had become a Thursday night fixture by enthusiastically embracing producer Mike Leander's belief that "glam rock was all about putting on a show." As a result, "the records too were constructed to be seen," he pointed out, "whereas in the Sixties they were constructed to be heard" (qtd. in Hoskyns 41). Featuring stomping tribal rhythms and simple, repetitive riffs, peppered with teen crowd noises calling for the band to lead us into battle with our parents and possibly even older siblings, here was a less subtle, more easily digestible "Starman" ("Star-Teen," perhaps)—visceral and exciting, humorous, and fun, an all-inclusive, shouty call to arms. Yet, this being glam, there was strangeness too. I was certainly not alone in being fascinated at the sight and behavior of Sweet's bass guitarist, who wore women's clothes and heavy makeup, and whose voice, gestures and onstage moves compelled one to lock onto him whenever the studio camera picked him out (which it did a lot, of course). Yet, I do not recall ever being shocked by Steve Priest's appearance and camp antics; and neither can I remember any negative comments from my watching parents, even as Priest's performances seemed to grow more outrageous by the week. As far as I can recall, there were no playground assaults on Sweet fans. Perhaps because in just two years or so, Bowie and other glam acts had prepared the way for greater mainstream tolerance of the transgressive. Perhaps because what constituted the "normal" had dramatically shifted in the face of glam's counternormative challenges.

Warranting often little more than a footnote in rock history, we might conclude that glam's commercial success is what lies at the very root of this marginalization. Is it all so "obvious" that it simply does not deserve serious critical consideration? Is this why rock narratives appear to confound that truism about history being written by the "winners"? Certainly, at least insofar as the 1970s are concerned, it seems as if popular music history has been written by those who identify with its "losers"—ergo, the disproportionate critical attention paid to the likes of Nick Drake, the Krautrockers, and even the punks. By contrast, glam has found itself largely erased from this narrative—not "cool," too "pop," too British, a novelty, an unnatural aberration, "the rock that dare not speak its name" (Turner, *Glam Rock*, 10). But, of course, this is a version of history that simply does not tally with the pop life that I and millions of other young Brits lived out at the time. It is a version that we refuse to accept. Propelled by revisionist ire, then, *Glam Rock* investigates the origins, development, and impact of an undervalued and misunderstood musical genre that has for too long remained hidden in plain sight (and sound). Wedged between late '60s rock and late '70s punk, glam has failed to generate anywhere near the volume of studies that have emerged from these fabled and much-storied moments. This despite—or perhaps more pointedly *because of*—the fact that many millions of glam records—singles and albums—were sold. T. Rex reportedly shifted sixteen million of them in just eighteen months to the middle of 1972, representing an impressive, almost Beatles-esque 4 percent of *all* recorded music sold in the UK. Now, sales alone do not necessarily make this a tale worth telling; but at the very least they should add significant heft to the case for glam's inclusion in the pop grand narrative. Exploring it in relation to a range of key contexts (artistic, political, psychoemotional, sexual, demographic, and commercial), this book will treat glam to the full account that it surely deserves. Woven into the fabric of the pop everyday, it was "not just a highly successful trend in popular music—it became something like a cultural dominant . . . manifest as sensibility in all areas of British popular culture in the 1970s" (Auslander 49). As zeitgeisty, then, as the revered rock formations that immediately preceded it and those that would follow it. Arguably even more so, because of that long, wide reach. And, as the global reaction to David Bowie's death demonstrated, the story of glam is not only one of how it carved out a meaningful place for itself as a musical style in a specific time—but also of how it has continued to be received and understood by musicians, the industry, critics, and, most importantly of all, audiences.

Glam delivered an exhilarating, colorful, and sugary explosion of pop joy. In this respect, it was surely—to paraphrase Noel Coward—one of the most "potent" forms of "cheap music" yet witnessed. For the orthodox rock critic, it was evidently too much of a challenge to take such "potency" seriously—to acknowledge and try to understand the significance of performance and context. Instead, glam's critics winced at the fact that visuals were unashamedly integral to this most theatrical of genre's meaning and appeal. It was both telling and fitting that it should be a trio of memorable TV performances—of "Starman," which had followed on the stack heels of T. Rex's "Hot Love" and which would then precede Roxy Music's "Virginia Plain" by a mere six weeks—that would announce its arrival in such spectacular fashion. (Or, that on a more personal level, it should be Sweet performing "Teenage Rampage" a few years later that would baptize me into the joy of pop.) Glam, though, did not simply score some kind of Pyrrhic victory for style over content, for surface over depth. For style and surface read content and depth. More than a case of one-sized jumpsuit fits all, glam was musically diverse—ranging as it did from the complex art-rock of Roxy Music to the artless thump, grunt, and grind of Gary Glitter. Yet, as a Sparks newspaper ad for a bass player who—it was stipulated— "must be beard-free and exciting" indicated, here was a joyful reboot for music that had of late so grimly embraced denim-clad seriousness. "Glam's allure"—so says a perceptive Jon Savage—was built on many things: "outrage, gang solidarity, rapid motion, androgyny, *but most of all glee*" (Savage, "Kiss," 82, my italics). Of all these ingredients, it is the last here that will truly unite all the glams discussed in this book.

Busting out at the tail end of 1970 with T. Rex's "Ride a White Swan," glam gate-crashed a house divided. It then set about transforming a landscape split asunder by what appeared to be an unbridgeable schism between rock and pop that had been embraced nowhere more enthusiastically than in the States. Here glam found itself dismissed as a parochial pop novelty by those who believed that rock should purvey truth and authenticity. "Like all glam bands," wrote Lester Bangs with the humorlessness of the true believer, "Roxy Music are more interested in getting their names on the social register and trying on different kinds of clothes than doing anything about real rock and roll." His conclusion that "in Roxy Music, you see the triumph of artifice, because what they are about is that they are not about anything" (qtd. in Stump 75) encapsulates the critical default position on an entire genre. No great surprise then to find that Dave Marsh—founder of *Creem*, contributor to *Rolling Stone* and *Village Voice*, and biographer of such canonical rock figures as Elvis Presley, the Who, and Bruce Springsteen—should only include three glam tracks out of the one thousand and one listed in a book that claims to identify the "greatest singles ever made." T. Rex's "Get It On" (1971), Alice Cooper's "School's Out" (1972), and an eighties hip-hop reworking by Planet Patrol of Gary Glitter's "I Didn't Know I Loved You till I Saw You Rock and Roll" (1972) represents a scandalous return that ultimately reflects poorly on the compiler-critic. "Singles," Marsh writes, "are the essence of rock 'n' roll" (Marsh ix). (Spot on, Mr. Marsh. In fact, you share this belief with glam. Although, it would put its fervently held faith in the single into practice at a time when the rock mainstream you lionize would not.) To include so few glam 45s might lead us to conclude that it is perhaps *American* singles that we are talking about here. After all, even the rock critic's go-to whipping boy, disco, gets more entries than glam! While any list is of course subjective, it is at the very least revealing of its curator's values. Subscribing to the classic rock ideology, much like Bangs, Marsh apparently only has eyes and ears for the authentic. That said, you didn't have to be American to adopt this position on glam. "If you wanna hear a rock and roll band," wrote a staffer in the UK music weekly *Melody Maker*, "wipe off that bloody silly make-up and go see Zeppelin" (qtd. in Bayles 255).

Its faint presence in American-penned Best-Ofs might well suggest that the glam story was both time and particularly place specific—confined to Britain in the first half of the 1970s, to the "holy trinity" composed of Marc Bolan, David Bowie, and Roxy Music, to the multi-million-selling glam-pop of the likes of Slade, Sweet, and the Bay City Rollers. However, it would also ultimately prove to be an unstoppable transatlantic phenomenon. "British," only insofar as any pop music style can be attributed and then restricted to a single geocultural location. It was the product of cross-fertilization, of a familiar transatlantic trade. Not least because it was so thoroughly obsessed and fueled by America. In the US, resistance that had initially limited its draw to localized, metropolitan scenes would be eventually overcome through the combined efforts of homegrown acts with proven box office appeal (Alice Cooper and KISS) and the high visibility first-generation British glamsters achieved through regular touring and sporadic Billboard successes, but chiefly via a number of—often British—stadium rock acts that consciously adopted many of glam's ingredients on the way to becoming some of the decade's biggest stars (Rolling Stones, Elton John, Wings,

Queen, ELO). As Peter Doggett observed, "Eventually, everyone who still believed in the power of pop jumped aboard the glam bandwagon" (*Shock*, 430).

Measured against the typical mayfly life span of some pop moments, glam's five years or so is not too shabby at all. Similar in longevity to first-wave rock 'n' roll or grunge; longer lived than acid rock or punk. Time enough then to refresh, reinvigorate, and redirect. The "high" glam years cover the half decade between 1971 and 1976—from "Hot Love" to "Bohemian Rhapsody"; but there have been a number of significant pop hybrids that have evidently drawn deeply from its sweet well in the forty years since Queen uttered their final multitracked "scaramoosh"—from glitter funk and disco (Parliament-Funkadelic, Labelle, Chic) to punk and New Wave (New York Dolls, the Tubes, Blondie), New Romanticism (Duran Duran, Depeche Mode, Human League) to "hair metal" (Van Halen, Mötley Crüe, Twisted Sister), grunge (Nirvana) to Brit-pop (Oasis, Suede), to the twenty-first-century synth-pop of self-conscious changelings like Marilyn Manson. (And, whether we like it or not, there would probably be no MTV without glam.) The critical default is to apply the "glam" label in a narrow fashion, to refer to a relatively brief time period and to a relatively small number of acts. Thereby implying—if not flat-out stating—that it had very little if any broader significance; that it blazed a bubbleheaded trail that would see post-'60s pop culture sliding into self-indulgence and excess; that it constituted a sort of pop regency. Perhaps it needs to be explained this way to fit that dominant narrative. You know, the one that has punk cleansing the palate. From "Lady Stardust" to Lady Gaga, this book will not only tell the story of how glam influenced its times and how those times influenced it, but also of how we all continue to live in a world shaped by glam.

I

"CHILDREN OF THE REVOLUTION"

Glam's explosive arrival in the first few months of the first year of the new decade invites us to see and hear it as some kind of clean break, as a full-scale popular musical regime change, "a total blam blam!" It is inevitable, then, that it should find itself defined—as it so often has—in counterpoint to the much-fabled '60s. In this dominant reading, glam's performers and its audiences are literally, as Marc Bolan described them, "children of the revolution." So, the standard line goes, to find out what became of the '60s, one only has to listen to glam; and, given the significance attached to that decade, this has meant that glam is more often than not understood as a set of negatives, a bratty musical offspring destined to disappoint. Yet, as what follows in this chapter will demonstrate, it was evidently as much a carrier of continuities in practice and of those sensibilities that fueled it, as it was a conscious reaction to and outright denial of so much of what that previous "golden" decade had held so dear. If glam is a "child" of the '60s, surely it must have some of it in its DNA? Tempting though it might be to view it as such, it is clearly not forged in the contextual vacuum of outer space. (And, anyway, which '60s are we talking about here?)

David Bowie released *Pin Ups* (UK no. 1, US no. 23) in November 1973, at the end of a year in which it would be no exaggeration to claim that glam had come to dominate British pop life. In addition to the thirty weeks its singles had spent at the top of the charts, six different glam albums had also been the nation's best-sellers for a total of eighteen weeks. The year 1973 was the genre's annus mirabilis. Strange, then, that this should be the moment that Bowie chose to put out an LP of '60s cover versions. Or maybe not. For some, *Pin Ups* was taken as a sign that David Bowie wanted "out," that he had somehow lost faith in the glam project he had done so much to drive at the very moment of its triumph. How else could one explain the most un-glam lead single "Sorrow" (UK no. 3)? It, like the rest of the album, was widely understood as a self-indulgent love letter to rock in a less complex time. Yet another of those seemingly ubiquitous exercises in nostalgia currently being undertaken right across the cultural dial, whose principal function appeared to be to offer everyone involved a warm and welcome escape from the troubled contemporary. What was surprising—and for just as many disappointing—was that this time, this familiar conservative message was being disseminated by pop's great modernizer. However, what was missed by nearly everyone at the time was that *Pin Ups* was as glam as Bowie's previous two releases, *The Rise and Fall of Ziggy Stardust and the Spiders from Mars* (1972) and *Aladdin Sane* (1973). It was, for example, entirely on point for glam that *Pin Ups* should not be an act of full-on Lennonesque personal revelation, but rather something closer to "an exercise in pop art: a reproduction and interpretation of work by other artists, intended for a mass audience" (Doggett, *Man*, 187)—a strategic and highly conscious mobilization of a past that speaks to and of the present. In this respect, *Pin Ups* is not a rock covers LP at all. It is a *glam* covers LP. The ethos and creative drivers that fuel each are strikingly different. As a culture of the "authentic," rock tends to view the cover version with suspicion. How can performing someone else's material reveal your "true" self and express your "truth"? The cover version must be little more than an ode to Onan. Pointless and self-indulgent. Self-abuse rather than self-revelation.

For others, *Pin Ups* was a brazenly cynical gesture, designed to allow an exhausted Bowie to rest up while continuing to separate the fans from their money. Admittedly, the case for the prosecution was a stronger one here. After all, the album was the product of just three speedy weeks labor in Paris in July; and recording nonoriginal material meant that Bowie's music publishers, with whom his management company was in dispute at the time, would get nothing from its sales. However, tempting though it might be to conclude that this represented the main reason for the album's appearance, it ignores its thoroughly glam-soaked content. In the fall of 1973 David Bowie is, inarguably, the UK's biggest rock star. Despite retiring his alter ego Ziggy Stardust in the summer, he simply has no need—at least because he is neither cash strapped nor creatively spent—to record an album of cover versions just a few months after the release of *Aladdin Sane*. *Pin Ups*, then, is no "place-holder project" (Reynolds, *Shock*, 366). Far from it. Delivered with absolute confidence by an artist who is neither floundering nor unsure of his next move, it is in fact shaped by the very sensibility that Bowie himself had done so much to forge and spread. So rather than being a cul-de-sac, an anomaly, a curio, it represents simply the next step in an extended project, whose beginnings lay with *The Man Who Sold the World* (1970) and which would only end with *Blackstar* (2016).

At the time of its release, Michael Watts's perceptive review in *Melody Maker* was one of very few to spot what might have been going on here. *Pin Ups*, he concluded, was "a pastiche that's as funny as it's marvellously insightful" (qtd. in *History 1973*, 143). Indeed, what makes its tracks—even "Sorrow"—"marvellously insightful" is the way in which they shed considerable light on glam's agenda, its modus operandi. As Bowie himself explained, "These are all [songs by] bands which I used to go and hear play down the Marquee [club] between 1964 and 1967" (qtd. in Reynolds, *Shock*, 367); and, in fact, with the single exception of his version of Pink Floyd's "See Emily Play" (1967), *Pin Ups* takes us back to the years 1964 through 1966—"to the very peak of 60s creativity, a time when Britain's pop culture was at its most optimistic and confident" (Turner, *Crisis?*, 148)—signaling that the decade's midpoint marked a defining moment for glam. Rather than giving us an insight into David Bowie the man, then, we are in fact learning more about what makes glam tick. This is what we value, says Bowie. Not because it tells you who I am or where I've come from. Because I'm still an actor, after all. *Pin Ups* was pointedly *not* fashioned out of material from the late sixties, and therefore, by design and execution, signaled a rejection of the dominant rock practice and values of that storied time. Far from being the "peculiar undertaking" (Reynolds, *Shock*, 366) that some have described, in a consciously anticanonical move, the LP mobilizes evidently valued source material to deliver a kind of glam primer or prehistory. "We had to develop a completely new vocabulary," Bowie explained "as indeed is done generation after generation." Something, he argued, which would be primarily achieved by "taking the recent past and restructuring it in a way that we felt we had authorship of" (qtd. in Du Noyer 77). This was an MO explicitly acknowledged in the Roxy Music song "Re-make/Re-model" (1972), and one that would come to guide their pop practice as much as Bowie's.

Perhaps feeling compelled to comment on *Pin Ups* because it featured two of his own compositions, the Who's Pete Townshend observed that "if someone like Bowie, who's only been a big star for 18 months or so, feels the need to start talking about his past influences, then obviously the roots are getting lost" (qtd. in Heylin, *Madmen*, 251). In proposing that there is something more going on here than mere water-treading, Townshend has at least seen and heard more than the vast majority of the album's reviewers then and now. With *Pin Ups*, Bowie is indeed in search of "roots." Though not, however, as Townshend implies, in the sense of this being a desperate act of pop musical archaeology, driven by the artist's disconnection from a creatively barren present. For the songs on *Pin Ups* are not presented as museum pieces, as dead objects, or as artifacts that in their recovering/y signal a desire to live in the past. Covers albums are typically viewed as emerging from a "bad place"—being either the product of a dearth of ideas or hubris (or both). But this does not explain *Pin Ups* at all. "Sorrow" aside, it bristles with life, energy, and joy. While never disrespectful, its confident reworkings are hardly timid or reverential. So, all very glam then. Much in the way Bowie's cover of the Rolling Stones' "Let's Spend the Night Together" on *Aladdin Sane* succeeded in giving it a thorough glam make-over—as vampy piano work, a camp spoken-word interlude culminating in an orgasmic yelp, and a Stylophone conspire to deliver a more lascivious, more louche version than the original.

Pin Ups kicks off with "Rosalyn." At under two and a half minutes, it is a suitably (s)punky shot in what is, appropriately enough given glam's love of the format, a collection of twelve 45s. "Rosalyn" is the first in a series of conscious throwbacks that are only *throwaway* in the sense that the best pop is and always should be. There is plenty of frantic energy and swagger here in the dosing of a simple Bo Diddley riff but also a palpable jittery anxiety that, while evident in the nervy, snotty, and hormonal garage rock of the original, might suggest that Bowie's present has shaped this reworking of one of British beat group the Pretty Things' earliest singles. Elsewhere on the album, there is plenty more nervy joy to be found. As when, for example, the cover of the Mojos' 1964 single "Everything's Alright"—which has been every bit as chaotic, teetering on the verge of collapse, and ramshackle as the original—closes with a Beatles-patented vocal climax and chord sequence recalling "She Loves You." But there is much more neurosis too. Exceeding even the skittish "Rosalyn," Bowie's vocal histrionics on the garage rock staple "Here Comes the Night"—on which he also plays some appropriately ragged saxophone—render it borderline hysterical; while the half-speed, squealing-sax-filled cover of the Who's "I Can't Explain" helps transform a lyric featuring a "worried man" who is "dizzy in the head" from a song about the intoxicating effect of love into a Poe-esque tale of mental decline. In common with a number of tracks, "Friday on My Mind" has been criticized for its mannered and arch delivery. Surely, though, that is the point here? In tandem with what Simon Reynolds describes as the "sickly glace sheen" (*Shock*, 368) of its production, this is what makes it a living glam performance rather than a rictus-stiff act of reverence. This is true of all bar one of the album's tracks. Only Bowie's cover of "Sorrow"—a 1966 Merseys single that was itself a version of a song originally recorded by American garage band the McCoys—is the least glam cover on *Pin Ups*. Certainly, it has none of the histrionics but also none of the effervescence that mark the other eleven pieces. By far the most reverent track on the record, it is somewhat out of step with the lively irreverence that characterizes the rest of it.

Glam sought to plug into and then channel the visceral, hyperthyroidal energy of rock 'n' roll—its very essence, its life force. On *Pin Ups*, Bowie's cover of "Don't Bring Me Down" would thicken the archetypal gutbucket, rhythm 'n' blues riffing of the Pretty Things' original to take us back to a moment in the mid-1960s when rock was still urgent and fun. However, glam would frequently reach back further still in its quest for these essential ingredients in looking to rock 'n' roll's mid-1950s "golden age" for inspiration. In its heyday, so-called classic rock 'n' roll was perceived and received by supporters and opponents alike as an apocalyptic force, barbaric and uncouth, a direct threat to propriety and taste. Backed by its noise, its rhetoric would instruct its young fans to "rip it up," to behave antisocially, to resist, to challenge social control. Inchoate and impulsive though it was, it could be mightily disruptive. And, of course, it was not through the music alone that this message could be delivered. Classic rock 'n' roll existed as a mad package of both sound and vision, relying on the latter for maximum hedonistic effect to deliver pop that was "titanic, idolatrous, unsane, a theatre of inflamed artifice and grandiose gestures" (Reynolds, *Shock*, 2). Now vigorously pursuing what seemed in many respects to be a similar project—albeit this time in the face of an opposition led somewhat ironically by a disapproving rock mainstream rather than an alliance of educators, parents, and racists—glam could not help but feel like the sound *and sight* of a highly self-conscious regime change, as it reached out to those younger siblings of '60s rock fans who "never got it off on that revolution stuff" and who, in fact, found it all to be rather "a drag" ("All the Young Dudes").

In November 1973—the very same month in which *Pin Ups* was released—America's New York Dolls made their first UK TV appearance on the BBC's late-night rock show *The Old Grey Whistle Test*. Dressed in full glam glad rags—women's blouses, lurid-colored satin pants, boas and scarves, stack heels—and wearing generous amounts of makeup, the band lip-synched to two garagey songs from their debut album. A year earlier, the Dolls' lead singer David Johansen had told *Melody Maker* that the band "felt something was lacking in music. It wasn't exciting any more to us. . . . Everyone's hanging about on stage, being morose as well," and the Dolls, he stated, simply "didn't dig that." So, like the kid in "Looking for a Kiss"—one of the tracks they performed that night—they were not gonna be "obsessed with gloom." "The thing about rock today," Johansen continued, "is that you have to impress somebody—it lost a lot when it became just like that. They forgot that you also have to entertain people" (qtd. in *History 1972*, 97). Unfortunately for the Dolls, however, the forces of rock conservativism were much closer than they might have imagined that November night. Present in the *Whistle Test* studio, in the form of the show's presenter, Bob Harris. As the New York Dolls bravely walked their very campy walk, Harris famously branded them "mock rock" in a sniggering outro to a performance that he—as spokesman for the rock orthodoxy—evidently mistrusted. Harris, then, could only see and hear the Dolls as fake. An impression the band themselves admittedly did little to challenge, in choosing with typical disregard for rock sincerity to lip-synch on pretty much the only TV show at that time that provided a platform for live performance. A more obvious home for the Dolls might have been *Top of the Pops*, on which everyone lip-synched; but the New

York Dolls had not yet placed a single on the UK charts and so no invitation had been forthcoming.

In the early 1970s, rock's critical consensus—represented in the UK by the presenters and loyal but relatively small audience of *The Old Grey Whistle Test*—was characterized by a default hyperromanticism that resulted in a real reluctance to "let go" of the late sixties. His onstage behavior might well have done Marc Bolan few favors in North America; but, in the "land of rock," his would always be a hard act to swallow. Not least because that was exactly what it was, so obviously, so unashamedly, an "act." Like the many glam artists who followed in its perfumed wake, T. Rex represented a highly conscious affront to a carefully cultivated, much-cherished, and jealously guarded rock naturalism. Something David Bowie himself acknowledged, when he pointed out that "realism, honesty and all these things that came out of the late 60s had got really boring to many jaded people going into the early 70s" (qtd. in Doggett, *Man*, 143–44). To no great surprise, Bowie would find an ally in opposition to this tiresome worship of all things "real" in Roxy Music's Bryan Ferry, who told *New Musical Express* that the "whole 60s presentation of rock music, and the implied honesty that went with it, was kind of bizarre and was always alien to me" (qtd. in Stump 73). Yet, while the words and deeds of its three principal architects illustrate the extent to which glam would set itself at odds to the orthodoxy, Bob Harris's contemptuous and patronizing attitude toward the New York Dolls indicated that the rock mainstream and its many believers were not about to take such heresy lying down. It is clear, for instance, that a commitment to—what Carys Wyn Jones has termed— the "classic rock ideology" fueled British music journalist Nick Kent's review of the *Ziggy Stardust* LP. Writing in the countercultural publication *Oz*, Kent observed/complained that Bowie was trying "to hype himself as something he isn't" (qtd. in Doggett, *Man*, 151). Like so many in the transatlantic rock press at the time, Kent demonstrated not only that he didn't "get it" but that he didn't "like it." He seemed constitutionally unable to accept that irony, humor, and fiction could be valid elements of rock praxis. In the same year, Kent would also judge T. Rex's *The Slider* to be "bogus," a "crass package of synthetic rock and roll music"; and two years later he would abandon even any pretense of critical objectivity and fairness in simply dismissing Queen's eponymous debut LP as a "bucket of urine."

These hard-line views originate in the late 1960s. As Andrew Blake points out, this was the moment

> at which a canon of (largely white, male) "rock" performers emerged, seeking new musical values and distancing themselves from the commercial hurly-burly of chart pop—and with them grew a school of journalism which was eager to canonise both their work and its own. The Rock Musician is shadowed by the Rock Writer. (Blake 125)

In a simultaneously aggrandizing and self-aggrandizing move, then, "rock writing romanticises both its subjects and the writers themselves" (125–26). By the early 1970s, the rise and rise of the professional rock critic—an American-led phenomenon—had contributed greatly to rock's exaggerated sense of its own self-importance, playing a major role in both enshrining and then actively disseminating its accepted "truths." In October 1970, *Sounds* had joined *NME* and *Melody Maker* in the UK music weekly marketplace. Its pro-rock agenda proved so successful that it effectively forced its two main rivals to freshen up their rosters with young hipsters like the aforementioned Nick Kent, and, in so doing, to pretty much turn away from "pop" altogether.

Although fully aware of how rock *should* work—"one of the principles in rock [is] that it's the person himself expressing what he really and truly feels"—David Bowie told any rock writer who bothered to ask that he "always saw it as a theatrical experience" (qtd. in Heylin, *Madmen*, 209). In so publicly committing to it as "theater," he would lead glam's charge on rock's precious commitment to sincerity and authenticity, inevitably running into considerable opposition from an openly contemptuous rock elite, quick to brand it "mock rock."

In one crucial, ostensibly contradictory, respect, it could be argued that glam sought to move rock forward by invoking and, in many cases, actively mobilizing its past. Specifically, the classic rock 'n' roll of the mid-1950s appealed not only because it was untroubled by "sincerity" and seriousness, but also because it embraced the theatrical without any trace of guilt. In its purest—some would say most rudimentary—form, glam's revivalist impulse was evident in a drapes-and-crepes act like Showaddywaddy or in the Gene Vincent shtick of Alvin Stardust; but it was also caught in the musical and lyrical echoes found right across the generic spectrum—in Wizzard's "Angel Fingers (A Teen Ballad)" (1973), for example, or in T. Rex's and Queen's direct quoting of Chuck

Berry's "Little Queenie" in "Get It On" (1971) and "Now I'm Here" (1975), respectively. Of all the first-wave rock 'n' rollers, it was Little Richard who exerted the greatest influence on future glam stars. To young Brits, he sounded, looked, and behaved like no one else. As a kid growing up in the London suburbs, David Bowie had sent off for signed pictures of his idol and subsequently confirmed that, more than any single performer, it was Little Richard who inspired him to form his first band. Prominent in set lists, Little Richard covers would become glam staples—simultaneously functioning as acts of homage and statements of intent. It was no coincidence, then, that Slade's first hit single should be a cover of Little Richard's "Get Down and Get with It."

When glam emerged in 1971, the best-selling album on both sides of the Atlantic was Simon and Garfunkel's *Bridge over Troubled Water*—a fine piece of work, for sure, but one that could hardly be said to have bottled the fizz and kick that made rock 'n' roll such an intoxicating brew back in the 1950s. About as far from Little Richard as you could get, *Bridge over Troubled Water* was serious, "grown-up" worthy, and, if truth be told, in its solemnity ultimately a little dull. It was, though, indicative of where rock music found itself at the beginning of the new decade. However, while it was quintessential, to find out why, we must travel back several years to the mid-1960s. To the summer of 1965, in fact, and to the moment that gunfire crack of a snare shot ushered in "Like a Rolling Stone." For Bob Dylan would lead rock 'n' roll down a path that would undeniably deliver all kinds of riches, but that would also—for the time being at least—cut off the supply line to some of the "good stuff" it had been offering up to this point. Achieving previously unimagined status as a means through which the world might be interpreted, rock music—as it would soon come to be titled—would be seen and heard as capable of many things; but fun, excitement, and glamour would not be among these. This was, of course, a realization that drove Bowie's enthusiastic reanimations of those mid-sixties songs on *Pin Ups*. His choices were significant. Jon Savage has identified 1966 as pivotal and transformative—a year, which he argues, "began in pop and ended with rock." It was, he wrote, "the last year when the '45 [rpm record] was the principal pop music form, before the full advent of the album as a creative and commercial force" (*1966*, ix–x). Yet, while it seems that we can all agree on *what* happened, it is impossible to reach broad agreement on exactly *when*. So, for what it's worth, I am with Phillip

Ennis, Andrew Grant Jackson, and Greil Marcus among others in hom-
ing in on the summer of 1965, when Bob Dylan "proved it was possible
to have both artistic freedom and a hit." With "Like a Rolling Stone,"
Dylan "liberated his peers to write about anything they wanted," thus
making 1965 a "unique ground zero moment when the monochrome
door opened onto a kaleidoscopic Oz waiting on the other side" (Jackson 2, 8). Where I and, more importantly, glam depart from Jackson
and the rest of the pro-'65 lobby, though, is in not sharing the view that
what lay ahead was somehow 100 percent better than what had already
been. For, as Nik Cohn points out, "with respect came the first stirrings
of self-importance" (4); and while Dylan could certainly be wry and
witty in song, what followed in his wake tended to be short on humor.
Henceforth, the joyous inarticulacy that characterized rock 'n' roll
would largely be confined to pop; rock, by contrast, would seem to favor
the joylessly articulate. Bruce Springsteen described the six-minute-
plus "Like a Rolling Stone" as "revolutionary." It "freed your mind," he
said, "the way Elvis freed your body." It marked the moment when
something as previously ephemeral and trivial as pop mutated into
something enduring and significant. As Ennis calls it, '65 saw rock 'n'
roll "maturing into rock," achieving "a minimal level of maturity when it
stretched beyond its teenage concerns and constituency, past the trau-
ma of puppy love and the problems of parental authority" (313). There
are gains, for sure; but it is possible to argue that this "maturity" came at
a price. Not least in rock outgrowing its teen audience, and so abandon-
ing the very folks who made it.

As the 1960s ended, we could argue that another chapter of that
familiar popular music cycle—one that begins with innovation and experimentation but that ends with standardization and homogeniza-
tion—had been played out. As rock 'n' roll morphed into rock, it was
subjected to a classic pincer movement—"internal," artist-driven pressure to ramp up its seriousness on one side, more familiar industry
moves to control and contain on the other. Where Dylan led, others
followed. "He showed all of us," acknowledged a grateful Paul McCartney, "that it was possible to go a little further" (qtd. in Inglis 72). The
years 1964 through 1967—the very years Bowie had mined for songs to
cover on *Pin Ups*—had witnessed a spike in guitar sales, with some
surveys conducted at the time suggesting that nearly two-thirds of
young males under twenty-three were band active. During this time,

garage rock—the brand of music performed by most of these amateur outfits and exactly the kind of music that would come to fuel *Pin Ups*—kept the rock 'n' roll spirit alive. Spontaneous, amateurish, basic, but energetic, it was (im)precisely the kind of music-making that could easily be taken as a snotty measure of discontent with the finely chiseled "rock" now being expertly crafted by the likes of Dylan and the Beatles. At the same time, the music industry that seemed hell-bent on extinguishing this flame—largely through simply ignoring it—now found an unlikely ally in the form of a rapidly professionalizing rock mainstream, whose rising sense of self-importance and increasing engagement with "serious" subject matter would make garage rock's less "adult" concerns and unrepentant lack of proficiency seem regressive. "We can do things that please us without conforming to the standard pop idea," explained George Harrison. "We are not only involved in pop music but all music" (qtd. in Heylin, *Act*, 113). So, this was a time when rock acts were, often under the influence of psychedelics, stretching themselves lyrically and musically, and when many were flexing their cultural power by demonstrating varying degrees of countercultural engagement. Increasing creative autonomy was obviously a "good thing," but in the wrong hands it could be a license for pretension and pomposity.

The nail in the coffin for garage—driven in hard by both rock acts and the business—was a shift in emphasis from the single to the album format. This, of course, suited rock's recent musical developments to a tee. Acid rock, hard rock, and nascent progressive rock, for instance, would all flourish in long-player form. Two summers after Dylan had shown what might be possible with *Highway 61 Revisited*—which had featured "Like a Rolling Stone" and the eleven-minute "Desolation Row"—the rock LP arguably came of age, its status as an artistic document cemented by the June '67 release of the Beatles' *Sgt. Pepper's Lonely Hearts Club Band*. Here was an album whose success not only ushered in the era of album-oriented rock—and so radically reshaped how popular music would work economically—but which also confirmed that rock LPs would be taken seriously by not just the musicians, the business, and the fans but by the critics and reviewers too, who in turn would play their part in conferring the status of "art" upon them. Held in the same month, the Monterey Festival was envisioned by its organizers as an event that might validate rock music as an art form comparable to jazz and folk. While it is debatable that the festival achieved this aim, Monterey unequivocally signified the arrival of rock music as "big," if not "show," business. Something confirmed by the attendance of A&R men from all the major record labels, armed with checkbooks, and eager to sign up rock acts to their companies' rosters.

The net result of all this was to effect a concurrent hardening and widening of the difference and distance between both rock and pop, and rock and rock 'n' roll. These were divisions that the likes of Bowie, Bolan, and Ferry would eventually come to straddle and, in some cases, even collapse. However, this seemed very unlikely, if not impossible, in the late 1960s. Two very distinct markets had emerged by 1968—different arenas in which popular music would be both produced and consumed. This was the year in which—in the United States—sales of albums surpassed sales of singles for the very first time. This was a commercial watershed, for sure, but it also indicated that the album had now become rock music's natural format. It even had another powerful ally in the form of the many FM radio stations springing up across the country that would happily play album tracks, that would not refuse to play anything more than four minutes long. All this left garage rock in a difficult place. It was the very antithesis of what the industry wanted. Not least because major-label rock acts shifted more LPs. By 1970, then, garage is dead in the water. Killed off by a lethal combination of factors that include: rock's increasing stress on virtuosity, technical chops, or, at the very least, proficiency; that widespread and widely shared assumption that only the album is the true test of a musician's worth; the fact that the album is now established as the industry's format of choice; and, as previously noted, the growing number of FM radio stations willing to playlist album tracks, and on which the music of the rock mainstream will invariably sound "better" than ragged garage. So, garage finds itself on the "wrong side" of the divide—that is, the one *not* with rock—banished to the pop musical hinterland by the perfect storm of factors outlined above. In hindsight, that it should find itself out in the cold should not have been a surprise. Paths that had, if not crossed, then certainly ran closely adjacent back in the mid-1960s, were now well and truly divergent. Symptomatic of the many degrees of separation between rock—significant and weighty—and pop—ephemeral and trivial. The former was built to last; the latter was built for speed.

So, what did this weighty rock music look and, more importantly perhaps, sound like as the 1970s dawned? Although there was variety enough under the "rock" header to warrant the identification of four distinct substyles, it was still the case that each of these channeled common feelings of disappointment and disillusionment, that each expressed a shared desire to withdraw or retreat, and that each typically wrapped this all up in a musical package marked by its unmistakable seriousness. Given the drivers that contributed to it, perhaps we should not have been surprised by such a state of affairs. For these compose a "litany" that has subsequently come to be almost as familiar as that which explains the death of rock 'n' roll at the tail end of the 1950s. It includes, then, the untimely deaths of some of its principal players (Jimi Hendrix, Janis Joplin, Jim Morrison); the assassinations of public figures who personified progressiveness and hope (Martin Luther King Jr., Robert Kennedy); the escalation of the Vietnam War; the damage caused by the widespread availability of hard drugs; the psychic cost and bitter symbolism of events in the summer of 1969 at Altamont and in the Hollywood Hills; and even the complicity of the music industry itself. It is in and out of this context, then, that rock's (re)turn to and (re)discovery of musical "roots" becomes entirely understandable. This can be heard in the country stylings of Bob Dylan on *John Wesley Harding* (1968) and *Nashville Skyline* (1969), of the Byrds on *Sweetheart of the Rodeo* (1968) and *Dr. Byrds and Mr. Hyde* (1969), and of the Band on *Music from Big Pink* (1968) and *The Band* (1969).

The singer-songwriter or troubadour turn, hymning an acoustic and introspective "comedown" and typified by the output of Joni Mitchell, Neil Young, James Taylor, and Crosby, Stills & Nash also led rock down a path marked by retreat, retrenchment, and withdrawal. Crosby, Stills & Nash's material was characterized by its high seriousness, its self-importance even, and by its sometime weary commitment to "Carry On" (1970), the track "Almost Cut My Hair"—from the US number one album *Déjà vu* (1970)—reaffirming the band's dogged commitment to the countercultural sixties. The quasi-hymnal transatlantic number one single "Bridge over Troubled Water" (1970), by Simon and Garfunkel, fellow travelers down this path, memorably bottled this post-1960s comedown, singing of "weary" lives being lived out in some kind of postapocalyptic world. All the acts noted here, then, represented the high-profile vanguard of the introspective, solipsistic, and confessional

mode of the singer-songwriter that would enjoy huge commercial success in the early 1970s. It was also evidently a long way from rock 'n'
roll, something that might not have been said of the third path taken by
rock music at the time—hard rock. Concurrent with those acoustic
delicacies, some music simply got harder and heavier, its sound typified
by British groups like Led Zeppelin, Black Sabbath, and Deep Purple.
Yet, it too was undertaken in all seriousness and treated with equal
reverence by its many millions of fans. Similarly, the emerging style of
progressive rock was also very appealing to musicians, fans, and the
business alike, who would all benefit from its emphasis on virtuosity and
tendency toward pretension. Like heads-down hard rock, it could be
said to have packaged withdrawal in a different form. In this case, via
solipsism on a grand scale.

As the seventies dawned, this was a rock landscape recognizably
"made in the USA." Now back in charge after the blip that was the
British Invasion, American record companies appeared to be in full
command of what constituted rock music, enthusiastically supported in
this by the rock press. As Gillett notes, Columbia, Capitol, and Warner
Brothers had "followed the natural instincts of major organisations to
try to stabilise their market, to lengthen the careers and spread the
appeal of their artists" (402). This meant that the major labels would
treat "pop" as distinctly second class at best. Rock was where the big
money was: in album sales and long, lucrative careers. So it seemed that
"the industry [had] finally won its battle to stabilise the elusive ingredients of popular music, and more-or-less abandoned the young teenagers" (399). And this was a business model that had apparently gained
considerable traction in the UK too. Just twelve months after it happened in the States, the UK would report that in 1969 sales of LPs had
finally eclipsed those of singles. However, all was not what it seemed. In
sharp and audible contrast with the American scene (and so with the
market that measured it), it sometimes appeared as if the UK had an
entirely different understanding of what constituted rock music. A
quick comparison of the two nation's singles charts in 1973, for example, indicates as much. In this year, glam dominated the British listings,
while the upper reaches of the Billboard Hot 100 told a very different
story. While three singles by ex-Beatles—George Harrison's "Give Me
Love," Ringo Starr's "Photograph," and Paul McCartney's "My Love"—
and "Angie" by the Rolling Stones made number one in the States,

none of these representative offerings of the rock mainstream could manage a similar feat in the UK. So, as Gillett (377) points out:

> Although there were many parallels between the development of music in Britain and in America in this period, there was one fundamental difference which had repercussions that lasted for at least the next fifteen years. In America, the leading underground bands all signed direct to major record companies, enabling those companies to reinforce their hold on the American record industry and effectively drive out virtually all the independent companies. The result was a drift into conformity, sterility and repetition that destroyed much of the momentum of the previous fifteen years.

In Britain, however, a similar lockdown did not occur. Here, the four majors—Decca, EMI, Philips, and Pye—were not only challenged by overseas competitors like CBS and Polydor, they were also "undermined from below by independent managers and producers" (Gillett 377). The scope and scale of this challenge can be demonstrated by focusing once again on the situation in 1973 and, specifically, on glam in that year. While the UK majors did have glam acts on their books—notably, Bowie at RCA and T. Rex at EMI—"overseas competitors" CBS and Polydor had Mott the Hoople and the year's biggest pop act, Slade, respectively. Second only to Slade in terms of singles chart success in '73, Sweet was signed to RCA, but had done so before they "glammed up." Otherwise, the year's hottest musical style was the preserve of the independent labels or imprints—Gary Glitter and the Glitter Band at Bell, Suzi Quatro and Mud at RAK, Roxy Music and Sparks at Island, Wizzard at Harvest. Furthermore, the glam-pop acts would rely on independent writing and production teams to keep the hits coming—like Chinn and Chapman who worked with Sweet, Mud, and Suzi Quatro. All this demonstrates why and how major-label market dominance failed to materialize in the UK. Of course, this was partly a result of industry failures of foresight and faith; but it also happened because Britain's popular music "scene" was genuinely resistant to the application of corporate intelligence. Simply put, it was nowhere near as predictable as the North American "scene." Dave Haslam has identified 1970s Britain as "the subculture capital of the world"—"land of a thousand fashions and a thousand dances [where] ideas, especially those disseminated through music, moved quickly" (118). Although there was a sizable audience for mainstream rock, principally among college-age males, British teens—and young girls in particular—rejected this music (and the values it encoded) in favor of something they might call their own. Whereas in the US the industry—aided and abetted by the rock mainstream—had managed to reduce things down to a product that could be packaged for most, the UK stewed in a "febrile atmosphere of innovation" (Miller 298) supported by an infrastructure that could make it all happen. There were three all-powerful music weeklies—*New Musical Express*, *Melody Maker*, and *Sounds*—with a combined readership of hundreds of thousands, together with a limited network of radio and TV outlets with a reach of millions. Size, then, did matter. This distinctive scale and scope—marked by a compact music market and the power of a centralized media—allowed for the rapid and widespread dissemination of all these trends and sounds, affording potentially blanket coverage, thus offering both a persuasive explanation for how and why glam should take off so spectacularly in Britain and how and why it should have so singularly failed to fly in the States. Visiting the UK in 1972, a bemused but presumably envious Iggy Pop declared, "This country is weird, man. It's unreal" (qtd. in Turner, *Glam Rock*, 91). It was unusual, too, that the country's music business should service this "weirdness" rather than seeking to actively extinguish or simply ignore it.

Just as their American peers did, music writers at the British weeklies tended to champion mainstream rock. However, although they may well have disliked what they saw and heard emerging from "the land of a thousand fashions and dances," they found it hard to ignore and duly reported on it. Furthermore, on UK radio—still broadcasting on the AM frequency—it was pop pretty much all the way. In contrast to the situation in the States, where the industry enthusiastically backed it and the numerous FM stations would play it, there were comparatively few outlets for rock. As for national TV, in prime time at least, it was also all about pop. *Top of the Pops*.

Taking this into account, it should come as no surprise to learn that Elvis Presley's "The Wonder of You" was the UK's biggest-selling single of 1970. Hardly classic rock 'n' roll, of course, but then obviously not classic rock either. Neither was it a novelty record. Although we should not have been surprised if the year's best-seller had been a pop novelty, since the UK did binge on these with addictive regularity in the late

1960s and early 1970s. In 1970, Presley would be pushed hard by TV artist-entertainer Rolf Harris's single "Two Little Boys," whose six-week run as the nation's best-seller had begun in December 1969 and had followed directly on from the Archies' two-month tenure at the top of the UK chart with "Sugar Sugar." There then followed number one singles for the England soccer team's World Cup sing-along "Back Home," and two indigenous bubblegum tracks in the shape of Christie's "Yellow River" and Edison Lighthouse's "Love Grows." Each in its frothy optimism was a counterpoint to rock's miserabilist dominant, subscribers to which would have presumably found even less comfort and even more despair in the following year's singles chart. For 1971 would deliver UK number ones for TV sitcom actor Clive Dunn ("Grandad"), comedian Benny Hill ("Ernie"), and once again two bubblegum hits for Middle of the Road ("Chirpy Chirpy Cheep Cheep") and Tony Orlando ("Knock Three Times"). Flighty and "gimmicky" or lively and vibrant. The state of the UK's pop scene might help explain the enthusiasm for rock 'n' roll revivalism that was evident in the early 1970s. So, while Presley has 1970's best-seller, a younger generation of Brit-rockers are embracing the kind of music he introduced to their older siblings a decade and half or so earlier. In December 1970, for example, Dave Edmunds enjoyed a six-week run at number one with a cover of a 1952 Smiley Lewis track called "I Hear You Knockin'"—a song whose title seemed apt for the popular music putsch that was only a matter of weeks away now and which was presaged by the song that would tuck in just behind it at number two on the chart, T. Rex's "Ride a White Swan."

Regardless of whether they were British or American, the album was everything to most rock musicians, rock fans, and record executives. Rock groups could sell millions of records; and, for as long as it was albums that were being sold, they would avoid the critics' condemnation and scorn. Albums were the product of artistic endeavor, undertaken in all seriousness. Therefore, multiplatinum successes did not constitute "selling out." This format was associated with credibility. By contrast, singles were mere vehicles for "pop," only fit for parents and children. Yet, of the two formats, it is the 45 rpm single that will matter most to the story of glam. Responsive and light on its feet, the single has always been a bellwether for the UK's subcultural verve, where it can be most keenly felt. It is also the case that a vinyl disc's volume level is dependent on two factors: the length of its sides and the depth of its grooves. The more songs, the quieter the sound. Singles then are just noisier, palpably more exciting.

While high summer's high-profile Isle of Wight Festival, with its stellar lineup of '60s-made rock superstars like Hendrix, the Who, the Doors, and Emerson, Lake & Palmer, might have suggested otherwise, by 1970 Britain and America were—with apologies to Winston Churchill—two pop nations divided by a common language. Although the two album markets are more in sync—there are six transatlantic number ones in 1970 (*Abbey Road*, *Let It Be*, *Led Zeppelin II*, *Led Zeppelin III*, Creedence Clearwater Revival's *Cosmo's Factory*, and *Bridge over Troubled Water*)—this disconnect is particularly evident in relation to the singles market. Here, there would be just two shared number one singles all year—"Bridge over Troubled Water" and the rereleased "Tears of a Clown." This is a divide that will only widen through the years to come; one that, in the short term, glam will play a lead role in sustaining. For, in being neither what the music industry nor the rock mainstream wanted, glam was a counterculture—representative of a gulf that opens on *intra*generational lines, one that typically separated older and younger siblings rather than parents and their kids. "My brother's back at home with *his* Beatles and *his* Stones / I never got it off on that revolution stuff" ("All the Young Dudes"). This countermessage is expressed visually on the cover of *Pin Ups*, in which David Bowie and the model Twiggy stare out at you with a cold replicant gaze—the thousand-yard stare of the '60s survivor perhaps. And what has become of the '60s poster girl? Twiggy, the face and body of swinging London, is now recast, reframed, and re-presented in 1973 as neither unchanged nor a museum piece. Like the music within, she has been glammed up. She is not nostalgically offered to us. She—like Bowie—is pinned up, pinned back, and pinned down, like a plastic surgeon's patient-victim with the job half-done. The contrast in skin tones here makes her face appear as though it has been sewn back onto her skull like a mask. It is all very unsettling, a visual staging of disconnection that offers further evidence of distancing from "that" '60s.

Glam is forged by drivers that are specific to the UK. As the new decade dawned, British music fans were faced with a straight, simple choice of either rock or pop. However, as Thompson notes, this meant that while "eight-year-olds were catered for by the bubble-gum boom

[and] eighteen-year-olds by the longhairs playing the colleges" (22), many Brits of high school age felt poorly served. Through its direct address and appeal to a disenfranchised teen constituency, glam simultaneously drove a wedge and plugged a gap—a dual function found as a subtext in pretty much all its songs, but which is more overtly enacted in tracks like "Cum On Feel the Noize" (1973), "The Sixteens" (1974), "Teenage Dream" (1974), "Teenage Lament" (1974), "Teenage Rampage" (1974), and of course "All the Young Dudes" (1972). All these (self-)consciously reach out to speak both to and for those Marc Bolan referred to as "the children of the revolution." These are the same "children" Bowie invited to "boogie" in "Starman," of course, but in whom the rock mainstream had apparently no interest at all. When asked in 1972 whether the Stones appealed to the younger teenage T. Rex fan, Mick Jagger told *Melody Maker*, with a mixture of relief and disdain, that "we don't have to go back to those people" (qtd. in *History 1972*, 75). Although he was aware of a significant difference between the band's US and UK audiences—in America it is fifteen-year-olds who "dig" the Stones, whereas it is "students" who do the same in the band's homeland—Jagger is adamant that he will not be attempting to woo those pesky glam kids anytime soon. "I'm not interested in going back to small English towns and turning on the 10-year-olds. I've done all that" (qtd. in *History 1972*, 75). (Two years later, he and his band will court the glam fan on vinyl [*It's Only Rock 'n' Roll*] and in live performance.) By contrast, David Bowie was genuinely reaching out to "those people." He was more than happy to be associated with teenage fans, frequently expressing his respect for that demographic in interviews. Such declarations help us to understand why glam would take the single so seriously, and possibly why the dividing line between it and "teeny-bopper" pop could sometimes appear indistinct. As Slade's plain-speaking lead singer, Noddy Holder, explained, "We don't want no underground leftovers. We are after the kids" (qtd. in Reynolds, *Shock*, 163)—a statement that enables us to get a measure of glam's unashamed and strenuous commitment to a young audience.

Yet, for all its quarrels with rock, glam's roots do not lie exclusively in those prelapsarian days before rock 'n' roll morphed into the more grown-up variant. This is demonstrated on *Pin Ups*, on which Bowie's version of Pink Floyd's 1967 psych-rock single "See Emily Play" would perhaps initially seem to be out of place in a collection of songs otherwise drawn from the British beat boom of 1964 to 1966. Of course, it is significant that the Floyd original was a single, and a stand-alone thing of near-garagey pop beauty at that. "Interstellar Overdrive" it is not. Furthermore, as with the tracks on the rest of the album, to call the Bowie version a "cover" is to do it a disservice. For it might lead us to presume that we are to be presented with a faithful—for which read rather lifeless—copy. When in fact what we have is a reworking, a glam makeover, if you will. Far from being unrepresentative, then, Bowie's version of "See Emily Play" could well be the most on message of all the tracks on *Pin Ups*. While the queasy vari-speed vocal—reminiscent of Bowie's own "Bewlay Brothers" from his 1971 album *Hunky Dory*—recalls the original, some busy Moonesque drumming and guitarist Mick Ronson's distinctive figures and riffs, together with Mike Garson's angular piano lines, all contribute to the making of a full-on, rather gonzo baroque affair that is far from preserved in aspic. Presumably, intended as a criticism, Simon Reynolds describes the track as "hope-lessly mannered, almost comic" (*Shock*, 368). I would, however, suggest that, while it is undeniably "mannered" and could quite easily be re-garded as "comic," this is surely the point. (Here, Reynolds's judgment on "See Emily Play" should come as no great surprise, given that his epic glam history often comes across as an apologia—as if the genre is only worthy of consideration by dint of what it might have drawn from the past and, even more importantly, what it gave to the music that followed. In this respect, Ian Penman is correct when he calls *Shock and Awe* a "pre-punk book to go with [Reynolds's] post-punk opus *Rip It Up and Start Again*" [25]. Indeed, strange as it might sound—and particularly so of a six-hundred-page monster—it often reads like a book in a hurry to get to what comes after glam.)

Bowie's version of "See Emily Play," then, demonstrates the live links that existed between glam and the rock music of the late 1960s. His admission that Syd Barrett empowered him to sing in his own voice—or at least to adopt a range of recognizably British voices—rather than offer an approximation of an American one, for example, helps prove this point. Barrett, explained Bowie, was "the first guy I'd heard sing pop or rock with a British accent. His impact on my thinking was enormous" (qtd. in Heylin, *Madmen*, 199–200). Perhaps more con-tentiously, photographer Mick Rock has claimed that Bowie "wor-shipped" Floyd's Syd Barrett, even going as far as to suggest Ziggy's androgyny was inspired by the British psych-rock eccentric. Intended as stinging criticism, John Lennon's appraisal of the 1960s as a time when everyone dressed up but nothing changed surely misses the point. "Dressing up" could be political, and the knowledge that it did not necessarily have to be an empty gesture was something glam rockers shared with the likes of Barrett. Marc Bolan's exposure as the schoolboy Mark Feld to a biography of the Georgian dandy Beau Brummell would "encourag[e] him to take flight from the habits and conventions of his environment" (Paytress, *Bolan*, 16). In the late 1960s, dandyism also worked in a similar (no pun) fashion for members of the more playful, less conventionally political British underground, thus making it a meeting point for the counterculture and glam. The dandy, writes Hawkins,

> is a bewildering construction: a creature of alluring elegance, vanity and irony, who plays around with conventions to his own end. At the same time, he is someone whose transient tastes never shirk from excess, protest or rebellion. . . . From mannerisms to ways of posing and performing, the dandy revels in artifice simply for style's sake as a mischievous play with masks of calculated elegance. All the same, dandifying one's act is linked to self-thinking, sensibility and narcissism that exudes a put-on sense of social elevation. . . . All the great dandies have been outsiders; they have been intellectual figures, artists, and disaffected young men, eager to make themselves publicly visible through a conceit that is deemed their birth-right. (15)

For those of a countercultural persuasion, glam was often their worst nightmare. This despite there being some obvious common ground. Dandyism could, of course, be easily detected in any of those first-wave rock 'n' rollers lionized by glam musicians and fans. It was surely personified in that favorite-of-all-favorites, Little Richard. However, in the second half of the 1960s, there were none more dandy than those darlings of the counterculture, the Rolling Stones. So, it should not really have been a surprise to anyone, then, when the Stones belatedly embraced glam in the mid-'70s. In fact, given the band's campy theatrics, narcissism, and rampant hedonism, perhaps the only surprise should have been that this embrace came as late as it did. Glam would launch a campy assault on rock—via gender play operating on a variety of levels from androgyny through transvestism and drag to queering. Back in the late '60s, though, the Stones had never shied away from striking such poses as blows—as when, for instance, cross-dressing in the promotional film for "Have You Seen Your Mother" (1966) or consciously mobilizing dandyism to attack a repressive British establishment in the promo for "We Love You" (1967). *Rock and Roll Circus* (1968) saw the band leading from the front, showcasing the kind of campy theatrics that arguably suited the band better—and so represented a "truer" picture of them—than the crude politicking (wrongly) assumed to feature in a track like "Street Fighting Man" (1968). Of course, it was this latter imprint of the band that the counterculture would come to worship, conveniently ignoring the persistent dandyism that can even be discerned on "Street Fighting Man."

Just as there had been with the late '60s "underground" (and the music that spread its word), there was more to glam than met the eye; it arguably represented "the first pop flowering of an increasingly confident gay culture: five years after its partial decriminalisation, Bowie injected homosexuality into the British pop mainstream." As the reception of "Starman" had demonstrated then, it "both empowered uncertain teens and gave the more resolutely heterosexual a wider palette in which to trip the light fantastic" (Savage, "Kiss," 82). While the late 1960s had witnessed an increase in public displays of sexuality, sparked by a series of liberal reforms, it was glam that would effectively "carry the news" into the mainstream, helping to process liberal and progressive ideas for mass consumption.

Although Bowie had included a cover of "Where Have All the Good Times Gone" on *Pin Ups*, it was another Kinks song that would make a more obvious point of reference for those keen to unearth glam's prehistory. The skeptical "Dedicated Follower of Fashion" (1966) had attacked foppery, making Ray Davies a rather unlikely advocate; but "Lola" (1970) would take gender confusion into the upper reaches of the pop charts (UK no. 2, US no. 5) and onto the nation's TV screens—declaring that "Girls will be boys and boys will be girls / It's a mixed up, muddled up, shook up world." Purportedly based on Davies's date with Candy Darling—a transsexual who would be subsequently immortalized in Lou Reed's Bowie-produced "Walk on the Wild Side" (1972)—the song is lyrically uncompromising. Lola "walk[s] like a woman and talk[s] like a man"; and an encounter with her leaves the narrator questioning his own sexuality—"I almost fell for my Lola." However, although it is all very confusing, it is made clear that Lola knows who she is—"It's a mixed up, muddled up, shook up world, *except for* Lola." She alone here is comfortable in her skin; and our narrator evidently admires, even worships, her for this—"I got down on my knees and I looked at her and she looked at me / That's the way that I want it to stay." That Lola is a good person—and most definitely not some kind of freak—is confirmed by the full title of the album on which the song would feature, *Lola vs. Powerman and the Money-Go-Round* (1970). "Lola," then, might well be heard as a kind of pop outrider, injecting a new conception of politics into the cultural mainstream that would more fully emerge in the early 1970s: a politics in which the "personal is political," and therefore anticipated ways in which—in typically inchoate style—glam would and could come to have a big role to play.

In *Fire and Rain*, David Browne claims that the story of the Beatles, Simon and Garfunkel, James Taylor, and Crosby, Stills, Nash & Young in 1970 was a "lost" one. But can this be true? *Fire and Rain* offers a fascinating account of these artists in context, for sure, but their story was never remotely in danger of being "lost." After all, these canonical acts represent the rock motherlode. Perhaps if one is looking for the real "lost" story of 1970—and of the years that immediately follow— then one should look no further than glam? Browne persuasively identifies 1970 as a "year of upheaval and collapse, tension and release, endings and beginnings" (3). Yet, while he notes that it saw the opening of a "generation gap that cracked rock and roll apart, separating the older fans from the newer, next-generation ones, [that] was now an entrenched part of the culture" (333), rather oddly, his focus remains determinedly fixed on the old guard. Even in the more orthodox US, though, there were signs that other stories were emerging. Stories such as Alice Cooper. However, wedded to the classic rock ideology, the rock press persistently looked to dismiss Alice Cooper as a fraud. Appealing to a largely high school–age demographic, Alice Cooper's music had little or nothing in common with mainstream rock's then-dominant strains; and the band's—and particularly its lead singer's—appearance and behavior jarred too. Wearing "macabre black make-up" and dressed in "a pink ballerina dress, topped off with a black leather jacket," the man his parents knew as Vincent Furnier would "prowl the stage, contort his body, and [spit] newspaper directly onto incensed hippie onlookers" (Cagle 108). After recording two albums for Frank

Zappa's Straight Records—*Pretties for You* (1969) and *Easy Action* (1970)—the band had signed with Warner Bros. Initially released as a B-side in North America in June 1970, "Eighteen" benefited from generous Canadian radio-play to become a sizable US hit in early 1971 (no. 21). As its title made explicit, "Eighteen" self-consciously reached out to a different audience—to "betweeners" who were typically neither college-age rock fans nor teenyboppers, those the UK rock press would sneeringly dismiss as the "punk and pimply" (qtd. in Hepworth 252). "Eighteen," then, was a proto-glam anthem—"And I just don't know what I want . . . / I get confused every day," living in "the middle of doubt," but "I'm eighteen and I like it." Alice Cooper combined its antihippie rhetoric—most often characterized by a kind of late-teen nihilism—with an outrageous theatricality. According to critics Cooper and Gaines, the band's *Killer* tour offered fans "the first dramatized rock and roll show with a story concept" (qtd. in Cagle 124), its songs "accompanied by intensified theatrics and extreme special effects" (Cagle 125). The tour would help the *Killer* album go platinum and garner plenty of press coverage, including three *Rolling Stone* cover stories and pieces in *Time*, *Newsweek*, and *Playboy*.

As the first rock act to incorporate grandiose theatrical sets and to adopt a conceptual approach to all aspects of performance including characterization, Alice Cooper has a role to play in the genre's creation. In November 1971, David Bowie would take his newly formed band along to an Alice Cooper London show to try to persuade the reluctant Spiders from Mars to follow him and "glam up." Eighteen or so months earlier, he had told the music press that he was "determined to be an entertainer: clubs, cabaret, concerts, the lot" (qtd. in Doggett, *Man*, 78), and had begun to make strenuous efforts to put this commitment to entertainment into practice via a new musical project. Having run through alternatives like "Harry the Butcher" and "David Bowie's Imagination," he eventually fixed on the name Hype because—as he explained—"now no one can say they're being conned" (qtd. in Heylin, *Madmen*, 138–39). Producer and fellow band member Tony Visconti has claimed that Hype's debut on March 28, 1970—at the Roundhouse, the capitol's countercultural bastion—was "the very first night of glam rock." "We were derided a lot during [it]," he recalled, "but photographer Ray Stevenson showed me a photograph he took of Marc Bolan resting his head on his folded arms watching the entire performance"

("Hype," 65). Visconti has also identified Bowie's 1971 album *The Man Who Sold the World*—the bulk of which was recorded in those early months of 1970—as important to the birth of glam. There is, however, very little in *The Man Who Sold the World* to suggest that this is where glam on vinyl might begin. As Visconti himself acknowledged, "David's new songs were darker and much heavier" ("Hype," 65). So, in this, then, arguably more attuned to the rock dominant du jour. Featuring riffs reminiscent of Led Zeppelin or even Black Sabbath, a track like the eight-minutes-plus "Width of a Circle," with its lumpy tempo shifts, "movements," and humor-free portentous lyrics, is simply not as light on its feet as tracks found on *Ziggy Stardust*. While the record marked the inaugural extended workout for the musicians who would comprise the Spiders from Mars, the most "glam" thing about it could be found on the cover of its UK version, which featured Bowie reclining on a sofa, holding a queen of hearts playing card, wearing a dress. Nevertheless, "Width of a Circle" was on the set list for the Hype shows—along with the more apt "Prettiest Star" and, rather less appropriately, a cover of Van Morrison's "Cypress Avenue." Evidently, at this point, the music had yet to catch up with what must have been quite a startling look. Bowie described Hype as his first costume band, featuring as they did plenty of cartoonish role-playing and "glitter everywhere" (Bowie qtd. in Doggett, *Man*, 79). Tony Visconti, on the bass guitar, was "Hypeman" with a big "H" emblazoned on his long-sleeved white T-shirt. As "Rainbowman," a silver-blue-haired Bowie was dressed in a metallic, collarless shirt with tights and thigh-length boots. Drummer John Cambridge wore a cowboy hat, while lead guitarist Mick Ronson had borrowed a gold satin jacket from Bowie to become "Gangsterman." It was, recalled Roundhouse booking agent Jeff Dexter, "comic book rock 'n' roll in a nice way" (qtd. in Trynka 65). Not a bad first pass at defining glam.

Glam is not defined by a single musical style or sound. Pre–rock 'n' roll Hollywood glamour and flamboyance mixes with kitschy manufactured Brit-rock from the early 1960s; British beat groups, the baroque Beatles, and the freaky Stones mix with the scuzzy, boho garage rock of the Velvet Underground and the Stooges, while transatlantic bubblegum and Brit-pop novelties are also fair game. Being typically flighty and promiscuous, glam did not confine its referents to all points west either; also in the mix could be European torch songs and Weimar cabaret. Together, these demonstrate that "the very heart of glam was a desire to play with ideas of drama and decadence, sexuality and showmanship" (Turner, *Glam Rock*, 21), making it, therefore, a conscious reaction to the rock ideology forged in the second half of the 1960s—one borne of and speaking to the intragenerational discontent and frustration felt by the younger siblings of mainstream rock fans. Yet—as has been noted—although it can offer us some pretty big clues as to what became of the sixties, it was never representative of a wholesale break. Both in practice and sensibility, there were continuities that were clearly "made in the '60s." However, true pop music is proprietorial, drawing much of its power, impact, and appeal from the simple fact that it is "ours" and not "theirs"—whether "they" are your parents or your elder siblings. As Peter Doggett has pointed out, by the early 1970s many established artists were "using rock to explore the crises of privileged adulthood." This, he suggests, meant dealing with "preoccupations" that "were distant from those of the traditional rock 'n' roll audience: teenagers." These teenagers "wanted to believe in the majesty and transcendent power of rock 'n' roll, because it still raised them up, took them away from the tedium of the everyday, provided the rhythm of their daily lives and filled their minds with fantasies of rebellion and stardom." As Doggett correctly asserts, "Adolescents wanted heroes who were rebellious and carefree; only adults could afford to sympathise with the decadent and jaded" (Doggett, *Shock*, 422–23). *We* wanted the pop thrill of "Ballroom Blitz," then, not the sanctimonious "Almost Cut My Hair."

If all this makes glam sound rather frivolous and reactionary, then by conventional yardsticks perhaps it was. Yet it represented a different kind of politics made for a different time. Particularly in its emphasis on roles and transforming identities; in its challenges to the rock mainstream; and in its "shock value [and] confrontation with conformity through the use of flamboyant costumes and cosmetics that delighted teenage fans precisely because it annoyed an older generation" (Turner, *Glam Rock*, 12–13). It enacted a rock 'n' roll reboot, for sure; but it was also representative of the more fluid politics of the 1970s. Reviewing *the audience* at a Bowie show at New York's Carnegie Hall in September 1972, Roy Hollingworth captured something of this when he concluded:

I've never seen quite such a strange gathering of people who resembled Christmas trees on legs. There was much glitter, and several men dressed as ladies. As somebody quite rightly said, "The 60s are well and truly over." (Qtd. in Cagle 163)

Such tableaux vivant would, of course, be replicated not only at other Bowie shows, but also at Roxy Music gigs and at many other glam shows thereafter. Wedged between the supposedly more creative, liberating, and liberated 1960s and the conservative neoliberal reformation of the 1980s, the 1970s—particularly its first half—are routinely dismissed as a regressive era of cheesy style and political stagnation. A liminal vacuum of a "space between," best forgotten. Yet look and listen closely. These turbulent and tumultuous years generated dynamic and transformative cultural expression that is easily the equal of anything produced in those more storied times. Vibrant, conflictual, and quintessential, glam demonstrates the "unstable nature" of an era whose "very ambiguity" supplies "its generative and disruptive influences." If, for example, the '70s "constitute a laboratory for experimentation with self-creation," then clearly this music is very much on point (Waldrep 4, 2). So, "get" glam and you go a long way toward "getting" the seventies.

At a more local level, this drive to self-invent can help explain glam's "big bang." Through 1970, David Bowie had demonstrated that the genre was in a developmental stage—principally with those Hype shows, but also via "mission statements" that would emerge during interviews. On the evidence of *The Man Who Sold the World*, though, his sound had not yet caught up with his vision. Inventions are, of course, often the product of several pioneers working independently of each other at the same time. It would then be another veteran of the British '60s popular music scene, Marc Bolan, who would win the race to bring glam into the world. "What I've been trying to do," Bolan explained, "is recapture the feeling, the energy, behind old rock music without actually doing it the same technically" (qtd. in Doggett, *Shock*, 428). Fittingly for what was T. Rex's breakout single, "Ride a White Swan" offered a perfect demonstration of glam's Janus-faced, irresistible blending of rock and pop, old and new, counterculture and mainstream. In this, it therefore represented an obvious contrast to the 45 that would ultimately keep it off the top spot. While it might not have sold as many copies as Dave Edmunds's straightforwardly retro-revivalist, reverential, and "archaeological" version of "I Hear You Knockin',"

"Ride a White Swan" possessed something that its unidirectional rival clearly did not have. In the words of T. Rex's publicist B. P. Fallon, "There was too much gray. What was needed," he proclaimed with a characteristic mix of hucksterism and perceptiveness,

> was something flash and loud and vulgar, and, to some people, annoying. Marc [Bolan] was very shiny. He brought that in, and it actually opened the door for Bowie. Suddenly men were checking their eye make-up. And the music was much more forthright and jumping, much more below the belt. (Qtd. in Hoskyns 5–6)

Recorded on July 1, 1970, "Ride a White Swan" was simple, repetitive stuff. Just three chords courtesy of Chuck and Eddie, a blink-and-you-miss-it lead solo, handclaps on the offbeat, a barely walking bass line, low-key Tony Visconti–arranged strings, and a dozen or so lines of hardly deep (albeit evidently counterculture-soaked) lyric. At a shade over two minutes, it was a bold, Technicolor statement in pop economy, advocating the guiltless pursuit of pleasure via lines full of "spells" and "stars" that were at once both absurd and joyous—instructing listeners to "wear [their] hair long," to "wear a tall hat like a druid in the old days" and "a tattooed gown," and, perhaps most oddly of all, to "take a black cat and put in on [their] shoulder." Released in October, "Ride a White Swan" would eventually peak at number two on the UK singles chart at Christmastime. Glam was up and running.

2

"GET IT ON"

T. Rex would build an all-conquering eighteen months on the success of "Ride a White Swan." During this time, as Slade would prove, glam was not just about one act. However, 1971 was undeniably Bolan's year; and it is for this reason that he and his band are at the very heart of a chapter exploring glam's first full calendar year. As subsequent chapters will demonstrate, though, while a single act could be said to headline each of the glam years to come—so, David Bowie in 1972 or Roxy Music in 1973—there will of course be other acts orbiting around them. The year 1971, for example, witnessed the release of two Bowie albums (*The Man Who Sold the World* and *Hunky Dory*), the first number one single from Slade ("Coz I Luv You"), and the morphing of Sweet from bubblegum act into a bona fide glam outfit. All told, glam singles would be the UK's best-sellers for an impressive fourteen weeks; and although often disregarded (and dismissed) as a genre ill suited to the longer format, T. Rex's *Electric Warrior* would spend a month and a half at number one and go on to be the year's biggest-selling album in the UK. George Harrison's "My Sweet Lord" might have sold more copies, but its five weeks at number one represented one fewer than T. Rex's "Hot Love," which would enjoy the year's longest residency at the top of the chart and so contribute to the band's unrivaled status as the UK's biggest-selling singles act of 1971.

So the metrics are impressive; but they are only statistical markers pointing to Bolan's deeper cultural significance—a significance that did not go unnoticed by a few shrewd contemporaries. "The most important person in Europe and England today," David Bowie told *Creem* magazine, "is Marc Bolan, not because of what he says but because he is the first person who has latched on to the energy of the young once again" (qtd. in Heylin, *Madmen*, 166). Serving up an appreciation of his friend and rival's achievements with just the merest hint of jealousy, Bowie—as is perhaps to be expected—clearly understood what lay at the heart of Bolan's appeal. And if this is not all about the music, then what of it? Even some of Marc Bolan's most loyal supporters—then and now—have described him as an opportunist, a "musical chancer" (Doggett, *Shock*, 429). Such judgments, though, usually result from the application of criteria that derive from a rock orthodoxy that can only value artists deemed to be "authentic" and "true." Glam, as we know, would choose not to play by such rules. As Jeff Dexter said of Bolan, he "never talked about being a musician. He wanted to be a star"—possessing a proto-glam (self-)consciousness that was evident as early as October 1965, when the then-unknown singer told the *London Evening Standard's* Maureen Cleave that "the prospect of being immortal doesn't excite me, but the prospect of being a materialistic idol for four years does appeal" (qtd. in Paytress, *Bolan*, 31, 50).

Bolan was nothing if not consistently open in his commitment to stardom. Honestly insincere, one might say. Indeed, in his earliest encounter with the British media three years earlier—which indicatively had absolutely nothing to do with music-making but much to do with being a dandy—the then-fourteen-year-old Mark Feld had told *Town* magazine:

> I've got 10 suits, eight sports jackets, 15 pairs of slacks, 30 to 35 good shirts, about 20 jumpers, three leather jackets, two suede jackets, five or six pairs of shoes and 30 exceptionally good ties. (Qtd. in Paytress, *Bolan*, 17)

In the same feature, young Mark was asked for his opinion on politics and, specifically, on demonstrations. Coming across very much like a glamster-in-the-making—and, not coincidentally, expressing near-identical views to those rock imperialist Mick Jagger would offer up in the wake of rioting in central London in the spring of '68—Feld/Bolan noted that it was "all exhibitionist," and therefore that he was "all for that" (qtd. in Paytress, *Bolan*, 24). For the mod—for the subculture with which he was then affiliated—clothes and style *were* politics. As

Paytress explains, "It was consumption, and shameless consumption at that, but in pampering an essentially ungratified self it provided a perfect boost to troubled egos," since "staying sharp was, on one level, a symbolic refusal of their class position, the drive to become an ace face simply old-fashioned upward mobility in (literally) new clothing." Furthermore, one could arguably map the distinctive gender/sexual "politics" of mod onto those of glam, particularly so since

> the world of the urban modernist, individualist and hipster had much in common with elements within the gay community. Defying conventions through the wardrobe; the willingness to use cosmetics to enhance the sense of disguise; the emphasis on consumption; and the abnormal amount of attention devoted to self-image. All, in the eyes of the mainstream, were regarded as "feminine" pursuits. (Paytress, *Bolan*, 18, 25, 43)

As an arch-mod in the early '60s, then, fashion was far more important than music to whom the young Mark Feld believed he was. However, by the middle of the decade, it was evident that a pop world now radically transformed by the likes of the Beatles and Bob Dylan could provide similarly genuine opportunities for youthful self-expression. In the late summer of 1965, perhaps directly inspired by Dylan's very public metamorphosis from folksinger to rock star, Mark Feld became Marc Bolan. There has been much debate as to the derivation of this new name. Did it, for example, come from his friendship with the British actor James Bolam? Or from his record company's suggestion of "Bowland"? Or even from a voguish French fashion designer called Marc Bohan? It might, of course, have simply been plucked out of thin air. However, given both his formative mod history and recent musical discovery, the theory that it emerged from a fusion of Euro-glamour ("Marc") with his new idol—"Bo(b Dy)lan"—seems highly plausible. Whatever the truth about its provenance, the record shows that in August 1965, Marc Bolan was offered a one-single deal with Decca Records. "The Wizard" was released in November. With an arrangement by future Gary Glitter producer Mike Leander, the track—at barely one minute, forty-five seconds—was a blink-and-you-miss-it piece of folk-pop whimsy. While Bolan approximated Dylan's characteristically nasal vocal delivery, the song possessed none of the latter's bite or wit. Publicity shots at the time showed him in full beatnik garb—

all stevedore jackets and black polo-neck sweaters—but, if anything, the lyrics of "The Wizard" suggested a different affiliation. "Walking in the woods one day," he "met a man who was magic" with a "pointed hat on his head," who "turned and melted in the sky." Apparently without the aid of powerful lysergics, Bolan had managed to preempt the lyrical concerns of the UK underground. Indeed, some have even viewed "The Wizard" as the movement's first vinyl outing.

Possibly because it was so ahead of its time, "The Wizard" failed to chart. However, Bolan was not deterred by its lack of commercial success—so utterly convinced as he was that he would be a star—and a track like "Observations" (1966) would seem to have represented a much stronger vehicle to realize his dream. Hindsight is a wonderful thing, of course, but one never has to look and listen too hard to catch the glamness in Bolan's pre-glam output. There are all manner of continuities that—if nothing else—counter those accusations that Bolan was a "sellout," a chancer, an opportunist. Closer now to the wordy Dylan of "Subterranean Homesick Blues" (1965), "Observations" is a straightforward talking blues featuring just an acoustic guitar and solo voice. Yet, it is its lyric—more than the simplicity of its musical frame—that is of major interest here, and particularly in its anticipation of the Technicolor palette of T. Rex in its glam pomp. With its references to "boppin'" and shoppin'," "jivin'" and "groovin'," this hip picaresque "Day in the Life" name-dropped with lively intertextual abandon—whether it be places (Brighton and Maida Vale), celebrities (Barbra Streisand), or rock 'n' roll songs ("See Ya Later, Alligator"). At one point, Bolan even orders us to "throw away [our] zip gun." Eight years later, T. Rex would release a single, "Zip Gun Boogie" (1974), from an album called *Bolan's Zip Gun* (1975). The exhortation of "Observations" to "make like a rocker" also helps explain how and why Bolan could briefly serve as a guitarist in the psych-rock group John's Children. Released as a single in 1967, the Bolan-penned "Desdemona" did not chart, but did gain a certain rock 'n' roll cachet when the BBC banned it for the line "lift up your skirt and fly."

Nevertheless, while all this suggests that Bolan's journey to pop glory might well have been undertaken in full view, it is perhaps the case that it becomes less easy to spot the glam way-markers the closer one gets to home. For, after his flirtation with garage rock, Bolan settles into life in an acoustic duo, alongside percussionist Steve Peregrin Took. Between

1967 and 1970, as Tyrannosaurus Rex, the duo would not sell many records, but their four albums would see them become "darlings of Britain's hippie underground" (Stanley 328). Enthusiastically championed by the Radio One DJ John Peel, who would play their records and often insist that they be booked as support for his own gigs, Tyrannosaurus Rex achieved cult status. Marc Bolan might well have been a "limited musician" who "only knew seven chords," but as Tony Visconti notes, "he was mesmerising and his audience was fiercely loyal" (qtd. in Chapman, "Waiting," 49). It was Visconti who, in July 1968, produced the duo's first LP, *My People Were Fair and Had Sky in Their Hair . . . but Now They're Content to Wear Stars on Their Brows*. Recorded in just four days, the album seemed to capture the very psych-folk essence of Tyrannosaurus Rex on tracks like the six-minute closer "Frowning Atahuallpa (My Inca Love)," which featured John Peel reading a Bolan-penned children's story and plenty of Hare Krishna chanting. Yet, the LP opened with the decidedly unchilled "Hot Rod Mama," a basic blues rocker recounting a familiar blues story of ill treatment at the hands of a woman that made reference to "mustangs," "motorcycles," and "steel chrome." Elsewhere on the record, "Chateau in Virginia Waters" was arguably more on message in its gentle parochialism and pastoralism; but then "Mustang Ford" returned to an apparently life-long fascination with "carburetors" and "alligator leather" that would have made Chuck Berry proud. Add bass, drums, and electric guitar, and clearly neither this track nor "Hot Rod Mama" would have been out of place on *Electric Warrior* (1971) or *The Slider* (1972).

October 1968 saw the release of *Prophets, Seers and Sages: The Angels of the Ages*. It took just eighteen days to record. Unlike the previous LP, which had managed to scrape into the UK Top 20, this one failed to chart. Even the underground scene appeared to be (in) a different place in late 1968. So, if Bolan was such an opportunist, so desperate to be a star at all costs, one might ask why he persevered with this style of music. On *Prophets, Seers and Sages*, Peregrin Took played bongos, African drums, kazoos, and a Chinese gong on songs such as "Salamanda Palaganda," "Trelawny Lawn," "Aznageel the Mage," and "Juniper Suction"! Commercial fortunes improved, however, with the May 1969 release of the noticeably less lo-fi—although by no means less "away with the fairies"—*Unicorn* (UK no. 12). "Cat Black (The Wizard's Hat)" featured a piano, double-tracked vocals, and some emphatic drumming; while the droney groove of "She Was Born to Be My Unicorn" offered yet more evidence of the proto-glam in Bolan's late '60s material. These roots were also on show on the positively fuzz-drenched, anthemic single "King of the Rumbling Spires" (UK no. 44, summer 1969)—which featured Bolan on electric guitar for the very first time and Peregrin Took hammering out an Adam and the Ants–style tribal stomp on a full drum kit.

March 1970's *A Beard of Stars* was the first Tyrannosaurus Rex LP to make extensive, albeit often rudimentary use of the electric guitar (e.g., "Woodland Bop," "Lofty Skies," "Pavilions of Sun"); and so, while many consider it to be Bolan's last long-form underground offering, there is still plenty here to suggest that a fuller musical reboot was already under way and possibly imminent. At one minute thirty-nine seconds, "Woodland Bop" might have been the shortest of the fourteen tracks on the album; but they were all—with the exception of "Elemental Child"—very brief indeed and, in this respect, indicative of a pop sensibility at work. As David Hepworth points out, even as an acoustic duo Tyrannosaurus Rex "always had hooks." In his view, though, what was noteworthy was that from 1970 onward, Bolan "places these hooks in the shop window" (185). While plugging in helped achieve this, though, this crucial shift in musical practice was nowhere near as abrupt as Hepworth suggests. Still, there could be no denying that 1970 witnessed a number of highly significant "moments" that quickened the pace of change. In September, explaining what looked like a hurried change of label, Bolan declared:

> People associated us with Flower Power, and that was a long-gone era. I wanted people to look at the thing in a new light, and the only way to do that was to have a label change. *Change the music and change the name but not lose any identity.* (Qtd. in Paytress, *Bolan*, 165, my italics)

Such statements make it hard to disagree with the widely held view that the final months of 1970 "marked a brutal, crucial break with the past" (Paytress, *Bolan*, 165): with "Ride a White Swan" set for release (and presumably constituting that musical "change" Bolan refers to); with the band name now shortened to T. Rex; and with Steve Peregrin Took now permanently ousted by the supposedly more photogenic Mickey Finn. Yet, if December's *T. Rex* LP did mark a giant leap toward fully fledged glam, it could not be said to signal that "brutal, crucial break" identified by Mark Paytress and many others. For glam was already in the bloodstream, and those underground ties continued to bind. "Children of Rarn" kicks off the album with a message for the "heads" and the hip, reaching out to "seekers of space" with its reference to "our master's face that is young and gold and silvery old"; "Diamond Meadows" is delicate, orchestral stuff; "Root of Star" sees the narrator addressing "thee" and singing about a "shield of bronze"; "The Visit" features archetypal acoustic strumming; while "The Time of Love Is Now" has minimal amplified input but plenty of bongos. So far, so Tyrannosaurus Rex. Perhaps this is how and why, despite undeniable changes in other respects, Bolan could claim that the band would not "lose any identity"? Elsewhere, though, the new T. Rex is on show. "Childe," for example, captures the essence of glam in a Bolan-franked two-line mission statement: "I want to give every child the chance to dance / I want to spread my feet in the silver heat." T. Rex is still a two-piece at this point, and so the music is not thickened out by a full rock lineup, but "Childe" still manages to showcase a number of Bolan's glam signatures—that minimal, crunchy lead guitar with its economical solo, those wailing banshee BVs (backing vocals), and handclaps. "One Inch Rock" had appeared as a single in 1968 and was now reworked into a chugging boogie. "Is It Love?" features a classic "1-2-3-4" count-in, the repeated line "We're gonna rock," and combines some fuzzy electric guitar with an effective but brief solo. Like "One Inch Rock," it is barely more than a jam. Most glam of all, though, chiefly courtesy of what would subsequently become a very familiar string arrangement, was "Beltane Walk"—a genuinely catchy two-and-a-half-minute strut that builds to a fuzzy crescendo.

In the view of onetime Pink Floyd manager Patrick Jenner, Marc Bolan was a sellout and a fraud:

> [He] was a complete arsehole, the way he turned over Peel and everything else. Quite clearly he was just a very ambitious little kid who wanted to become a pop star. . . . He sussed that the way through for him was by being a little hippie. He used me and he used John Peel. (Qtd. in Paytress, *Bolan*, 191–92)

If this is true, then Bolan surely played a very long game indeed. He was, concluded John Peel, "just a quite ambitious lad with a small gift

and a lot of good reference points who enjoyed being mildly famous"
(qtd. in Hoskyns 16). Was this characteristically laconic but no less
withering assessment from a supposed friend the product of Peel's status as a classic rock ideologue? From the late 1960s, effectively operating as BBC Radio's in-house "freak," Peel had been given license to
play underground music—music that he lived and breathed but which
evidently Bolan now no longer did. Like Jenner, he too felt betrayed.
(Although, he did perhaps have more personal cause for grievance here,
as Bolan is said to have failed to return the DJ's calls when he became a
star.) For the believers, it seemed that Bolan was "mock[ing] the coun-
ter-culture's emphasis on the value of spontaneity, and"—much to their
disgust—in the process laying "the foundations for a new kind of rock
performance that courted overt theatricality" (Auslander 98). Yet, he
would never become totally disconnected from his underground past.
Indeed, full-blown glam works like *Electric Warrior* (1971) and *The
Slider* (1972) would continue to channel some of its colors and flavors.
Bolan did not feel it necessary to sever his ties with the UK underground because—much more so than the North American variant—it
was essentially optimistic and celebratory. Its politics were of the predominantly cultural kind, firmly fixed on the quest for personal freedom
rather than any desire to smash "the system." Furthermore, it was also
the case that the "velvets, lace and dandyism of the original London
underground had shifted [its] focus away from the disgraced statements
of political and social liberation towards sexual liberation" (Thompson
20). In 1967 homosexuality had been decriminalized, and this had been
followed by further relaxations in censorship. In this liberalizing context, one could argue that Bolan was one of the "first to take all these
elements—sexual ambiguity, sartorial sensuality, literary art and theatrical cinema—and blend them into a cohesive whole" (Thompson 22).

Of course, this was completely missed at the time. Instead the focus
was often on the band's perplexing, if not downright shocking, regres-
sion. For many, this represented, at best, a rather contrary move in
these days of rock virtuosity. "T. Rex are a strange band," wrote the
NME's Roy Carr:

> When electrified, they encompass the basic rudiments of rock. . . .
> They emit a naïve enthusiasm one would expect from a bunch of
> blokes who had just acquired their first instruments and were having

a good old blow down the local church hall or someone's front room.
(Qtd. in Paytress, *Bolan*, 186)

If this made T. Rex sound like a garage band, then Bolan was not in the least bit fazed. For him, it would be taken as a compliment. He did, after all, share in garage rock's then-unfashionable faith in the 45 rpm disc. "You can sell all the albums you like," he told a reporter in August 1971, "but until you get a hit single, you don't feel successful," adding for good measure that he "always wanted to be a rock 'n' roll star" (qtd. in Paytress, *Bolan*, 171). Hit singles would make this happen, but achieving such status also required a major rethink in other areas. Speaking to *Beat Instrumental*, Bolan declared that

> reaching a wider public is what we wanted. If "underground" means being on a show screened at midnight and watched by 15 people—then we're out of it. If we're asked to do *Top of the Pops* we do it, and if we're asked to do John Peel we do it. (Qtd. in Paytress, *Bolan*, 172)

This newfound commitment to "reaching a wider public"—by which he meant teenagers, of course—did not only extend to enthusiastically accepting all offers to appear on prime-time TV, or even in teen magazines for that matter. When the revamped T. Rex went out on tour in the fall of 1970, ticket prices were set at an affordable ten shillings (fifty pence). As Bolan himself pointed out to *Disc*, "The low admission at our shows has meant the younger kids can come—the teenybop heads" (qtd. in Paytress, *Bolan*, 167). Such statements suggest that there is (a frankly undeniable) icy cynicism at work here. Yet, they also illustrate the warm pop-intelligence that would lie behind so much of T. Rex and glam's phenomenal success—both in its evident respect for and genuine desire to speak to "the teenybop heads." It was, then, with a characteristic mix of sincerity and market consciousness that Bolan declared: "If there's going to be a revolution in pop, it must come from the young people, and if you ignore them you are cutting yourself off from the life supply of the rock music force" (qtd. in Hoskyns 17).

However, more ammunition would be needed if T. Rex was to lead this pop revolution. In mid-January 1971, the band went in to the studio to record the follow-up to "Ride a White Swan." David Hepworth deems "Hot Love" (UK no. 1) to be "a title which had previously seemed about as likely to be applied to a Tyrannosaurus Rex song as to a Virginia Woolf novel" (186). This is an amusing line from a fine writer; but perhaps his rock classicism had led him to overlook 1960s tracks like "Hot Rod Mama," "Beltane Walk," and "Is It Love?" Nevertheless, as a piece of dessert-only pop replete with both moments of direct address and opportunities for expression and release, "Hot Love" would make the kind of definitive musical statement that could be—and in fact was—taken as proof of a clean break with the past. Yet, in their more graphic illustrations of some of what went into the creation of the A-side, the two tracks on the B-side are worth some brief consideration here. So, the Cochranesque, 12-bar workout "Woodland Rock"—with its exhortation to "Let it all hang out / Everybody shout 'Do the rock'"—was either derivative and regressive or a bold homage, depending on your position on such matters. Although its deployment of backward guitar and cello did elevate the track above mere (if enjoyable) revival-ism. Similarly, reminiscent then of those psych-folk acoustic days, "King of the Mountain Cometh" can best be described as the kind of trippy fare that seemed to (semi-)consciously nod toward "the Heads"—fea-turing, as it did, elves and a "changeling son from Mars [who] played a Fender guitar." "Hot Love" would take something from each of these. "I know it's exactly like a million other songs," Bolan confessed, "but I hope it's got a little touch of me in it too. It was done as a happy record" (qtd. in Paytress, *Bolan*, 174). Based on a 12-bar blue(s)print, it made full use of sixteen-track recording to enhance elements found on previ-ous tracks like "Beltane Walk" and "Ride a White Swan"—such as the use of distinctive backing vocals, strings, and on-the-beat handclaps—to deliver a massive dose of "happy." "Hot Love" was Bolan's "She Loves You." No subsequent T. Rex single would so effectively bottle joy. Its embrace was warm and total. It was inclusive and connective. "I don't need to be bold, but may I hold your hand?" By no stretch of the imagination is it lyrically deep—"most" is rhymed with "coast," "gold" with "bold" and "old." But then neither was "She Loves You" nor "I Want to Hold Your Hand." However, like them, "Hot Love" invites the listener to join the party, and it does so well before the halfway mark. The "la-las" comprise nearly three minutes of this five-minute song. Plenty of time, then, to work its hypnotic magic. (One suspects that David Bowie took note. "Starman" would, of course, make effective use of the lengthy sing-along fade-out a year later.)

As the new single demonstrated, Bolan was aware that teenage participation was key to any success the now acutely pop-conscious T. Rex might have. As we know, the band was open to invitations to bring its new material to a prime-time audience. A new sound required a new look, and the T. Rex "deal" was well and truly sealed by a momentous appearance on *Top of the Pops* on March 24, 1971. On this evening, with (in hindsight quite modest) dabs of glitter under his eyes and dressed in a silver lamé top, Bolan presented a vision of androgyny that had never been seen before on British TV and so marked the moment when glam began. Emboldened by the success of "Hot Love," subsequent performances would see him wearing ostrich boas, satin pants, and embroidered jackets—clothes sourced from her favorite London boutiques by his manager's wife, Chelita Secunda, who had also dabbed his cheeks with glitter for that very first TV performance. Secunda can take some credit, then, for giving Bolan a makeover, her restyling working in tandem with the fact that by this time most British homes had color TV to maximize glam's impact. "Hot Love" would spend six weeks at the top of the UK singles chart. By May, the British media—and not just the music press—were talking about a new phenomenon, "Trexstasy."

That spring, with now-characteristic immodesty, Marc Bolan announced that he had "suddenly tuned into that mental channel which makes a record a hit and [that he felt] at present as though [he] could go on writing number ones forever." "The secret ingredient," he then went on to perhaps rather injudiciously identify, was "energy" (qtd. in Stanley 329). However, for the time being at least, any writing of hits—no matter how easy it came—would have to be undertaken while touring. Unsurprisingly, much younger, female-dominated audiences would be in attendance at T. Rex's spring and summer UK gigs. On live recordings of the tour, Radio One DJ Bob Harris can barely be heard above teen screaming reminiscent of Beatlemania. Tellingly, on the set list are "One-Inch Rock" and "Beltane Walk"—both included presumably because they represent good fits for the glam-pop star and his glam-pop audience. Together with new tracks like "Hot Love," these were songs that now "sound-tracked the youth club dances of the kids who were born in 1958 every bit as well as 'Satisfaction' had done for the people who'd been born in 1950" (Hepworth 190). One year later, and this would also be true for Gary Glitter's breakthrough single "Rock 'n' Roll,

Part One." It had initially failed to make the UK chart, but then had become a hit when its near-instrumental B-side was played in dance halls, discos, and even fairgrounds up and down the country.

The songs that were eventually gathered together on *Electric Warrior* were recorded while T. Rex was on tour in the States. The album was a kind of glam field recording, with producer Tony Visconti working with the band in the limited studio time carved out between live dates. "Monolith" was recorded in New York, "Get It On" in Los Angeles. Wherever the work was done, it was done quickly. According to Visconti, "What I did in America when we cut the album was not rehearse the band, just go in and make everything live and play. . . . We recorded [it] like the early Sun records" (qtd. in Paytress, *Bolan*, 177). Typically, then, songs would move very swiftly from Bolan's initial solo demo to full band take. This is a band now well established as a four-piece unit, with Steve Currie on bass and Bill Legend on drums. At the heart of *Electric Warrior* sits "Get It On" (UK no. 1). Neither hard rock nor soft bubblegum pop, it is quintessential T. Rex, built on one of the century's most memorable riffs. Like much of the LP, it radiated a genuine affinity for rock 'n' roll. Here, this reverence is reinforced by Bolan's direct quoting of a line from Chuck Berry's "Little Queenie" in the song's fade-out—"And meanwhile, I'm still thinkin'"—which proves that Bolan clearly knew his classic rock 'n' roll. "There is very little that I don't know about rock 'n' roll on any level," he boasted to Charles Shaar Murray (qtd. in *Shots*, 31). He was both a fan and a scholar. After all, he was "Born to Boogie" (*Tanx*). For some reason, though, Bolan's rock 'n' roll references and reverence irritated the rock orthodoxy. This was particularly hypocritical, given that a musician like Chuck Berry, for example, was so evidently key to the music of the much-lionized Rolling Stones. How could the Stones get away with their "plagiarising, revivalist tendencies" (Paytress, *Bolan*, 184), when T. Rex could not? An appearance by the latter at the "Festival of Progressive Music" held over the August bank holiday weekend in the seaside town of Clacton would provide, if not necessarily a clear explanation for, then certainly a clear demonstration of this inconsistency. T. Rex was appearing on a bill featuring the likes of music press favorites Rory Gallagher, Lindisfarne, Colosseum, and the Faces, who had reportedly played a storming set immediately prior to Bolan and his band taking the stage. In his Chuck Berry T-shirt, Bolan was heckled so badly by a crowd of classic rock ideologues that he lost his cool—"Why don't you fuck off. . . . If you don't want to listen, then I'll leave" (qtd. in Paytress, *Bolan*, 185).

All pop music is a "synthesis," noted Charles Shaar Murray in an uncharacteristically sympathetic piece written on T. Rex when the band was at its peak:

> In Bolan's head, Tolkien and Berry are collaborating on songs. . . . Does it work? Make up your own mind. It's worked in that someone has revived the single as an art form. Any imbecile can furzle around for 17 minutes and come up with some good licks, but to lay it all down in 2:15 or 3:38 or whatever is a dying trade. . . . We're suffering from a surfeit of amazingly tedious long-players so anyone with a gift for producing listenable music in a concise form is very welcome. . . . T. Rex are the best singles band we've got. The art of making singles as opposed to albums is no more odious than that of the short-story writer as opposed to the novelist. (*Shots*, 26–27)

That said, Shaar Murray judged most of *Electric Warrior* to be subpar, describing "Lean Woman Blues" as "clumsy," dismissing "Planet Queen" as "indifferent," and somewhat grudgingly declaring "Rip Off" to be a "mess but entertaining" (*Shots*, 27). Even though he recognized T. Rex as masters of the single, presumably the band still had much to learn if it was to master the album. However, released on September 24, 1971, *Electric Warrior*—the genre's first extended statement— would demonstrate that glam was *not* just about the single. It was a "proper" LP, with a unity of purpose and effect that defied its on-the-fly production and which, appropriately enough for a long-form glam work, was reinforced by its packaging. The iconic front cover—from an original concept proposed by Bolan's wife, June, then realized by photographer Kieron Murphy and Hipgnosis's Aubrey Powell—featured a guitar-wielding Bolan in heroic silhouette, encircled by a full-body halo that also surrounds his similarly impressive amp and which presumably emanated from within this godlike being. The cover of *My People Were Fair and Had Sky in Their Hair* had featured a fantastical scene illustrated by George Underwood that clearly chimed with the mythic address of songs like "Graceful Fat Sheba" and "Knight." *Prophets, Seers and Sages* had featured a photograph of a becaped Peregrin Took and a (perhaps surprisingly) less theatrically attired Bolan staring rather shyly into the camera. Doing away with any sartorial flamboyance—Bolan, for example, is dressed in a simple yellow vest—the next Tyrannosaurus Rex LP *Unicorn* had merely presented a modest portrait of the duo. For *A Beard of Stars*, Steve Peregrin Took had evidently been deemed surplus to requirements for cover duty. This time we just have a Pre-Raphaelite Bolan, striking a Romantic pose dressed in what would appear to be a sort of ruff. Perhaps tellingly, a photo of the new duo of Bolan and Mickey Finn takes up two-thirds of the cover of the transitional *T. Rex*. The remaining third is composed of a pillar of red with the band's now-shortened name in bold yellow-gold type in the top-right corner. In the photograph, the foregrounded Bolan does have an electric guitar, but he is not handling it with any conviction. Indeed, it is almost as if it is the first time he has picked one up. What a contrast, then, with the cover of *Electric Warrior*.

At the time of the album's release, in September 1971, Bolan told *Rolling Stone* —somewhat unnecessarily, one feels—that he did not "wanna be James Taylor" because he was "feeling a lot more aggressive in my outlook towards the world." A month earlier, he had explained to *Melody Maker*'s Chris Welch that "there was a quiet period, flowers and peaceful but I don't feel that way anymore. It's not a peaceful world. I want to boogie, but with good words as well" (qtd. in Paytress, *Bolan*, 187). Of all the tracks on *Electric Warrior*, perhaps only its closer "Rip Off" could be said to have channeled this mood swing. It is certainly more musically abrasive, even angular, than other up-tempo songs on the album. It even features some free jazz–style sax parps toward the end. Yet, if "Rip Off" is—as Mark Paytress has suggested—"vitriol-filled" and found Bolan "rag[ing] . . . against the iniquities of the music business" (*Bolan*, 189), there is arguably much for the listener to do here to draw this message out of what is a typically opaque, allusive lyric—"Rockin' in the nude feelin' such a dude / It's a rip off" or "Dancin' in the dark with the tramps in the park / It's a rip off." Even the line "If it's hers then it must be mine" is nonspecific.

Reflecting on T. Rex's phenomenal twelve months in a piece in *Creem*, Charles Shaar Murray concluded:

> All that happened was that Bolan added more and more technology, more and more instruments, more and more sounds and presentation, and when the necessary level of electrical energy had been built up, all hell broke loose. Rock and roll madness, verily. (reprinted in *Shots*, 14)

Of course, to really "Get It On," in addition to all this "electrical energy" and all that extensive overdubbing made possible via Trident Studio's sixteen-track "technology," there needed to be that essential ingredient of joy. And indeed, the record shows that Bolan would reign supreme for as long as this held true. Furthermore, *Electric Warrior* also possessed what Bob Stanley describes as a "strange magic"—a "magic" attributable to both its sometime "reliance on acoustic guitars and restraint" (as on "Cosmic Dancer" and "Life's a Gas," for example) and to the fact that it is one of the "most sexually charged albums ever released in Britain." So, it "audibly pants, yet also leans on cellos and the eerie banshee backing vocals of ex-Turtles Flo and Eddie for its power" (Stanley 329). The glam ballad "Life's a Gas" was fragile and reflective, while the similarly meditative, haunting "Cosmic Dancer," its arresting time-shifting lyric taking us from "womb" to "tomb," went even deeper into distinctly un-pop existential territory—asking, "Is it wrong to understand the fear that lies inside a man?" and "What's it like to be alone?" to a musical accompaniment featuring a plangent cello and an eerie effects-treated guitar solo. Although ostensibly more familiar to fans of "Hot Love," the up-tempo boogie "Jeepster"—which placed Finn's bongos very high in the mix—was still lyrically unconventional for teen pop. In this respect, much like "Get It On" with its reference to "the teeth of the Hydra," "Jeepster" seemed to speak of (and possibly to) Bolan's not-too-distant past. As producer Tony Visconti points out, "Even when we were making the pop albums and the Flower Children were no more [Marc] said we had to include some special effects like flanging and phasing for 'the Heads'" (qtd. in Chapman, "Waiting," 49). And if "special effects" were to be included for this demographic, why not lyrics too? "Jeepster" rather quaintly addressed a woman with "the universe reclining in [her] hair" as "pleasing to behold" and politely, chivalrously, enquired as to whether she might be called "Jaguar, if I may be so bold." Then, toward the end, things became rather more "adult" with the close-to-the-knuckle promise to "suck ya," as "Hot Love's" "two-penny prince" morphed into a predatory vampire. Even at the peak of Trexstasy, Bolan often appeared to make few, if any, concessions to his growing teen audience. His landmark show at the Empire Pool Wembley in March 1972 featured lengthy, noodling jams complete with cross-legged acoustic strumming and extended workouts of the hits—"Get It On," for example, ran to fully eleven minutes. At

Stoke-on-Trent, on the band's summer '71 UK tour, a faithful low-amp version the very first Tyrannosaurus Rex single "Debora" (1968) was followed by a lengthy Bolan monologue stressing how little T. Rex had changed. All that had happened was that "we've just grown a little."

Such apparent defensiveness was understandable. Even generally positive reviews for *Electric Warrior* had tended to come across as condescending if not downright grudging. "He has developed the knack for writing good, original pop," wrote *Melody Maker*'s Chris Welch, "and with the aid of producer Toni Visconti is developing an amazing studio sound with its roots in the Fifties" (qtd. in Paytress, *Bolan*, 197). Of course, one of the downsides of having a signature sound, no matter how exciting and engaging, was that almost inevitably it opened Bolan to charges that all T. Rex tracks were essentially the same. The 12-bar blues "Lean Woman Blues" did, of course, bear an undeniable family resemblance to other tracks on the album, while even the ballad "Girl" sounded like "Cosmic Dancer," which sounded like "Life's a Gas." In hindsight, perhaps this helps explain T. Rex's finite shelf life. If the songs were interchangeable, then Bolan's prospects for longevity were not good, particularly as more inventive challengers would emerge and ultimately outgun him. Yet, while he may well have been, in Visconti's words, a "limited musician," *Electric Warrior* showcased an unusual, idiosyncratic way with the pop couplet. Album opener and—with its riff, strings, and BVs—quintessential T. Rex track "Mambo Sun" includes the lines "I got stars in my beard / And I feel real weird," while its near twin "Planet Queen" features Bolan exhorting a "flying saucer to take [him] away" and figures the Queen herself using his "head like a revolver." Sitting somewhere between those up-tempo rockers and the ballads, "Monolith" is arguably one of the strongest album tracks—with its stoner groove and proportionate, wah-wah-infused solo. Too often, though, non-singles can sound like fragments or studio jams with very little of interest. Some, like "The Motivator," for example, are barely songs at all. Perhaps all this is not surprising, given that Tony Visconti admitted that with *Electric Warrior* "what we were probably doing was amassing singles" (qtd. in Paytress, "Yeah," 83).

At the end of the year, there seemed very little for Marc Bolan and T. Rex to worry about. Far from it. The band's third single, "Jeepster," had peaked at number two, and so contributed to their unrivaled status as the top-selling singles act of 1971, while *Electric Warrior* had reached number one on the UK album chart just before Christmas, and would go on to enjoy an impressive two-month run as the nation's best-seller. Easy to believe, then, how T. Rex could account for an estimated 4 percent of all recorded music sold in Britain that year. Particularly when such impressive sales figures were backed by similarly Beatles-esque scenes around the country on the band's fall tour. A police escort was now required to get the band in and out of venues, with shows accompanied by piercing teen screams. No longer merely a "local" matter for the music press, the nationals took note and "Trextasy" was duly coined. T. Rex—it was claimed—could also be credited for the spike in ratings for *Top of the Pops*, increased sales of the pop-orientated week-lies, and even for the proliferation of magazines aimed at teenage girls in which Bolan became something of a fixture. *Jackie*, for example, was receiving around eight hundred letters each week by the end of 1971. As its editor Nina Myskow explains:

> We went to inordinate lengths to print three-page pin-ups of [Marc Bolan]. Little girls like non-threatening, not overtly sexual boys [and Bolan had] that boyish quality, that cute cheekiness . . . in spades. (Qtd. in Paytress, *Bolan*, 186–87)

Bolan's "androgynous beauty," then, "his peculiar outfits and manner-isms and that aspect of his narcissism that revealed itself as childlike vulnerability," constructed the near-perfect teen idol (Paytress, *Bolan*, 199).

Inevitably, where T. Rex led, others were sure to follow. However, as '71 drew to a close, the only credible (albeit at this point still distant) rival to Bolan and his band was Slade. With seventeen consecutive Top 20 hits including six number ones, Slade would eventually eclipse T. Rex and in the process become the decade's most successful singles act. None of this, though, seemed likely on New Year's Day 1971, when the band played a "homecoming" show at Wolverhampton Civic Hall, the first of what would be more than 150 gigs that year. Starting out as the 'N Betweens in 1966, Slade would still be playing venues like Dudley Zoo five years later. During this time, the band had experienced a number of false starts in the studio. In 1969, they had signed with Fontana Records on the condition that they change their name, and so, as Ambrose Slade, recorded a debut LP, *Beginnings*. Like the instru-mental single "Genesis," it flopped. However, it was at this point that

Chas Chandler, former bassist with the Animals and ex-manager of Jimi Hendrix, became the band's manager. Chandler encouraged them to write their own material and—presumably because it was then one of the UK's more high-profile youth movements—to embrace the skinhead look. By 1970 the name had also been trimmed to Slade. Two singles, though—"Shape of Things" and "Know Who You Are"—failed to chart, as did the LP *Play It Loud*; but then, acting on Chandler's suggestion, the band recorded a thoroughly road-tested cover of Little Richard's "Get Down and Get With It." Although a studio recording, the intention was to capture something of the excitement the band generated live. Five years of touring had been a slog, but the band had never lost its desire to entertain, typically climaxing its crowd-pleasing set of mostly covers with a rabble-rousing version of "Get Down and Get With It." According to lead vocalist Noddy Holder, "The stamping, clapping, [and] the vocal sound" on the record worked a treat. "The other day, I heard someone say it sounds like hooligan Spector. That's exactly what it was" (qtd. in Harris, "Whatever," 51). "Get Down and Get With It" made the UK Top 20 in the summer of 1971.

As with Bowie and T. Rex, Slade's success would be sealed by TV appearances made memorable by the visual impact of its two flamboyant front men—lead vocalist Noddy Holder and lead guitarist Dave Hill. Never remotely androgynous, the band did, however, appreciate the value of putting on a show. A commitment to generosity in and through performance, then, made the band undeniably glam. "It was all about major impact to me," Hill explained. "If I was on *Top of the Pops*, I was going to be more noticed than anybody else. I knew what I was doing" (qtd. in Harris, "Whatever," 52). True to his word, on the TV show to promote "Get Down and Get With It," Hill wore a woman's pink coat with diamond-studded dungarees; and subsequent appearances—and there would, of course, be many as Slade became glam's most prolific hit makers—saw the guitarist ramp up the sartorial outrageousness with costumes and looks that were typically debuted on *Top of the Pops* for maximum impact. Visuals were arguably as important to Slade as they would be to Bowie, just as the pop single was as important to the band as it was to Bolan.

With a hit single finally under their belt, Slade went into Command Studios in London to record a similarly "live-sounding" set of songs for the *Slade Alive!* album. On October 30, a new single "Coz I Luv You" was released. It would spend a full month as the nation's best-seller, and was the first of a spectacular run of twelve consecutive UK Top Five singles that would include five more number ones. Although self-composed, the song did bear a not-altogether-surprising family resemblance to the straightforward stomp of "Get Down and Get With It." However, classically trained multi-instrumentalist Jimmy Lea's snaky violin—in tandem with its minor key—would supply the track with distinctiveness. Originally titled "I Love You," according to Lea it sounded "too weedy" and so was misspelled to capture "the yobby thing we'd got into the records" (qtd. in Harris, "Whatever," 50). There could be something simultaneously cynical and naïve about such a strategy, of course, but it is also very glam in its desire to connect with its audience. So, while there is always a danger that it could be read as being rooted in a rather patronizing assumption about teen intelligence (or lack of), here, though, Slade is simply talking *to* rather than down to its audience. Those misspellings—"Coz I Luv You," "Take Me Bak 'Ome," "Gudbuy T'Jane," "Cum On Feel the Noize" and so on—reinforced a sense of ownership and identification generated by songs consciously crafted with participation in mind. This is why the relationship between Slade and its audience was frequently likened to the fierce and noisy tribalism that characterized British soccer in the 1970s.

Writing in the *Times* in early 1972, Richard Williams observed that "after a couple of years devoted to worthy but dull earnestness, rock 'n' roll's back where it belongs: in the streets, in the sweaty ballroom, the paperboy's whistle" (qtd. in Turner, *Glam Rock*, 54). Something for which the uberdemocratic glam could be held responsible. At the time, though, glam was essentially two—albeit very big—acts, T. Rex and Slade. However, others were emerging. In 1971, Sweet, for example, had taken significant steps toward glam and away from the sugary bubblegum pop the band had been peddling up to that point. Two years earlier, as Sweetshop, both "Lollipop Man" and "All You Ever Get from Me" had failed to chart. In 1970, now rebadged as Sweet but still obviously bubblegum, the band released a cover of the Archies' "Get on the Line." It too failed to chart. Sweet, though, made its TV debut in December 1970; and it is from this point on, appropriately enough, that fortunes improve. Significant singles chart success is finally achieved in the spring of 1971, when the Nicky-Chinn-and-Mike-Chapman-produced "Funny Funny" makes the UK Top 20. The follow-up, "Co Co," is even more successful, peaking at number two in the summer. In both cases, these are still recognizably bubblegum tracks, marked, for instance, by the absence of the band themselves in all but vocals. In contrast to T. Rex, Bowie, and even Slade, who would all journey from the world of rock with its countercultural associations, Sweet's provenance as a bubblegum act means of course that it will come at glam from an entirely different direction. Yet Sweet's (hi)story is as glam as T. Rex's. Indeed, taken together, the life cycle of these two acts can tell us much about where glam sits and fits, and about what makes it tick. Sweet's pre-glam history is as illustrative and instructive as Bolan's. It tells us, for example, that glam is inescapably rooted in "pop." If it were not, then Sweet would (and could) not have played such a major role in recalibrating it for those in their mid- to late teens to enjoy. In the mid-'70s, in an act of perhaps understandable overcompensation designed to wipe the band's pop past, Sweet would look to reinvent itself as a hard rock act. That "shameful" history, though, undoubtedly served the band well when it came to fashioning some of the purest-grade glam. However, we are getting ahead of ourselves. At the end of 1971, Sweet had a third single of the year in the chart. Stalling at a relatively lowly number thirty-three, "Alexander Graham Bell," a copy-homage to Slade's "Coz I Luv You," would seem to indicate that momentum had been lost.

Perhaps thinking of those three Sweet singles, Dave Haslam has described 1971 as a "good year for bad records" (50). This is neither accurate nor fair, even if we confine ourselves to the world of the pop single. Any year in which "Hot Love," "Get It On," "My Sweet Lord," "Double Barrel," "I'm Still Waiting," "Hey Girl, Don't Bother Me," "Maggie May," and "Coz I Luv You" can occupy the top spot for a combined total of thirty-three weeks cannot be all bad. There was novelty, of course. An uninterrupted ten weeks of it, for example, in the summer, as first Tony Orlando and Dawn with "Knock Three Times" and then middle of the road with "Chirpy Chirpy Cheep Cheep" made number one. The year had also been neatly bookended by actor Clive Dunn's "Grandad" and comedian Benny Hill's "Ernie." Of all these, Haslam seems particularly disappointed at the success of the "tame" "Grandad," which he finds "absurd" at a time "up to its throat in despair, violence and extremism" (50). Yet, there is surely no mystery here. It had been released for the Christmas market, Dunn was then a major star in a long-running and very popular TV sitcom called *Dads'*

Army, and, most important of all, the song's mawkish nostalgia played particularly strongly to a nation desperately in need of some midwinter cheer from all that "despair, violence and extremism."

For David Bowie, 1971 would turn out to be a tale of three LPs— *The Man Who Sold the World*, *Hunky Dory*, and *The Rise and Fall of Ziggy Stardust and the Spiders from Mars*. Although recorded in 1970, business disputes had delayed the release of *The Man Who Sold the World* until early '71. As noted earlier, this album represented a stuttering move to full-on glam. If the music was predominantly brooding, often rather leaden-footed hard rock, bordering on the proggy at times, then the visual message relayed by the record's UK cover provided a big clue as to the direction in which—whether he knew it himself at the time—he was headed, featuring as it did a reclining, dress-wearing Bowie holding a queen of hearts card.

Recorded in just two weeks in the summer of 1971, *Hunky Dory* is perhaps usefully understood as Bowie's *T. Rex* (where *Ziggy Stardust* might well be his *Electric Warrior*). In the US, *Billboard* carried an advertisement for the album that boasted of Bowie: "He has the genius to be to the 70s what Lennon, McCartney, Jagger and Dylan were to the 60s." Clearly, then, RCA believed that it had a rock "classicist" on its books; and, to be fair, there was plenty on the album to back this up, particularly in the strong, then-voguish singer-songwriter flavors of the first three tracks—"Changes," "Oh! You Pretty Things," and "Eight Line Poem." Yet, by the time of *Hunky Dory*'s winter release—in an echo of what had happened to him between it and *The Man Who Sold the World*—Bowie had already moved on to explore musical territory that would this time indicate much less continuity with those illustrious '60s forebears. This was a direction signposted most clearly by tracks like "Andy Warhol" and "Queen Bitch"; but, in their focus on identity, the piano-led "Changes" and "Oh! You Pretty Things" both addressed thematic concerns that would come to be closely associated with glam.

The garagey, raunchy, yet campy "Queen Bitch" featured Bowie as the song's narrator, possibly attacking his old friend and rival, the now highly successful Marc Bolan. As Bowie himself would later admit, "We fell out for about six months" (qtd. in Doggett, *Man*, 119). So, the song might have taken the form of a kind of bitchy character assassination. Indeed, Peter Doggett has suggested that Bolanesque flourishes abound here—such as the use of a quirky descriptor for a hat ("bippetyboppety"), for instance—and the track signs off with a decidedly green narrator-Bowie letting us know that he "could do better than that." Throughout, "Queen Bitch" also has a rather simple, propulsive arrangement that is very reminiscent of T. Rex.

While it might well have been, in large measure, a "votive offering to the RCA A and R department to prove he could write a tune, and craft a radio-friendly album" (Heylin, *Madmen*, 172), Bowie had already written *and* recorded the bulk of his next album by the time of *Hunky Dory*'s release in December 1971. Indeed, he had been talking up a Ziggy-style project as far back as February—telling *Rolling Stone* of his intention to create a stage caricature of the rock star and explaining that his "performances" had "to be theatrical experiences for [him] as well as for the audience" (qtd. in Heylin, *Madmen*, 202). Bowie had made these comments during his first, eye-opening if not life-changing, trip to the United States—an experience that would push him further toward his own glam makeover. "I think I've been in prison for the last 24 years," he said. "I think coming to America has opened one door."

> I didn't believe it till I came here, got off the plane from England, America merely symbolises something, it doesn't actually exist. And when you get off the plane and find there actually is a country called America, it becomes very important then. (Qtd. in Doggett, *Man*, 103)

The scenes and characters he encountered undoubtedly lit a creative fuse. New songs flowed. On this trip, he saw both the Velvet Underground and the Stooges play live, while the former's *Loaded* album, featuring tracks like "Sweet Jane" and "Rock and Roll," supplied an appropriate soundtrack. Keen to claim it for America, Cagle views glam's commitment to the "notion that fame could result from the self-creation of a particular style and persona (posing)" as distinctly Warholian (99). For Bowie at least, there can be no denying that this was a factor. However, even in his case, there is a danger that Warhol's influence can be overplayed. As for other glam acts, there is no evidence to suggest that Marc Bolan, for example, consciously drew on this "distinctly Warholian" concept of fame. There were—as we have seen—a host of ingredients in the mix, many of them sourced from much closer to home. For Cagle, though, Bowie was simply "a rock and roll Warhol," taking "most of his aesthetic and philosophical cues" from the artist, "particularly as the self-invented, media manipulating Ziggy Stardust" (13, 11). It is Cagle's contention, then, that Andy Warhol, the Factory, and the Velvet Underground effectively birthed glam, in supplying its "primary themes of flamboyance, style and image construction, poly-morphous sexuality and multi-media montage" (96). With Bowie, of course, the music often appeared to lend weight to this argument. Listening to "Queen Bitch" or "Suffragette City" or his cover of "White Light White Heat," we can understand how and why he agreed with Charles Shaar Murray's suggestion that "[Lou] Reed was to you as Chuck Berry was to the Stones" (qtd. in *History 1972*, 86). Yet, even in 1971 and 1972, it was evident that Bowie's reference points and re-sources were being drawn from a much deeper well—from the wider world of rock and pop, certainly, but just as likely to come from "out-side" even that world, from mainstream entertainment or from stage and screen.

Still, through 1971, there were undoubtedly plenty of direct engage-ments with that Warholian milieu. In September, Bowie was back in the USA, meeting Lou Reed, Iggy Pop, and even Andy Warhol for the first time. On this trip, he also signed a three-album deal with RCA. This gave Bowie what seemed to be a rather modest $37,500 advance per LP. However, the terms of the contract included the record compa-ny's agreement to underwrite both the cost of all PR campaigns and, crucially, of the stage shows too. This would provide important financial backing in areas that would be key for Bowie—and for glam—in the years to come. At the end of the month, he was back home and playing to just 250 people at Aylesbury Friars, performing a set that included "Queen Bitch" and "Andy Warhol" from the as-yet-unreleased *Hunky Dory*. Yet within a matter of weeks and before that LP came out, Bowie's attention would turn to recording a new batch of songs. The bulk of *Ziggy Stardust* was, in fact, recorded over the course of a single week in November 1971. Of the nine tracks recorded at this time, six—of the eventual total of eight that would appear on the final album—would tell the Ziggy story. Although, at this early stage in the project, "Lady Stardust" was penciled in to bring the Ziggy story arc—and hence the album—to a close. By mid-December, then, a provisional track listing had emerged that had the record opening with "Five Years," then "Soul Love," and then "Moonage Daydream." Three songs from these late '71 sessions—two cover versions and an original—would not, however, make the final cut. Several of the songs that would feature on the *Ziggy Stardust* LP had, in fact, even predated the July *Hunky Dory* sessions. Versions of "Hang On to Yourself" and "Moonage Daydream" had been recorded at the beginning of the year, "Lady Stardust" and "Ziggy Stardust" in March, and "Star" in May. According to Clinton Heylin, these tracks were shelved at the time because they communicated "quite a different message, and targeted a wholly different audience" (*Madmen*, 172). In the summer of 1971, as disappointing sales of *The Man Who Sold the World* had demonstrated, Bowie did not really have an audience at all. What he did now have, however, was a concept, a product; and if he felt he could not personally deliver the perfect rock 'n' roll star package, then perhaps someone else could front it for him. Songs like "Hang On to Yourself" and "Moonage Daydream" would be vehicles for an imaginary star. This would allow Bowie to "test out the potency of his dream, without risking" what "reputation" he might still have (Doggett, *Man*, 111). With this mind, a nineteen-year-old fashion designer, Freddie Burretti, was handpicked as lead singer for a "ghost" band Bowie called Arnold Corns. Unfortunately, Burretti, though nice to look at, could not sing. A single flopped, and the project was dead in the water. Bowie would have to do it himself.

In January 1972, Bowie told *Disc*: "It's the youth that are feeling the boredom most; they are crying out for leadership to such an extent that they will even resort to following the words of some guitar hero." *Ziggy Stardust* would be tauter and tighter. Teen focused and teen friendly. Guitar driven, where *Hunky Dory* had been piano led and largely orthodox in its "grown-up" rock stylings. A song like "Hang On to Yourself" possesses an almost punky swagger that would not have been out of place down in CBGB four or five years later. With its lyrical steal from the Velvet Underground's "Sweet Jane," Cochranesque chords and "c'mons," it was immediate and accessible without talking down to its younger demographic. Glam.

3

"HANG ON TO YOURSELF"

In 1972, T. Rex would continue to rule the land, but it would be David Bowie who would take glam to another level. Although under attack from Slade and glam newcomers like Sweet, Roxy Music, Mott the Hoople, and of course Bowie himself, the T. Rex *palmares* for '72 was in fact nearly identical to that of the previous year. As was the case in 1971, there are two number one singles ("Telegram Sam" and "Metal Guru") and two 45s that peak at number two ("Children of the Revolution" and "Solid Gold, Easy Action"); and, while *The Slider* would not perform as well as its predecessor in the UK—where it could only reach number four on the album chart—sales in the US would comfortably outstrip those for *Electric Warrior*.

Yet, the year's first significant glam moment concerned neither its reigning monarch nor did it play out musically, on vinyl or live. David Bowie would lay the groundwork for his rise to glam superstar status in a January 22, 1972, interview that featured in the pages of the British music weekly *Melody Maker*. Appropriately enough, though, this was still very much a "performance." True to glam, it might seem that what Bowie wore for this interview was almost as important as what he said in it. Introduced to readers as "rock's swishiest outrage," Bowie is described by Michael Watts as "looking yummy":

> He'd slipped into an elegant patterned type of combat suit, very tight around the legs, with the shirt unbuttoned to reveal a full expanse of white torso. The trousers were turned up at the calves to allow a better glimpse of a huge pair of red plastic boots with at least three-

inch rubber soles; and the hair was Vidal Sassooned into such impeccable shape that one held one's breath in case the slight breeze from the window dared to ripple it. I wish you could have been there to vada him; he was so super. (Qtd. in *History 1972*, 13)

This description of how he looks is then followed by a consideration of what it might all mean that pulls few punches:

[His] present image is to come on like a swishy queen, a gorgeously effeminate boy. He's as camp as a row of tents, with his limp hand and trolling vocabulary. "I'm gay," he says, "and always have been, even when I was David Jones." But there's a sly jollity about how he says it, a secret smile at the corners of his mouth. He knows that in these times it's permissible to act like a male tart, and that to shock and outrage, which pop has always striven to do throughout its history, is a balls-breaking process. And if he's not an outrage, he is, at the least, an amusement. The expression of his sexual ambivalence establishes a fascinating game: is he or isn't he? In a period of conflicting sexual identity he shrewdly exploits the confusion surrounding male and female roles. (Qtd. in *History 1972*, 15)

According to Van Cagle, the interviewer was shocked by Bowie's frank declaration of his sexuality. There is, however, absolutely nothing in the interview to support this conclusion. In fact, unlike most journalists at the time, Watts would prove to be a very perceptive reader of (and so be receptive to) the whole Ziggy project. In a review of a gig that took place a few weeks later at London's Imperial College, he concluded that Bowie was "dedicated to bringing theatrics back to rock music" (qtd. in *History 1972*, 7); his review of the *Ziggy* LP also indicated that he was wise to Bowie's "act." Indeed, in the January interview, Watts identifies Bowie's "acute ear for parody [that] doubtless stems from an innate sense of theatre," those "theatrics that will make the ablest thespians gnaw on their sticks of eyeliner in envy." It is such "theatrics," he implies, that also underpin Bowie's statements about his own sexuality—"He's gay, he says. Mmmmmm" (14, 13). There is "sly jollity" and a "secret smile." In short, Watts gets it. "Outrage" and "amusement" are, of course, key to understanding glam. Yet, just because it might be "a fascinating game," the bravery and certainly the impact of Bowie's flamboyant, very public self-outing should not be underestimated. At the time, even for someone at Bowie's then-modest level of celebrity, it was a high-risk move. Indeed, for a career that had barely gotten off the ground, it might have permanently put an end to any hopes he might have had for mainstream pop success.

So, was he—as Watts seemed to be suggesting—guilty of using his sexuality as a PR stunt, of "shrewdly exploit[ing] the confusion surrounding male and female roles"? Possibly. It was delivered with a "swish," after all. This interview would certainly make a bigger splash than the recently released *Hunky Dory*. Although not immediately in terms of sales, it did have impact. For Boy George, for example, it was a public statement that represented an act of bravery on Bowie's part. It was "a risk that nobody else dared take and [which] in the process changed many lives," including his own (qtd. in Doggett, *Man*, 138). It also had force for heterosexual males like John Lydon. It was—he remembers,

> as challenging to the world as you could ever hope to be at that point, and that was a damn brave statement to make, and yobs, hooligans, basically working-class [guys] really liked him for the bravery, for the front of it. It was taking on the world, going that's what I am and fuck you! (Qtd. in Sounes 154–55)

While there is a sense in which—as part of team Bowie—she would have probably said it anyway, his wife Angie made the still credible assertion that "social ethics and structures started to change" in the wake of the interview. "Gay people breathed more easily, without fear of recrimination," she noted. "People were actually speaking about a subject that in the past had remained strictly taboo" (qtd. in Cagle 142). However, even though with glam it was sometimes difficult to separate the two, could Bowie walk the walk as he talked the talk? Later in the year, there would, of course, be that memorable prime-time TV performance of "Starman," in which he tenderly drew Mick Ronson to him as the two men harmonized into a shared mic. More explicitly—here, literally so—the erotic fantasy of new song "Moonage Daydream" did not bury its transgressive message somewhere in its outer reaches, its nether regions. "Place your space-face close to mine, love," Bowie sings, as he exalts the "church of man-love" as "such a holy place to be" and promises to be a "rock 'n' roll bitch for you." Indeed, at one point, reference is even made to a "pink monkey-bird," which was gay slang for a recipient of anal sex—the kind of activity that will presumably make song's narrator "jump into the air." So "Moonage Daydream," then, was a prime demonstration of the way in which glam could channel new takes on gender and sexuality. In the fall of 1972, the stand-alone single "John, I'm Only Dancing" (UK no. 12) would see Bowie revisiting this "holy place," presenting a tableau vivant of the gay club scene and—reputedly—name-checking actual and potential male lovers. These songs help illustrate the extent to which David Bowie saw himself—as others would see him—as genuinely transgressive. As he explained:

> We took ourselves for avant-garde explorers, the representatives of an embryonic form of postmodernism. [Whereas] the other form of glam-rock was directly borrowed from the rock tradition, the weird clothes and all that. To be quite honest, I think we were very elitist. (Qtd. in Heylin, *Madmen*, 203)

So, for Bowie, Marc Bolan and the rest were merely practitioners of end-of-the-pier campery. Yet of course—whether consciously invoked or not—a dandy is still a dandy, someone whose assault on convention is largely measured by the extent to which it encourages others to follow. Besides, as Bowie himself confirmed at the very end of "Rock 'n' Roll Suicide," we were "not alone." There was some further evidence to suggest that the times were a-changing. Two high-profile movie releases, for instance—one set in a dystopian future and one in a fin-de-siècle past but both appropriate to the present—served to demonstrate this much. January saw the UK theatrical release of Stanley Kubrick's controversial movie version of *A Clockwork Orange*. Its distinctive clothes and footwear would, of course, influence glam's wardrobe, while Bowie would use William/Wendy Carlos's version of "Ode to Joy" to presage his arrival onstage on the *Ziggy* tour. Later in the year, the Weimar-set *Cabaret* would arguably be even more influential in complementing, and in some cases directly impacting, the glam work of not only Bowie—on tracks such as "Time" and "Aladdin Sane," for example—but also of Roxy Music, Cockney Rebel, and Sparks.

In January 1972, the National Union of Mineworkers (NUM) called its first ever national strike. This precipitated a crisis that led to the UK government issuing the first of what would turn out to be several declarations of a state of emergency over the next few years. It heralded the beginning of a period in which the country seemed to be forever teetering on the brink of total collapse. In 1972, the total number of days lost to industrial action hit its highest level for nearly fifty years, unemployment was rapidly approaching one million, and there were five hundred deaths in Northern Ireland. In this context, what did it tell us that the year's biggest-selling single should be Judy Collins's version of the hymn "Amazing Grace," on which she was backed by the Band of the Royal Scots Dragoon Guards? Number one for five weeks in the spring, it could be dismissed as yet more evidence of the UK's seemingly unquenchable thirst for pop novelty. It was in bad company, after all. Chicory Tip's "Son of My Father," Lieutenant Pigeon's "Mouldy Old Dough," and Chuck Berry's "My Ding-a-Ling" formed a cheesy trinity of best-sellers that could all be straightforwardly (and understandably) read as escapist. Simply doing, then, what pop has always done. "Amazing Grace," however, is perhaps better grouped with two other UK number one singles from 1972—Harry Nilsson's melodramatic "Without You" and Don McLean's mournful "Vincent." Far from looking away, all three songs face the misery head-on, with "Amazing Grace" even offering the listener, in its promise of redemption, a way through it. This is how pop texts could be seen and heard to relate to their context. Rising and falling in these "difficult" times, glam could and would function in similar ways; and, while it would not engage in politics as '60s rock had done, this did not mean that it could not be, that it was not, politically engaged. As Bowie explained:

> In the 70s, people of my age group were disinclined to be a part of society. It was really hard to convince yourself that you were part of society. It's like, "OK, you've broken up the family unit, and you say you're trying to get out of your mind and expand yourself and all that. Fine. So now that you've left us, what are we left with? Cos here we are without our families, totally out of our heads, and we don't know where on earth we are." That was the feeling of the early 70s—nobody knew where they were. (Qtd. in Doggett, *Man*, 13)

While this "feeling of the early 70s" is perhaps not as instantly discernible in the work of Slade or T. Rex, it is understandably easier to catch in Bowie's, fueling pop in a time of what the novelist Jonathon Coe has described as "ungodly strangeness." On *The Rise and Fall of Ziggy Stardust and the Spiders from Mars*, the opening track "Five Years" is a glam-rock prophecy. Crisscrossing the Atlantic, its preapocalyptic scenarios jump from an English market square to a stylized urban America—all cops, Cadillac wheels, and ice cream parlors—but which together suggest the end is fairly nigh. The track has been described as journalistic; but while it is bringing us "the news," it is clearly not doing so in, say, the manner of a folk-protest song. Instead, it delivers (melo)dramatically, theatrically, cinematically. Here, pacing and arrangement are key. A simple drum part portentously fades in, to be joined as the picture and the emotion build by piano, acoustic guitar, bass, and finally strings. By the end of the song, Bowie is hysterical, on the edge, his "brain hurts a lot," screaming and shredding a vocal that had started out coolly documenting seemingly random scenes. Then, all that is left is for the returning solo drum part to take the listener out of the track. More than simply setting the tone, "Five Years" functions as a kind of overture for Ziggy's rise and fall.

Through the first half of 1972, glam gathers pace and traction. In addition to continued singles successes with "Look Wot You Dun" (UK no. 4) and "Take Me Bak 'Ome" (UK no. 1), *Slade Alive!* (UK no. 2) gives Slade its first hit LP, while the almost identical levels of transatlantic chart fortune achieved by the ostensibly non-glam but increasingly glittery Elton John with "Rocket Man" (UK no. 2, US no. 6) and Ringo Starr with his T. Rex homage "Back off Boogaloo" (UK and US Top 10) would only serve to demonstrate that it might be here to stay. It was, though, the arrival of two long-form glam works that settled any doubt. Kismetically, Bowie's *The Rise and Fall of Ziggy Stardust and the Spiders from Mars* and Roxy Music's eponymous debut were both released on June 16. These two albums simultaneously broaden and deepen the genre; but, importantly, they would do so without leading it away from the pop mainstream. This constituted a rather unfamiliar trajectory. Such "stretch" more often than not has the effect of moving things in the opposite direction; but with glam, as has already been suggested, things were different. *Ziggy Stardust* would eventually peak at number five in the UK and spend more than two years on the album chart. It was glam's first, coherent long-form statement. Something, however engaging it might have been, *Electric Warrior* could never claim to be. *Ziggy Stardust* can be considered quintessential because it is about stardom, because it is "an essay on fame" (McKay 28). The working title for "Lady Stardust," for instance, was "A Song for Marc." It makes reference to a long-haired performer with makeup on *his* face and an "animal grace," whom people cannot help gawking at. It could, of course, have been about Bowie himself; but its original title suggests otherwise. Besides, when Bowie tells us that "the song went on forever," it could well be a bitchy dig at "Hot Love" with its lengthy sing-along fade-out. It could also be that Bolan is on Bowie's mind at the end of the next track on the album, "Star," when he exhorts us to "get it on."

Originally conceived as a song cycle documenting the life of a rock star, it falls some way short of being a fully realized concept album. As Bowie himself confessed, "There [had been] a bit of a narrative, a slight arc and my intention was to fill it in more later . . . [but] I never got round to it" (qtd. in Heylin, *Madmen*, 205). Perhaps conscious of the need to "sell" the project/product a little harder, he told US radio:

> What you have . . . is a story which doesn't really take place. It's just a few little scenes from the life of a band called Ziggy Stardust and the Spiders from Mars, which could feasibly be the last band on earth. (Qtd. in Heylin, *Madmen*, 206)

Sitting side by side, "Star" and "Hang On to Yourself" do work very effectively as ruminations on fame. On what it might take to achieve ("I can make a transformation as a rock 'n' roll star"), what it might offer ("so inviting, so enticing to play the part"), and what ultimately it might cost. Much of this price is graphically demonstrated in the fate of Ziggy Stardust, and specifically in the song that is up next on the album and which, of course, bears his name. The character of Ziggy was believed to have been constructed from Bowie's knowledge of an unholy trinity of larger-than-life rock casualties—Stooges front man Iggy Pop, the Legendary Stardust Cowboy, and Vince Taylor. He had come across the Legendary Stardust Cowboy—a Texas-born pioneer of psychobilly with an obsession for space travel—when the two had been on the same record label in the late 1960s. Featuring an odd array of instruments including dobro and bugle and an even odder vocal performance, the Cowboy's 1968 antisong "Paralyzed" had evidently intrigued Bowie. "I immediately fell in love with his music," he later recalled on bowie.net. "Well, actually the idea of his music" (qtd. in bowiewonderworld.com). Yet, of the three outsized characters, it was undoubtedly the delusional Taylor—an LSD casualty who once told a French audience that he was the Messiah—who would prove the single most influential (rock and) role model. As Bowie explained: "He always stayed in my mind as an example of what can happen in rock and roll. I'm not sure if I held him up as an idol or as something not to become. Bit of both, probably" (qtd. in Heylin, *Madmen*, 22). Ziggy is a "special man," a "leper messiah," the priapic rock-star-as-savior, "the Naz" with "snow-white tan" and "god-given ass," but someone who will ultimately take "it all too far," and so meet his fate at the hands of the very "kids" who worship him.

In January 1972, Bowie had told *Disc*'s Dai Davies that it was "the youth that are feeling the boredom most; they are crying out for leadership to such an extent that they will even resort to following the words of some guitar hero." Was Ziggy sounding the end of days? Was he offering a way out or through it? Whatever the "message" here—and however muddled—it surely represented something more intriguing and thought provoking than that being delivered by T. Rex. "At this point," explained Bowie, "I had a passion for the idea of the rock star as meteor" (qtd. in Heylin, *Madmen*, 218); and, as Ziggy's story indicated, this arc would not end well. For meteors burn bright, travel at great speed, and then just as surely crash and burn. So it is that in the album's curtain call, "Rock 'n' Roll Suicide," as prophesied, our hero meets a sticky end at the hands of his own adoring fans. Technically, then, not a "suicide." More an act of (self-)sacrifice or martyrdom that does not appear to be in vain, as, in true glam spirit, the expiring Ziggy extends an invitation to his "wonderful" audience to join ("gimme your hands")—the "leper messiah" offering "the kids" a real contact high. "You're not alone," he cries. "I'll help you with the pain," he promises. "Just turn on with me." It was a further, even more dramatic, and powerful illustration of that genre-defining bond between performer and audience that could be found in the superinclusive "Starman." With a sustained piano note recalling the Beatles' "A Day in the Life," as the song—and album—came to a close, it sealed a very glam moment of euphoric communion.

Unsurprisingly, even before related charges of irony and camp were taken into consideration, it was this shameless theatricality that was often the root cause of the poor critical reception the album received. Missing the point entirely, in *Oz*, Nick Kent, for example, complained that Bowie appeared to be trying to "hype himself as something he isn't." In *Sounds*, the reviewer noted that *Ziggy Stardust* "could have been the work of a competent plagiarist," concluding that "a lot of it sounds as if he didn't work on the ideas as much as he could have done." Typically, both reviews would do little more than betray the journalists' fealty to rock authenticity and naturalism. Only Michael Watts in *Melody Maker* appeared to be dialed in to what Bowie was trying to do and say. He noted that, while the album documented "the ascent and decline of a big rock figure," it left "the listener to fill in his own details." "In the process," Watts pointed out, Bowie was "also referring obliquely to his own role as a rock star and sending it up" (qtd. in Doggett, *Man*, 151). Perceptive reviews were the exception, though. In *New Musical Express*, Roy Carr pegged Bowie on the evidence presented on *The Rise and Fall of Ziggy Stardust and the Spiders from Mars* as all "hype and hoax," a "singing boutique who appeals to only freaks" (qtd. in Sandbrook, *State*, 353).

Such opinions tell us much more about the reviewer than they do about the musician and his work. That tiresome classic rock ideology might well have been "an inherently vague concept," but its grip was mighty powerful and "certain features" were "indisputable" (Wyn Jones 84). Above all, then, the critical consensus on glam—which had begun to form and rapidly harden in response to T. Rex's spectacular successes in the previous year and which was now very much in evidence in the majority of reviews of *Ziggy*—was undeniably shaped by what Barker and Taylor call the "spectre of authenticity" that had grabbed rock in a headlock in the mid-1960s and which showed few signs of loosening in the early '70s. Glam emerged at a time when rock music was widely understood as "a mode of performance characterised by a strong desire to stop acting and get real" (157). In an affront and open challenge to this much-prized article of faith, it would clearly revel in its inauthenticity. So, in fact, there is a case to be made for glam being ultimately *more* honest in brazenly celebrating the fact that rock—no different to pop—is a performance. Writing about the "problem of how self-consciousness affects performers," Barker and Taylor highlight the two ways in which performers look to negotiate "the gap between the person you think you are and the persona that others perceive." The artist-performer who strives to *minimize* this "gap"—and so tries to "project the authentic person and also live up to the persona that he projects"—is guaranteed to win favor with classic rock ideologues. He or she invariably looks to communicate a "simple honesty" about who he or she is, and so seeks to "avoid dishonesty by becoming the person that [he or she is] perceived to be"—traveling a righteous path that "leads to the quest for personal authenticity, integrity and sincerity in music." The alternative path, however, is the rock(y) road least traveled—one on which the artist-performer will "glorify the degree to which [he or she is] faking it" and so "theatrically celebrate [his or her] ability to perform a role, to take on a persona (or a series of personas) that is clearly not meant to reflect the real [self]." Such a "highly theatrical" approach is one that inevitably leads to accusations of "faking it." Yet, such charges are absurd. For one thing, "authenticity is rarely an issue with music for which the performer intentionally adopts a theatrical approach" (243–45).

If Bowie's *Ziggy Stardust* had given the rock orthodoxy palpitations, then an album released on the same day in June 1972 would threaten to induce a full-on nervous breakdown. Guest reviewing in *Melody Maker*, Slade's Dave Hill had described "Re-Make/Re-Model"—the opening track on Roxy Music's eponymous debut LP—as "very unusual" sounding, "like something from [King] Crimson," albeit with a bit of Rolling Stones in there too. Hill's conclusion was that, with "a lot of influences" on the album, Roxy Music "must be a very mixed-up band" (qtd. in *History 1972*, 68). He meant it as a compliment. Other reviewers would not be so generous. For starters, Roxy Music's name alone appeared guaranteed to rile rock's classicists. Music that was "roxy" was highly unlikely to be earthy and honest. Surely it would be flashy, kitschy even—like those movie houses up and down the land that bore the same name? Then there were statements such as this from the group's leader, Bryan Ferry, that seemed deliberately designed to annoy—"I don't honestly think that one has time these days to really be sincere about anything" (qtd. in Turner, *Glam Rock*, 75). More explicitly anti-rock in both word and deed than even David Bowie, Roxy Music's work was replete with intertextuality, actively collapsing both the high/low and rock/pop cultural divides. Almost alone among a rather hostile British rock journalist fraternity, *Melody Maker*'s Richard Williams declared *Roxy Music* to be an "extraordinary album from an extraordinary group." Music that "consciously displays echoes of pretty well every style of pop and rock" was not, he argued, "a hotch-potch," but was instead "contemporary [as the band] use their awareness of earlier modes to inform and reinforce their own unique ideas." If the word "postmodern" had then been in critical usage, it might well have represented a good fit for Roxy Music.

For Williams, "the adjectives—imaginative and intelligent—pretty much sum up where they score over the muddy morass of mediocre rockers truckin' nightly up and down the M1" (qtd. in *History 1972*, 69, 104). Indeed, only Roxy Music's drummer Paul Thompson came close to being the kind of dues-paying Brit-rock journeyman Williams had described. Even he, though, confessed that he had "always wanted to do something out of the ordinary. I can't stand the heavy bands that just play riffs. . . . I try to play melodically as well as rhythmically" (qtd. in *History 1972*, 105). Andy MacKay had been an oboist with the London Schools Symphony Orchestra, before taking up the saxophone while studying English at Reading University. Here he had played in both a soul band and the college orchestra, finding time to cultivate an interest in avant-garde music too. Guitarist Phil Manzanera acknowledged and channeled a range of musical influences, including Chuck Berry, George Harrison, and Lou Reed. "I think," he told *Melody Maker*, "people are getting fed up with long guitar solos. . . . I'm reacting the opposite way—getting into songs and simple rock 'n' roll music. I like to be economical" (qtd. in *History 1972*, 105). Brian Eno had grown up near a US Air Force base in East Anglia. This, of course, had exposed him to a particularly rich, eclectic popular music mix. He had then gone on to art school, where he had booked a succession of avant-garde performers in his capacity as president of Winchester's student union.

Roxy Music's debut album had been swiftly—and, at an estimated £5,000, cheaply—recorded in March 1972. This speedy dispatch could be put down to the fact that the band had been honing many of its songs for over a year before going into the studio. One benefit of not schlepping up and down the nation's M and A roads. The LP betrayed the band's distinctive prehistory: channeling the art school, prog rock, avant-garde electronica, and even classic rock 'n' roll; processing doo-wop, jazz improvisation, torch-song crooning, squawking sax, and Eno's synthy squeals and squelches, throbs and pulses. Sometimes it seemed that the band had attempted to deliver all this in a single song. "Ladytron," for instance, moved through a series of distinct musical acts in its four and half minutes—kicking off with a spacey 1950s B-movie mood piece, before going on to showcase a Spectoresque oboe solo and a section featuring synth-treated guitars. "We were interested in inventing different musical textures," Bryan Ferry explained, to create "pictures in sound" (qtd. in Doyle 47). Here, the vocabulary drawn from the world of art is both telling and appropriate. The richly textured "Re-Make/Re-Model" had even been titled after, and directly inspired by, a 1962 painting called *Rethink Re-entry* by the British pop artist Derek Boshier.

Yet, alongside this engagement with the visual arts, Ferry was always very willing to profess a love for pop music. It is worth noting that, while many of his peers were embracing psych-rock, the mid- to late 1960s found him playing in a seven-piece rhythm 'n' blues group called the Gas Board. Indicatively, he had hitched down to London in the "Summer of Love" not to check out the then-burgeoning underground scene but to see Otis Redding and the Stax Revue. This while studying art at Newcastle University, where he was taught by pop art pioneer—and *Beatles* cover designer—Richard Hamilton. Ferry, then, loved art as much as music—and so looked to find a way to integrate the two. His appreciation of pop art's mission to dissolve the boundaries between high and low culture, for example, would consistently find expression, an outlet, through his own music-making. Furthermore, it was clear that his was a manifesto that was shared by all the members of Roxy Music. "I saw the songs in the context of pop art," Brian Eno confirmed:

> One of the things we didn't like about bands that had preceded us was that they were so unironic, they were so serious about what they were doing. We were serious, but in a different way. We wanted to also say, "we know we're working in pop music, we know there is a history to it and we know it's a showbiz game." And knowing all that we're still going to try to do something new. (Qtd. in Hoskyns 58)

"Virginia Plain"—one of glam's foundational triad of singles together with "Hot Love" and "Starman"—would most likely not have happened were it not for the band's shared love of pop. Just as the other two had, it would also achieve much of its cultural power via a memorable TV performance beamed to millions. As Bryan Ferry admitted in an interview in July 1972, "Virginia Plain" was consciously created as a "a bid to get on *Top of The Pops* actually":

> I think a single is necessary: after all, most of the best things in pop have been done in that medium. We've always wanted to make

them. . . . There's nothing wrong with being commercial if it's good.
(Qtd. in *History 1972*, 104)

Indeed, at a shade under three minutes, "Virginia Plain" was a proper single—and arguably more radio friendly, more readily digestible, than anything found on the LP. This should come as no surprise. It was, after all, intentionally crafted as such. Initially peaking at a respectable number twenty-two, *Roxy Music* had done pretty well for a debut album. By the late summer of 1972, however, it was on the slide; and so—not hearing one on the LP—Island Records suggested the band write a bespoke single to hopefully reignite sales. Of course, Island was pushing against an open door here. The band was more than happy to oblige. Released in August, "Virginia Plain" would eventually top out at number four on the UK singles chart. Described by Stump as "bubblegum with brains" (60), "Virginia Plain" succeeds because it cannot be pigeonholed, because it operates—and so appeals—on a number of levels. It could be enjoyed as pop, but could offer the listener more if he or she wanted it. The song's stream-of-consciousness lyric had been inspired by a piece of graphic art Ferry had produced in the mid-'60s. This work had been constructed around a three-way visual pun, "quoting" an American cigarette brand together with the motif of a woman positioned at the end of a plain—making cigarettes, woman, and landscape all "Virginia plain." The song also featured plenty of what Ferry nonchalantly described as "little images and throwaway lines." "I felt it was time for a bit of verbal dexterity," he said (qtd. in *History 1972*, 104). And true to his word, "Virginia Plain" packed in a lot. It is soaked in Americana—what Ferry himself described as "that whole American Dream thing"—with its references to Las Vegas, Route 66, Studebakers, Robert E. Lee, Baby Jane Holzer, and movies *The Last Picture Show* and *Flying Down to Rio*. It is also "about" the glamour of travel—that jet-set life ("midnight blue casino floors") that happens someplace else, in Rio, Acapulco, and Havana—and the sheer effort required to join this exclusive club ("We've been around a long time / Just try try try tryin' to make the big time"). Yet, characteristically, it is not addressed without a degree of myth-busting irony and knowingness—"What's real and make-believe?" Ferry sings. "Throw me a line / I'm sinking fast." More ruminations on fame and stardom, then. Topics that, of course, make the song on message for glam.

"Virginia Plain" is a densely textured work, a genuine pop musical collage to which all band members contributed. There was Ferry's lyrical smarts and that most un-rock vocal delivery; Eno's weird, unnatural noises; MacKay's minstrel oboe; Manzanera's spiky guitar licks and improvised but brief solo; and Thompson's muscular drumming. Reminiscent of campy Spector epics like "Leader of the Pack," there were also handclaps and even the sound of a revving motorbike. "I'm still not quite sure whether I like them or not," wrote one reviewer. "There are so many different things on the album, that sometimes I get the feeling they're dabblers, playing with various forms without playing much music" (Peacock, n.p.). Roxy Music is disorientating, destabilizing, unsettling stuff. Perhaps laboring under the influence of that classic rock ideology, the reviewer appears unable to overcome the nagging feeling that the band are dilettantes who do not really mean it, man. A familiar suspicion that would prompt a similar response to Bowie and host of other glam acts.

As noted earlier, despite respectable LP sales and high-profile summer support slots with both Alice Cooper and David Bowie, it was the band's debut appearance on BBC's *Top of the Pops* that sealed the glam deal. "Virginia Plain" was a strong single, for sure, and did pick up radio play; but while hearing the band was—as Barney Hoskyns memorably put it—"like hearing a pop group from Neptune" (61), *seeing* this bunch of extraterrestrials was a whole different matter. Roxy Music was by far the oddest-looking act seen on *Top of The Pops* up to this point. David Bowie and Marc Bolan included. Of course, it could be argued that if it were not for Bolan and particularly Bowie, then Roxy Music would not have had this mainstream TV moment. On the back on his *Top of The Pops* debut as Ziggy Stardust, Bowie's "Starman" had peaked at number ten just a few weeks earlier. In many ways a less conventional and so more challenging pop song, "Virginia Plain" would ultimately go six places higher. As an instantly transfixed and smitten Dylan Jones recalled, "It was their clothes that really turned heads. Leopard- and snake-skin. Gold lamé. Pastel pink leather" (38–39). For this prime-time TV outing, Bryan Ferry took up a position stage left at a stand-up piano, looking for all the (other)world like a glam vampire in his iridescent jacket and glittery green eye shadow; with Brian Eno, stage right behind his synthesizer, threatening to outglam his band leader in ostrich feathers and purple eye shadow. These two effectively framed the less outrageously attired band members occupying the space between. Although there was still the small matter of Thompson's off-one-shoulder leopard-skin top, Manzanera's oversized bug-eyed shades, and MacKay's bottle-green, enormo-collared jacket. Among the ten-million-plus viewers that evening, there are many who have attested to the inspirational charge of this performance—including Bono, the Sex Pistols' Steve Jones, and Duran Duran's John Taylor.

As the band's TV performances demonstrated, Roxy Music was wholeheartedly committed to putting on a show. A commitment fueled by a love of the movies, familiarity with the world of art, a shared passion for classic rock 'n' roll, and—in Ferry's and MacKay's cases—formative experiences playing in soul revues. "On stage, we felt like we were getting into costume or getting into character" (qtd. in Doyle 47), Ferry explained, noting with some satisfaction that audiences—at least in the UK—"really do seem to appreciate the fact that [the band] perform rather than just play" (qtd. in *History 1972*, 107). The band's theatricality was, of course, anathema to the rock orthodoxy—which had witnessed first Bolan, then Bowie and now Roxy Music all "consciously celebrate their distance from the 1960s . . . with a mix of sensational gender blurring, teenage anthems, decadence, negativity and daft clothes" (Haslam 105). Yet, of glam's triumvirate of pioneering acts, it was Roxy that appeared keenest to put the most "distance" between itself and the sixties. In part, perhaps because—unlike Bolan or Bowie—its members were never part of that "scene." Although he was twenty-six in 1972—so in fact older than both Bolan and Bowie—Ferry explained:

> There was more affinity with Bowie than Bolan, but we felt very different even from him. He seemed to have been around a bit, and his band seemed very old-fashioned. It was all very straightforward music, even though he was dressed up in a very extreme way. (Qtd. in Hoskyns 57)

This is what makes Roxy Music simultaneously the *most* and *least* glam of acts. While the band do tick a number of boxes—via its camp attack on the rock mainstream, highly developed sense of the theatrical, and pop-oriented outlook—only one of Barney Hoskyns's glam "signatures" is applicable to them. Even then, only loosely, since the vibrato deployed by Ferry was rarely if ever "faux Cockney" (xii). So Roxy Music's brand of glam was more self-conscious, arch, cerebral, and "cooler" than the "hot" variant practiced by T. Rex and acts like Sweet, Mud, and Suzi Quatro.

When Brian Eno told Richard Williams in July 1972 that he "realised that there were certain areas of music you could enter without actually learning an instrument," he was demonstrating exactly the kind of heretical avant-gardist thinking guaranteed to raise the hackles of the mainstream rock cognoscenti. The self-declared Roxy project, then, was to break away from traditional rock—making it, as Stanley Hawkins has pointed out, a project that was unlikely to find favor in one key market in particular:

> It was as if everything that Roxy Music stood for was contra the serious-mindedness of American rock, as they altered the pop scene into a domain of soft velvet and swooning boys and girls intent on romance and fancy dress. (18)

On June 30, 1972, Alice Cooper had concluded its triumphant UK tour at the Empire Pool Wembley—then the largest indoor venue in the country. In a *Melody Maker* interview published the day after the gig, an admiring Roy Hollingworth pronounced the band to be a "complete break away from [the] sophisticated, lame policy of Stateside rock" (qtd. in *History 1972*, 82). In the interview, the band's leader Vincent Furnier—by this point well on the way to being identified as Alice—told Hollingworth that Alice Cooper was "a musical *Clockwork Orange*," that it was "a drama thing, I love drama." It was also to be understood as a very explicit challenge to "the state where music was the main thing," where bands "just stand and play music" (qtd. in *History 1972*, 83). On August 12, Alice Cooper's latest single "School's Out" would start a three-week run as the UK's best-seller. Unashamedly aimed at teens— as its title clearly indicated—rather than "serious" rock fans, its invitation to rumble plugged into all those classic rock 'n' roll anthems of the 1950s that had urged their high school audience to "rip it up." Neanderthal, for sure, but full of humor ("a word that rhymes" with "innocent" cannot be found!), life, and fun. "School's Out" was anthemic, but *glam* anthems did not come any more bespoke than a single released on the very day that Alice Cooper made number one. David Bowie had initially proposed Mott the Hoople record a version of "Suffragette City." He wrote "All the Young Dudes" when the band declined the offer to cover

a song that would, of course, soon be known to many. While Bowie—
who also produced the single, played rhythm guitar, and contributed
backing vocals—denied that "All the Young Dudes" was a hymn to
youth, the song undoubtedly functioned in precisely this way for the
overwhelming majority of its audience. So, in this respect, it was closer
to the inclusive "Starman" than the Bowie track with which it has sometimes been compared, "Rock 'n' Roll Suicide." Accused of being "juvenile delinquent wrecks," the "dudes"—the shoplifting Wendy, Jimmy
who "dresses like a queen" but can "kick like a mule," the suicidal Billy,
Freddy who has "spots from ripping off the stars on his face," and our
narrator—are all representative(s) of a glam community in which the
age bar has been set ("don't want to stay alive when you're 25") and
where the quarrel is not so much with the older generation as *within*
their own—"My brother's at home with his Beatles and Stones / We
never got it off on that revolution stuff." For the "dudes," the name-
checked T. Rex is where it's at, and TV, as opposed to, say, the turn-
table, is acknowledged as the natural habitat for this new sound and
vision. It is, though, in the song's typically lengthy fade-out where the
focus switches from telling us who the "dudes" are to an invitation to
join their growing ranks. This section features vocalist Ian Hunter's ad-
libbing, which is perhaps why the song's author disagreed with those
who heard the track as a hymn to youth. For—aside from the song's
distinctive opening guitar motif—this is where the band put its own
stamp on the song. With a throaty chuckle, Hunter reaches out to *all*
the young dudes—"I want to see, hear, and talk to you . . . all of you"—
and emphasizes this superinclusive embrace by enthusiastically singling
out someone wearing glasses and almost demanding, ordering even,
that they move to "the front." Here, then, the song becomes a glam
sermon with Hunter in the role of glam preacher leading a glam communion—"Oh yes, we can love." "All the Young Dudes" would very
effectively "carry the news." It reached number three in Britain, and, in
the fall, even made the Billboard Top 40. It outsold the more tentative
"Starman."

Though considerable, Bowie's successes would not yet make him a
genuine threat to T. Rex, whose crown showed little sign of slipping
through 1972. Having achieved commercial near saturation in their
native land, Marc Bolan and his band had inevitably turned their attention to the United States and embarked on a concerted campaign to

crack this prized market, for obvious financial but—at least to the musicians themselves—no less important artistic reasons. In January, "Get It
On"—renamed "Bang a Gong (Get it On)" so as not to be confused with
a similarly titled song still fresh in the memory by American jazz-rock-
ers Chase—reached the Billboard Top 10. In February, T. Rex embarked on a two-week US tour, with advance publicity proclaiming the
band to be "the new Beatles, the teen idols of the Seventies and the
biggest pop sensation in years" (qtd. in Paytress, *Bolan*, 204). However,
the tour did not go well. Meager forty-five-minute sets were often
greeted with indifference. Shows in Los Angeles and Detroit had been
well received; but in Chicago, where the band had been upstaged by its
hard rock support act Uriah Heep, the *Tribune* reported that "the se-
quins [Bolan] had pasted on his cheekbones sparkled more than his
music" (qtd. in Paytress, *Bolan*, 205). The American trip reached its
nadir, however, with the February 27 show at Carnegie Hall, where, as
manager Tony Secunda explained:

> We'd set up this hot media blast for the gig—searchlights lit up the
> Manhattan skyline, heavy faces were there to see the concert, and
> what does Marc do? Locks himself in the toilet with two bottles of
> champagne and gets out of his brain. He walked on stage wearing a
> T-shirt of himself and fell flat on his face. . . . It was so loud that no
> one could hear a damn thing—it was awful. (Qtd. in Paytress, *Bolan*,
> 206)

So, for Secunda—at least as far as T. Rex's North American hopes and
dreams were concerned—that was that. Bolan himself saw it differently. In May, when asked about the real picture in the US, he told a
British journalist that T. Rex was "very new, but very big. We've got a
gold single for 'Get It On' and [*Electric Warrior*] is gold this week. . . .
If the thing is done correctly," he pointed out, the rewards could be
"phenomenal there" (qtd. in *History 1972*, 66). Such comments typify a
characteristic mix of (over)confidence and delusion that would become
a very familiar feature of Bolan's public utterances as the year wore on.
Yet, it had all started off so well, with little indication of stormy skies
ahead and every good reason to be confident of continued, even greater, successes. "Telegram Sam"—the first release on Bolan's own imprint, T. Rex Wax Co.—had sold more than two hundred thousand
copies in just four days to become the band's third UK number one

single in less than twelve months when it held the top spot for two weeks in February. A glam-rap, featuring a cast of fictional characters ("Golden Nose Slim," "Purple Pie Pete," "Jungle-Face Jake," and the titular "Sam") and real people (Bob Dylan, Howlin' Wolf, and of course Bolan himself), "Telegram Sam" bore a family resemblance to "Get It On," deploying a similar riff albeit in a different key. If it ain't broke. There is much debate about who or what the song is "about." Was the "main man" Bolan's New York dealer? Was he referring to Tony Secunda? Or his accountant, Sam Alder, who had apparently been the first to give the band the news that "Get It On" had made number one? Of course, if the song must be about anyone, then it is surely about Bolan himself. Indeed, there is a Bo Diddleyesque degree of self-regard and self-mythologizing going on here—"I ain't no square with my corkscrew hair," "automatic shoes" and "3-D vision"—which simultaneously complements and fuels three minutes and forty-five seconds of full-on swagger and utter self-belief.

Bolan's Shea Stadium moment then arrived next month, in March, when he performed two shows on the eighteenth to sixteen thousand fans at London's Empire Pool Wembley. This was the first time that venue had been used for a pop or rock concert; and, for the British media at least, the gigs signaled not only that Trexstasy was a phenomenon that could now be seriously considered in the same breath as Beatlemania, but that it also marked the most visible and audible expression of a new youth movement—glam.

If further proof of this were needed, at over one hundred thousand, the band's follow-up to *Electric Warrior* had received advance orders of Fab proportions. The bulk of *The Slider* was recorded very quickly in the space of a week in Paris in April, with some overdubbing done in Copenhagen and LA. At the time, producer Tony Visconti had been aware that some of the "magic" had disappeared. "There was no innocence any more. We were making calculated T. Rex recordings. There was a formula." This was a "slide" that was presumably exacerbated by Bolan's emerging stimulant-fueled megalomania—"In the hit parade? What are you talking about, man? I am the hit parade" (qtd. in Paytress, *Bolan*, 86)—that, in turn, fed discontent in the ranks.

Kicking off the album, "Metal Guru"—which became the band's second UK number one of 1972—was reminiscent of Buddy Holly's "That'll Be the Day," and true to the obviously winning blueprint was as musically direct as any T. Rex single released thus far. Lyrically, it was also characteristic in its by now familiar, unique-to-Bolan wordplay— what exactly was a "silver stud sabre-tooth dream"? When quizzed, Bolan himself had this to say about the song's meaning:

> I relate "Metal Guru" to all the gods around. I believe in a god, but have no religion. With "Metal Guru" it's like someone special; it must be a god head. I thought how god would be; he'd be all alone without a telephone. I don't answer the phone anymore. I have codes where people ring up at certain times. (Qtd. in *History 1972*, 93)

This is a very revealing (self-)analysis. Does Bolan now think he is a "god head"? Is it he, not Bowie, who has "slid" into being Ziggy "making love with his ego"? "Lady Stardust" may well have been written about Bolan, but it would now seem that "Ziggy Stardust" was just as applicable. Mixing industrial-strength self-importance with some degree of astuteness, Bolan had also pronounced the Rolling Stones to be "just not that important anymore" because "they're finding it difficult to live within the context of 16-year-old kids" (qtd. in Paytress, *Bolan*, 210); and was even feeling confident—or possibly delusional—enough to take on the Beatles too. He told *Melody Maker*'s Welch and Watts that

> Lennon's thing for me was slightly too political. Rock 'n' roll is an up, and I like music to think to, obviously, and I don't listen to just anything, but I found [*Some Time in New York City*] slightly depressing as an album. . . . Rock 'n' roll is enough if you pick up a guitar and play it well, that's enough of a message. (Qtd. in *History 1972*, 66)

On the release of *The Slider* in July, Bolan proclaimed it to be "the only album in which I've said what I think I am" (qtd. in *History 1972*, 92). If so, what did it tell us about Marc Bolan? "There was a period when I covered everything in a very poetic style," he told Michael Watts. "The images were poetic. They're no less now, but they relate to people rather than the landscape of my head" (93). In its title at least, a track like "Main Man" might well have promised that here was a lyric that would indeed "relate to people." However, Bolan confessed that it too was "a song about me" (93). *The Slider*, then, was very much a case of business as usual, featuring that familiar menu of rock 'n' roll–sourced rhythms and motifs—in the case of the latter, for example, a surfeit of references to cars and car parts—lush strings, castrato BVs, and Bolan's unique Byron-in-outer-space lyrical take.

In the fall of '72, as the stand-alone single "Children of the Revolution"—a glam anthem neither as effective nor affective as "All the Young Dudes"—was climbing to number two on the UK chart, T. Rex had returned to the US for a longer, two-month tour. Lessons, though, had clearly not been learned. Still billed as "the new Beatles," extended solos and jams soon backfired, as the support act, the Doobies, consistently blew the headliners away. This time, furthermore, Bolan could not even take solace in his unrivaled status as the biggest star back home, as he had been able to do back in the spring. For now, there were a host of credible challengers at home—the Osmonds (whose glam-style single "Crazy Horses" would peak at number two later in the year), David Cassidy, Slade, Sweet, and Gary Glitter. Plus, of course, his old friend and rival David Bowie. On July 8, Bowie had played London's Royal Festival Hall, and a star was born. Writing in *Melody Maker*, Ray Coleman identified this as the moment "at which it's possible to declare: 'That's it—he's made it'" (qtd. in *History 1972*, 110). Exactly a week later, he played the Friars Aylesbury for the third time in a year. This time with American journalists in attendance. On the same day, Coleman's review of that Festival Hall show had appeared, signing off with the perceptive conclusion that "Bowie is going to be an old-fashioned, charismatic idol, for his show is full of glitter, panache and pace—a flashback to pop-star theatrics of about ten years ago" (110).

True to the emerging glam modus operandi that Bowie himself would play such a major part in defining, the *Ziggy* show was a conscious fusion of the popular and the avant-garde—constructing a space in which Broadway theater and classic rock 'n' roll fused with more avant-garde practices sourced from mime and that boho Warholian demimonde. Reviewing Bowie's August gig at London's Rainbow Theatre for *New Music Express*, Charles Shaar Murray was then at least half-right in describing it as a "spectacular in the grand tradition . . . your real old Busby Berkeley production. Bring on the dancing girls" (111). Half-right, for that disruption of conventional rock performance (which he acknowledged) was to be achieved via an eclectic mix of artistic forms and practices (which he evidently did not). That Shaar Murray should miss this is rather surprising, given that in a July 22 interview Bowie had told him that he "was not a musician" and that he did not "profess to have music as my big wheel," noting that "theatre and mime" were just as important (86). Perhaps Shaar Murray did not want to believe him? With their dry ice, scaffold towers, costume changes, choreography and mime, and portentous use of Beethoven's Ninth, the *Ziggy* shows were theatrical rock par excellence. "Perhaps the most astounding feature was the costuming"—writes Van Cagle—but

> the overall effect of the lighting, Bowie's precise movements, and the numerous changes in apparel was to provide audiences with visual images that aided in the overall creation of the bisexual/alien Ziggy character. (Cagle 165)

With Roxy Music as support act and Mick Jagger, Rod Stewart, and Elton John in attendance, the Rainbow Theatre show had featured the rolling, big-screen projection of stills of pop icons—Elvis Presley, Little Richard, and even Marc Bolan—implying that here was a starry pantheon to which Bowie/Ziggy could now be added. Theatrical moments abounded. However, one of the most powerful came at the very start of the show, when a spotlit Bowie sang "Lady Stardust" solo at the piano.

In the fall of 1972 Bowie took the *Ziggy* show to the US, opening on September 22 in Cleveland, moving on to Memphis on the twenty-fourth and then playing New York's Carnegie Hall on the twenty-eighth. While US media reaction was generally positive, it was also evident that, perhaps unsurprisingly, middle America was less enamored. In fact, Bowie would even fail to fill San Francisco's Winterland Ballroom. The tour was undertaken at a relatively stately pace, its schedule of twenty-one shows in sixteen cities over two and a half months giving Bowie the opportunity to immerse himself more fully in America. Most of the next LP, *Aladdin Sane*, was written on this tour—material that was clearly the product of a deep engagement with a country and culture that had fascinated him since childhood. This engagement was also evident in Bowie's personal and creative involvement with its citizens. Late in '72, Bowie would oversee the final mix of Iggy Pop's *Raw Power* LP. More noteworthy, however, August would find Bowie sprinkling some glitter over RCA label mate and artistic soul mate Lou Reed's second solo album, *Transformer*. As producer, Bowie has tended to receive much of the credit for the record's success. Certainly, in the UK and Europe at least, his name undoubtedly lent the project a fashionable glam sheen that must have helped Reed, whose debut solo effort had tanked. However, while Bowie had indeed spent some time in the control booth and contributed keyboards, acoustic guitar, and backing vocals to some tracks, he was less hands on than either engineer Ken Scott or Spiders guitarist Mick Ronson, who as coproducer, chief arranger, and musician had a much bigger part to play. The first single from the album, "Walk on the Wild Side," was an international hit—including reaching number sixteen on Billboard—despite the controversial nature of subject matter that it did nothing to hide—"But she never lost her head / Even when she was giving head." As Cagle points out, it was "the first American rock song to make explicit references to gay sexuality, prostitution, speed, hustling and transvestism" (152). Elsewhere on *Transformer*, "Make Up" managed to out-camp even "Walk on the Wild Side." Here, our narrator observes, with evident delight and unconcealed lust, his male lover's makeup regimen—"You're a slick little girl" and "Oooh! It's oh-so nice." Another visit to the "church of man-love." "Perfect Day" is, though, arguably the most overtly glam track on the album. Piano led and orchestral, theatrical in its tableau of images and musical construction, this inclusive, immersive anthem celebrated the transformative and transformational—"I thought I was someone else, someone good." Such audible glamness was complemented by the visual glamness of the record's cover art—on the front, an overexposed Mick Rock photo of a heavily mascaraed, androgynous Reed, and on the back, a photo of a man and woman by Karl Stoecker, who had shot the cover of the Roxy Music debut LP. Released in November, the LP would make the UK Top 20 and, perhaps more surprisingly, the US Top 30. In North America, critical reaction could be less than positive, even downright abusive. Nick Tosches in *Rolling Stone*, for example, dismissed most of *Transformer* as "artsy fartsy kind of homo stuff." Simply not manly enough, then. Robert Christgau gave it a "B–," while it was awarded just two stars in the *Chicago Tribune*.

By the end of a year in which he had become a credible rival to Bolan in the UK, David Bowie had still yet to crack either Billboard Top 40. *The Rise and Fall of Ziggy Stardust and the Spiders from Mars* had stalled at an underwhelming number seventy-five, while "Starman" had fared little better in reaching just ten places higher. Although Mott the Hoople's version of his "All the Young Dudes" had nudged into the Top 40 and he had production credits for his work with Lou Reed, Bowie's relative commercial failure in America might be largely put down to the fact that—as plenty of reviews confirmed—glam was so evidently *not* a continuation of classic, sixties rock. A fact confirmed in Stateside responses to other glam acts. Late in '72, Roxy Music had toured the US, supporting Jethro Tull and the Allman Brothers. Opening for Tull at Madison Square Garden proved to be a particularly traumatic experience for all involved. In a review that encapsulated the orthodox line on Roxy Music that would find its most ardent support(ers) in North America, Lester Bangs complained that the band's "vitality" was "severely limited" by its "artifice" (qtd. in Hoskyns 61). Prior to the tour, the British journalist Caroline Boucher had written in *Disc* that Roxy Music had "high hopes of America," betraying her own lack of appreciation of just how entrenched and conservative the US rock scene was when predicting that the band's "whole schmaltzy act should go down a bundle there" (n.p.). It did not. Perhaps because, as Steve Peacock pointed out in *Sounds*, the band members "don't really sound like a band—they tend to come over as a bunch of slightly eccentric people who play musical instruments, thrown together in a loose union that's straining at the seams with different ideas" (n.p.). There was also very little support from US radio, where the music was an uncomfortable fit for both FM and AM formats. Too flash for the former, too weird for the latter.

In a more receptive context, where the conditions were right, glam fared much, much better. In *New Musical Express*, Nick Logan pointed out that, with glam acts like Bolan and particularly Slade, British teenagers were "getting their first influential (in the sense of having the bread to influence trends) taste of rock music." Here were "the younger brothers and sisters of the Stones, Dylan and even Zeppelin fans; the kids who haven't been programmed and conditioned by the 'accepted' norms of snob rock behaviour." Just as "All the Young Dudes" had described. In his piece, Logan had also identified the gap in the market that the likes of Slade were filling with stunning efficiency. "What seems to have been neglected," he wrote,

> is the middle ground between the straight pop and progressive factions. Not all rock 'n' roll devotees are graduates hung up on John

Cale and Terry Reilly. Some are 16, just out of school and itching to boogie. (Qtd. in *History 1972*, 30)

Slade's constituency, then, was drawn from the "the same age range" as T. Rex, "anything from 10 to 15, with a concentration between 14 and 18." As front man Noddy Holder confirmed "these are the ardent fans." Nick Logan's tone could be patronizing; but he did correctly acknowledge that the band's "predominantly working-class audiences" could identify with Slade as "one of your mates made good" (qtd. in *History 1972*, 30). In September 1972, Holder had told *Melody Maker* that Slade's "records [were] good for discos and dancing, which is good." "We are playing to a new generation of fans," he continued, "to kids who don't know about the Beatles or the Stones. They might know about them, but they associate with the music that's coming out now" (31–32). Slade was an engaging, visceral experience on vinyl and particularly live. In the same month, reviewing the band's "stamping, crashing riotous stage act," *Melody Maker*'s Chris Charlesworth noted that "no one sits and listens." Instead, he likened the audience to "an unruly [soccer] mob" (33). Recorded over three nights in front of an invited audience of three hundred fan-club members, *Slade Alive!* (UK no. 2) was cannily built around the band's strengths as a live act. It would spend fifty-two weeks on the UK album chart. There were also four big hit singles in 1972—including two summer number ones, "Take Me Bak 'Ome" and the rabble-rousing "Mama Weer All Crazee Now." By the end of such a year, no one was surprised when the *Slayed?* album became only the second glam LP to reach number one.

December also saw the release of Sweet's "Blockbuster," marking the band's emergence as a fully fledged glam act and the end of a process of reinvention that had picked up considerable speed back in the summer with the single "Little Willy" (UK no. 4). Though still bubblegum flavored, "Little Willy" was clearly a more tangy proposition to the previous sugary efforts like "Funny Funny," "Co Co," and even "Papa Joe" (UK no. 11). Aside from the obvious entendre work going on, it featured a guitar riff "that signalled strutting sexuality not innocent childhood fun." Its follow-up, the Duane Eddy–riffing "Wig Wam Bam" (UK no. 4), would then signal Sweet's further distancing from bubblegum pop. This single—the first on which all band members would play—had a harder rock sound supplied by its "fusion of metal guitars and tribal drum-beats," and was accompanied by some memorable TV performances featuring Native American costumes and liberal amounts of glitter. As Peter Doggett describes it, the overall effect was "cartoonish, but not like the Archies," a parody of "sex, machismo, the pretensions of rock, ultimately adulthood—all in the spirit of pop. Here was irony, commerciality, artifice, compressed into an irresistible package" (Doggett, *Shock*, 427–28). Here was glam in excelsis.

As 1972 ended, David Bowie was six months into what would turn out to be a two-year reign as the UK's biggest rock star. And what did the man who had, by this point, wrested the glam throne from Marc Bolan think about his court and kingdom? In September, he was quoted as saying, "I think glam rock is a lovely way to categorise me, and it's even nicer to be one of the leaders of it" (qtd. in Doggett, *Man*, 154). This, at exactly the moment Bolan chose to distance himself from the whole glam thing. Looking to abdicate, perhaps because he knew that he had already lost his crown. Looking to retreat with as much dignity and self-respect as he could muster. "I don't feel involved in it, even if I started it. It's not my department anymore, and personally I find it embarrassing" (156). He can, though, barely disguise his jealousy.

4

"CUM ON FEEL THE NOIZE"

Coming to bury it in self-flagellating punk times, Charles Shaar Murray was forced to concede that glam "hit rock and roll like an unnaturally luminous tidal wave" (*Shots*, 223). Without a doubt, 1973 felt the full force of this glittery wash as it broke over Britain and made for a glam annus mirabilis. The year was top-and-tailed by two number one singles—Sweet's "Blockbuster" and Slade's "Merry Xmas Everybody." In between, there were seven further best-sellers. All told, glam acts occupied the top spot for a total of twenty-eight weeks. Slade's three number one singles all went straight to number one in their first week on release, something last seen in the UK in April 1969, when the Beatles' "Get Back" achieved the same. Furthermore, the genre's commercial success was not confined to the short-form format. Six different glam LPs made number one in 1973—two from David Bowie and Slade, one apiece from Alice Cooper and Roxy Music. Bowie would set a record for time spent on the UK chart in a calendar year, as his six albums racked up a combined total of 182 weeks.

There was, however, one notable absentee from this roll of honor. While intimations of decline had been evident toward the end of the previous year, 1973 would confirm that T. Rex's reign as the undisputed kings of glam was well and truly over, with the band's three single releases signaling both creative and commercial diminishing returns. Recorded on tour in Japan in December 1972, "20th Century Boy" was the equal to anything T. Rex had put out up to this point. "I move like a cat, charge like a ram, sting like a bee / Babe, I wanna be your man," its familiar musical and lyrical ingredients combining very effectively indeed. However, it would "only" reach three on the UK singles chart, breaking a two-year run of eight T. Rex hits that had either made number one or two. In the summer, crowded out by a host of glam 45s, "The Groover" (UK no. 4) would prove to be the last T. Rex single to make the Top 10 in Bolan's lifetime. As with "20th Century Boy," all those components that had served Bolan so well over the past thirty-six months were present and correct—the blazing self-regard ("Some call me Arnie, some call Slim / It don't make no difference 'cos I move right in"), the call to teenage arms ("the kids yell for more, more, more!"), all the sonic tricks and treats. Perhaps, though, the "kids" were getting tired of the formula—a conclusion that would be more confidently drawn when November release "Truck on Tyke" (UK no. 12) failed to make the Top 10. It demonstrated that T. Rex was running on empty. Bolan knew it and would admit as much at the time; and poor sales would suggest that the "kids" knew it too.

As Clinton Heylin persuasively argues, Marc Bolan's "ambition burned brighter but briefer than Bowie's because to him becoming the quintessential star was an end unto itself" (*Madmen*, 167). This was what made Bolan the quintessence of glam, of course. As Ziggy had powerfully demonstrated, stardom and fame were genre staples, obsessions even. Yet so were transformation and reinvention. Bolan, for instance, had appeared to pay little attention to his music in drawing from—draining?—a shallow well. This, though, was something that could not be said of one of glam's most successful newcomers, Wizzard, who would have two UK number one singles in 1973 ("See My Baby Jive" and "Angel Fingers"). Wizzard's Roy Wood clearly paid a great deal of attention to song craft. He "loved pop. He was a super-fan. He wanted to be all of pop, all at the same time" (Stanley 345). His songs were warm re-creations of Spector's Wall of Sound that plugged into the joyous melodramatic excess of pop music in more simple times. At the end of the year, Wizzard's "I Wish It Could Be Christmas Everyday" would provide a richer musical counterpoint to Slade's less sophisticated festive stomp. The latter easily outsold the former, but the Wizzard single still sold a million copies in these most glam of days.

It is a measure of glam's grip on British pop culture that even those who had ridden it to fame should now be lining up to attack it. Possibly raging against the dying light of his own superstardom, Marc Bolan pronounced glam rock to be "dead." "It was a great thing," he said. (Presumably, when T. Rex ruled.) "But now you have your Sweet, your Chicory Tip, your Gary Glitter. . . . What those guys are doing is circus and comedy" (qtd. in Haslam 128). Even the more secure David Bowie was not above disparaging his glittery fellow travelers. He was particularly bitchy about Sweet, who "were everything we loathed; they dressed themselves up as early seventies, but there was no sense of humor there" (qtd. in Heylin, *Madmen*, 202). However—perhaps for reasons discussed below—it could be argued that it was in fact Bowie who was suffering from a humor by-pass here. The campery of bands like Sweet was merely a pantomime, rather than proposing something genuinely transgressive. Yet, although the likes of Bowie favorites Mott the Hoople were—as Philip Auslander has pointed out—"clearly men who had adopted feminine decoration," their makeup taking "on something of the aura of such traditional male uses . . . as war paint" and so constituting more a "collision of male and female codes than a true subsumption of both to a third possibility" (62–63), this function should not be underestimated. The charge that the members of Sweet were bricklayers in makeup was neither inaccurate nor derogatory.

Bowie's "personal" attack on Sweet might well have been fueled by events in the early months of 1973, when his single "The Jean Genie" came off second best in a battle with Sweet's similar-sounding "Blockbuster." Recorded in New York in October, its title emerging from playing around with the name of mime-mentor Lindsay Kemp's hero, Jean Genet, "The Jean Genie" very effectively channeled the Velvet Underground sleaze that so evidently entranced Bowie. Written for Warhol scenester Cyrinda Foxe and loosely basing its main protagonist on Iggy Pop, it has an ur-glam riff that is reminiscent of the one deployed by the Yardbirds in their version of "I'm a Man." Soaked in Americana—"New York's a go-go" and "talkin' about Monroe"—it unequivocally celebrates the druggy, sexy, scuzzy demimonde of Gotham's cultural outsiders through some wry wordplay. The "outrageous" Genie "lives on his back," is motored by "Snow White," and "keeps all your dead hair for making up underwear."

Its adult content did not prevent "The Jean Genie" from climbing to number two on the UK chart. This made it Bowie's most successful single to date, exceeding even "Space Oddity," which had peaked at number five back in 1969. Had it not been for "Blockbuster," though,

"The Jean Genie" might well have made it all the way to number one. For fans of Bowie and indeed for the singer himself, the fact that the two songs shared a near-identical riff and chord sequence was particularly galling. Written and produced by Chinn and Chapman, "Blockbuster" would turn out to be Sweet's only UK best-seller, representing the very pinnacle of a sixteen-hit-single chart career. Between the summers of 1972 and 1974 the band enjoyed a run of seven consecutive Top 10 singles. Not one of these would feature on an album. As Andrew Collins—whose first purchased 45 was "Blockbuster"—pithily puts it, Sweet "knew if you couldn't suck it in three minutes and 13 seconds, it wasn't worth a fuck" (n.p.). Johnny Ramone once described his band's songs as "dessert-only." Unsurprisingly given Sweet's bubblegum provenance, this descriptor captures the essence of "Blockbuster" too. A three-minute-ten-second glam panto—a musical Hanna-Barbera animation where Bowie's picaresque tale of New York is more like an R. Crumb cartoon—"Blockbuster" was a fairground ride from first to last. All wailing sirens and wailing BVs, the theatrical build of guitars and drums, the stomp and thump, the bump and grind. All this in the opening half minute before the lead vocal comes in. When it does, that lyric is no less effective, arguably more *affective*, than Bowie's. It is, after all, yet another illustration of glam's superinclusive embrace. Indicatively, the word "you" is used eight times in the first of its short verses. While not as sleazy as "The Jean Genie," there is "definite dirt under its fingernails, [making it] the perfect blend of the spotless and spotty for your blooming generation" (Collins, n.p.). It can, however, compete with the Bowie track in its campness—especially so when bassist Steve Priest channels his best Blanche DuBois to interject hysterically, "We just haven't got a clue what to do!" and even outdoes "The Jean Genie" in its liberal dosing of humor and joy. Here then was a masterful glam confection—now mixing to perfection raw ingredients seen and heard on the previous two Sweet singles, "Little Willy" and "Wig Wam Bam."

"Blockbuster" was the UK's best-selling single for five weeks. In early March, it was overhauled by Slade's "Cum On Feel the Noize." Sweet might have been on a roll, but Slade were—as the *New Musical Express* noted in a review of a Glasgow gig later that year—"still the guv'nors when it comes to raising the masses" (qtd. in *History 1973*, 94). There was no better illustration of the band's preeminence than a single by a group called Geordie that made the UK Top 20 in the fall. "Can You Do It" featured future AC/DC vocalist Brian Johnson apparently trying to out-Noddy Noddy, while, lyrically and musically, the song could well have been written and performed by Slade, with its football terrace stomp and chant—"C'mon, c'mon. c'mon, c'mon, keep movin"—and very familiar couplet, "Can ya squeeze me? Can ya tease me?"

In 1973, the UK's major record labels did have some glam on their books. EMI had T. Rex, CBS had Mott the Hoople, Bowie and Sweet were both signed to RCA, and Slade was with Polydor. All, though, had been signed before glamming up, suggesting that luck more than conscious design or business smarts had delivered the rewards they were now reaping. A host of successful glam players were to be found on smaller, independent labels. On RAK and Bell, Suzi Quatro, Mud, Garry Glitter, and the Glitter Band offered a teen-friendly, unpretentious counterpoint to the rather po-faced pomp of often major-label, album-oriented acts like Pink Floyd. RAK was the UK's "House of Glam," and would have its first number one single when Suzi Quatro's "Can the Can" hit the top spot for a week in June. While its familiar tribal beat recalled the early Invasion hits of the Dave Clark Five, "Can the Can" could still offer greater musical and lyrical interest than, say, the meat-and-potatoes boogie of Status Quo. With its Alice Cooperesque guitar licks, fronted by a woman who was clearly in charge, it would speak directly to its female fans.

Analyzing the UK singles market over a twelve-month period from September 1972 to August 1973, during which time around 2,900 seven-inch discs were released, Simon Frith noted that the majors continued to issue them primarily to generate album sales. CBS, for example, had just fifteen hits from a total of 266 45s released, with approximately one in six of its singles functioning as high-profile "trails" for the artists' LPs. Even UK labels Island and Charisma operated similarly, experiencing comparable results in terms of the ratio of charting singles to total 45s released. Frith estimated that approximately a third of singles were treated in this way, leaving around two thousand that were presumably aimed squarely at achieving singles chart glory. Of this number, only 180 would be hits—a success-to-failure ratio of one in eleven. In Frith's view, then, to have one hit with every five singles released means a company is "doing extraordinarily well." In his sample period, the top-performing label was Bell (with a total of sixteen hits from sixty-nine releases), closely followed by MGM (eight from thirty-three), RAK (seven from twenty-one), and Motown (twelve from forty-six). All, as we can see, did better than "extraordinarily well." Indicatively, the UK's major labels did not do well at all. EMI posted a disastrous six for 166, while RCA—despite having Sweet and Bowie on the books—managed just fourteen high-charting singles from a total of 153 releases. Even with Slade on the roster, Polydor could only muster nine hits from 127 releases; and Capitol had the unenviable record of one for 33. Yet, guided by an imported business model, it was the "English pop giants"—EMI and Decca—that were clearly the worst performers, demonstrating that they were "out of touch with the pop market, misjudging taste, unable to sell." This was a market place dominated by "two movements on disco floors . . . smooth American soul and . . . rough British stomp." The latter—described by Frith as "crude and brash music for crude and brash dancing"—was now largely composed of glam acts like Slade, Sweet, Wizzard, Suzi Quatro, Mud, T. Rex, and David Bowie. Indeed, none came more "crude" and "brash" than Gary Glitter, whose supercompressed, Neanderthal stomp "I'm the Leader of the Gang (I Am)"—complete with revving motorbike, call-and-response chants, and invitation to join said "gang"—was a month-long UK summer number one. It was "a market that the knowing labels tapped." Glam acts, together with their canny, more responsive backroom teams, Frith concluded,

> know the fun, the excitement, the violence, even the green hair, belong to the kids. It's their exhilaration, and the records sound in the background as gestures, walls the dancers put up around themselves. New years, new steps. Glitter rock and glam rock, and all the teens won't last because the same dance gets boring. But it was the sound of 1972–3, there's no denying. (492)

Such wise words here are leavened by a classicist's obsession with longevity and the barely disguised, rather smug, implication that gaudy, gormless Mayfly pop musicians are not aware that they might have a limited shelf life. In his piece, Frith seemed to want to credit everyone except the performers themselves. Success, then, is down to "the kids," the business, and, of course, the media, because "even though it's important to know how records reach you, how they are released and promoted, marketed and distributed, once they've gone through this it's down to you." Frith also claimed that "one of the joys of singles . . . is the tension between what you like and what everyone else likes, the public struggle between your taste and everyone else's" (489–95). Surely, if true, this relates to album consumption, where it represents a somewhat rockist path to thin-lipped "joy"? Glam demonstrated that oftentimes substantive "joy" was to be found in the diametrical opposite, in consuming something that everyone else had and everyone else liked. Communal and participatory, it was about being "in the gang." Sweet's "Ballroom Blitz" (UK no. 2, fall '73) was supposedly based on the band being bottled off stage (pelted with bottles) at a gig in Scotland. While some—including bassist Steve Priest—attributed this as a response to the band's glam attire and makeup, it was more likely due to the audience's dissatisfaction with a set list reportedly short on Sweet's pop hits.

At once the most and least glam of acts, Roxy Music released their second LP *For Your Pleasure* in March 1973. According to Island's marketing director, Tim Clarke, the band "took something that might have been pop but actually had as much to do with King Crimson. It was not teeny bop" (qtd. in Hoskyns 60). Although by no means "teeny bop," opening track "Do the Strand"—described by Bryan Ferry as "purely a dancer" (qtd. in *History 1973*, 66)—was undeniably glam in its solipsistic commentary on dance crazes both real and imagined. Reminiscent of "Virginia Plain," in its furious pace, wordplay featuring un-rock-like vocabulary and references to "quadrilles," "Mona Lisa," "Lolita," and "Guernica," and campy good humor, "Do the Strand" jarred with much of the rest of an album that mined the vagaries of modern life and love in appropriately muted musical hues. Perhaps this is why it was released as a single in the States. This was also presumably the thinking behind selecting the album's only other upbeat track, "Editions of You," as its B-side. Commended by *Melody Maker*'s Roy Hollingworth as the product of "masterful thieving" (qtd. in *History 1973*) with an electric piano intro similar to the Stones' "Brown Sugar" and guitar parts apparently lifted from the Yardbirds' "Fortune Teller," "Editions of You" was the closest thing to rock to be found on *For Your Pleasure*. Yet, while musically familiar, its lyric explored decidedly un-rock territory. Typically Roxy.

No love is unique or special, sings Ferry, just as there is no one authoritative masterpiece or art object in the age of mechanical reproduction . . . there'll be another shag along in a minute, is basically Ferry's message. This is modern ("in modern times the modern way") and super-urban. (Stump 83)

No surprise, then, to learn that "Do the Strand" b/w "Editions of You" failed to chart in America.

Less novel, innovative, and experimental in its instrumental textures than the band's debut LP, *For Your Pleasure* came across as a more cohesive and confident piece of work. In part, this might be explained by the knowledge that Brian Eno was soon to leave the band. As "Editions of You" had demonstrated,

Eno's funny noise solo can't compensate for the increasing subordination of his tapes in the mix; the enjoyably metallic and abrasive clash of Ferry's electric piano and Manzanera's typically odd-ball rhythm guitar lines created a racket of its own without needing Eno's trickery to distress the surface. (Stump 82)

For Your Pleasure would be the last Roxy Music LP to feature Eno, the power struggle within the band resolving itself with Bryan Ferry emerging victorious. But not before listeners had been treated to "Bogus Man"—a nine-minute-plus improvisatory, sprawling jam about a sex pest that has been described by Brian Eno as like something German electro pioneers Can were doing at the time. Elsewhere, the glam torch song "Strictly Confidential" encapsulated the album's predominant mood. Moving from love letter to suicide note, for much of the track it seemed that only MacKay's mournful oboe accompanied Ferry on a journey into the pit of despair—"There is no light here / Is there no key?" Although a solid case could be made for any song on the album, "In Every Dream Home a Heartache" is rightly regarded as its standout track, perhaps because this sinister, unsettling ode to a blow-up sex doll succeeded in capturing a palpable sense of a nation at its lowest ebb in a time of great instability and high anxiety, a country tasting the bitter fruits of rising extremism, rupturing and unraveling. "Is there a heaven? I'd like to think so," but every step takes our narrator "further from heaven." In a *Melody Maker* interview at the time of the album's release, Ferry identified "In Every Dream Home a Heartache" as a "recitation rather than a song"—a status that his interviewer, Roy Hollingworth, looked to confirm when he declared it to be "one of those questioning pieces that throws one into a state of doomed confusion" (qtd. in *History 1973*, 66). For this reason, it is also archetypal, quintessential Roxy Music. In many ways, bottling what the band represented in the space of a single track. Like much of *For Your Pleasure,* it is about atomization, alienation, detachment, decline, and fall.

In his study of Britain in the early 1970s, the historian Dominic Sandbrook wrote that, at this moment, the country "stood on the brink of a profound transformation, caught between past and present,"

> its political consensus fragmenting under the pressure of social change, its economy struggling to cope with overseas competitors, its culture torn between the comforts of nostalgia and the excitement of change, its leaders groping to understand a landscape transformed by consumerism and social mobility. An old world was dying; a new was struggling to be born. (*State*, 13)

When excitement in these troubled times was often of the nervous kind, comparisons were frequently and seriously drawn between seventies Britain and thirties Germany; and while it has been said of David Bowie—notably on the evidence of Weimar-soaked tracks like "Time" and "Aladdin Sane"—that he spoke "directly to the chaos that was modern Britain," of "the failure of post-war dreams of progress" (Turner, *Crisis?*, 25), *For Your Pleasure*—released a few weeks before *Aladdin Sane*—suggested that there were others mining the same rich thematic vein. This was something Bowie himself acknowledged when his opinion of Roxy Music was sought in a *Melody Maker* interview in May. "Maybe they are the nearest thing to being decadent at the moment," he declared. "And I love them" (qtd. in *History 1973*, 103). Ramping up the decadence several notches, however, *Aladdin Sane* would give *For Your Pleasure* a run for its money. Indeed, the two works might well be viewed as cut from the same cloth—projects emerging from and responding to the same context.

In the early months of 1973, David Bowie had experienced marital meltdown, a punishing work schedule, a rising sense of personal alienation, and an increasing reliance on hard drugs. Unsurprisingly, this resulted in burnout. In the summer, Ziggy would be "retired," to be replaced by Aladdin Sane—a modified Ziggy perhaps inevitably shaped by this burnout, but also by Bowie's lengthy late '72 firsthand exposure to all things American. "In my mind," he explained, Aladdin Sane "was Ziggy Goes to Washington" (qtd. in Heylin, *Madmen*, 231). Released in April, the album came across as the diary of a madman; a journal charting explorations in a sometimes terrifying internal land that appeared to make it a more personal, more emotionally direct affair than his previous LP. The two-and-a-half-month US tour in the fall of 1972 had been undertaken at a relatively stately pace, which had enabled Bowie to immerse himself more fully in American life and culture than he had ever done before. Yet, while Ziggy had received a warm welcome in the nation's progressive oases—in its coastal cities, for example—"the leper Messiah" had been less well received in Middle America. *Aladdin Sane* was, then, fired by his unmediated engagement with the US, but it was also consciously tailored to win over more Americans. As Clinton Heylin has pointed out, it was "Bowie's idea of a landgrab," where "the territory in question was America" (*Madmen*, 232). As such, though, it did not appear to have been entirely successful. While it would give Bowie his first Billboard Top 20 album, by June it had only sold a respectable but hardly headline-grabbing 320,000 copies in the States.

Lead single "The Jean Genie" had posted advance warning, but the album's intent is clear to see and hear from the outset. With its now-familiar cast of characters, location, and vibe, opening track "Watch That Man" is, for example, close to a retread of "The Jean Genie." While Mick Ronson throws some recognizably Keith Richards–like guitar shapes, it told a rather hermetic tale that was as self-absorbed and self-mythologizing as anything the Rolling Stones were turning out at the time. Indeed, the murky mix of "Watch That Man," with its front-and-center wailing female BVs and barroom boogie piano work, is highly reminiscent of *Exile on Main Street* (1972). Inspired by Iggy Pop's stories of late '60s Detroit, recounted to him in October '72, "Panic in Detroit" offered a typically tongue-in-cheek Bowie take on the counterculture. Having drawn the comparison between White Panther leader John Sinclair and Che Guevara, the narrator then tries to secure the autograph of the former, who has—we are told—inspired him to trash a slot machine. Here, it is also worth noting the narrator's humorous fixation with the rebel leader's "diesel van." On message for glam, once again, we are witness to an ambiguous embrace of counterculture values in this far-from-earnest picaresque narrative. Moving us from Detroit to Los Angeles, the crunching rock of "Cracked Actor" provides an appropriate sonic accompaniment to a rumination on layers and levels of prostitution in Hollywood—on money for sex, sex for drugs, sex for fame. The fifty-year-old actor—once famous but now over the hill and so "stiff in his legend"—despises the drug-addled whore who, by turn, despises him. Seedy, sweaty, lewd, and antimythic, the song channels the kind of queasy decadence that would make Roxy proud. Released as a single to accompany the album's release, "Drive-In Saturday" (UK no. 3, US dnc) delivered a message from a postapocalyptic world of "fall out saturation" in which a version of the 1950s appears to be invoked as a prelapsarian time when people knew how to (make) love. This does not make it sound like an ideal pop single; but it is characteristically warm, humane, and humorous. Set in the postsexual future, the song advocates accessing old videotapes of movies—as a "crash-course for ravers"—that will teach the sex starved how to love again.

Aladdin Sane's five determinedly America-facing, noticeably more orthodox rock tracks—"Watch That Man," "Panic in Detroit," "Cracked Actor," "The Jean Genie" and the swaggering, sexually open cover of "Let's Spend the Night Together"—provide a sharp contrast to five songs facing a diametrically opposite direction, but which, in their fervid theatricality, their over-the-top-ness, are of course very glam indeed. Written on the ship back to Britain, "Aladdin Sane (1913–1938–197?)" highlighted significant dates in parentheses—two of which referred to the year immediately before the outbreak of World Wars I and II, while the third "197?" seemed to imply that a third world war was imminent. Pianist Mike Garson, a new addition to Bowie's band, would contribute much to the album, and particularly to this track, "Time," and "Lady Grinning Soul." Coming straight after "Watch That Man," "Aladdin Sane" offered a jarring musical contradistinction to the album opener's regular blues-rock. It was jazzy, avant-garde even, with its squawking sax and Garson's astonishing atonal wig-outs and messed-up misrenderings of the Great American Songbook. A companion piece to both the title track and, perhaps less obviously, "Lady Grinning Soul," "Time" has a Weimar vibe, redolent of Christopher Isherwood's tales of decadent, prewar Berlin. Replete with references to whores, wanking, "Quaaludes and red wine," Bowie's lyric— "love has left you dreamless"—is ably supported by Mike Garson's *Cabaret*-style glissandos, runs, and fills. On "Time," "the feeling of the words moving at different speeds—glamour and apocalypse, frivolity and war—was emphasised by the way the song was constructed. The verse represented a virtually identical theme over and over, while the accompaniment constantly shifted its ground, using chords that only a pianist could have conceived" (qtd. in Doggett, *Man*, 168).

Although it was perhaps the salesman in Bowie who had described the album as an "interpretation of what America means to me . . . a summation of my first American tour" (qtd. in Doggett, *Man*, 176), *Aladdin Sane* was more thematically ambitious than the musings of a rock star often to be found on that "difficult second album." It was about personal disintegration in a fragmenting world. In May 1973, Bowie confirmed as much when he told *Melody Maker*'s Roy Hollingworth that "after what I've seen of the state of the world, I've never been so damned scared in my life" (qtd. in *History 1973*, 102). True to glam, and very much in the Weimar spirit, it did practice a desperate hedonism as a coping mechanism to counter impending meltdown. Let's party like it's 1973. So, while it might have represented a concerted play for US success, this was possibly one explanation for the album being unlikely to propel Bowie to North American superstardom. The striking, uncompromisingly glam cover might well have been another. Brian Duffy's iconic image presented the singer as otherworldly, androgynous, artificial; his heavily made-up face bisected by a red-and-blue lightning bolt, his "snow-white tan" torso scarred by a single corrosive teardrop on his left-side collarbone.

Clearly, none of this bothered the Brits. Quite the opposite, in fact. Released in the UK on April 13, 1973, preorders of one hundred thousand helped propel *Aladdin Sane* straight to number one. It would be the nation's best-selling album for five weeks, and would then spend a further eighteen months on the chart. Critical reaction, though, was mixed. "How deep does it go?" inquired Chris Welch in *Melody Maker*, "is [Bowie] really saying anything much at all?" before proceeding to answer his own questions in declaring the LP to be "superficially stunning and ultimately frustrating" with "much to dazzle the eye and ear, but little to move the mind or heart." Charles Shaar Murray in *New Musical Express* begged to differ, concluding his review by stating: "One thing I know is that *Aladdin Sane* is probably the album of the year, and a worthy contribution to the most important body of musical work produced in this decade" (qtd. in *History 1973*, 69).

In January, David Bowie had played four gigs in the UK, made several TV appearances, and recorded the bulk of *Aladdin Sane*, before commencing his hundred-day world tour at New York's Radio City on the twenty-fifth of the month. The North American leg of the tour would end in Los Angeles on March 11, from where he would head to Japan, before returning to Britain in May. Through May and June, he then played sixty-one shows in fifty-three days—delivering two shows in a single night on eighteen separate occasions. On July 4 at the Hammersmith Odeon, on the tour's final date, Bowie abruptly announced his "retirement." By this point he had been on the road for eighteen months, touring the three albums' worth of material he had released in that same period. Understandably, Bowie was exhausted and not a little bored. In its July 14 edition, *New Musical Express* reported the "retirement" and quoted Bowie explaining that "from now on, I'll be concentrating on various activities that have very little to do with rock and pop" (qtd. in *History 1973*, 98). Yet, while his many distraught fans and a surprising number of presumably puzzled journalists took Bowie for his word, he was of course, in true glam fashion, simply "retiring" the Ziggy character. "Maybe I'm not into rock 'n' roll. Maybe I just use rock 'n' roll. . . . It's just an artist's materials" (qtd. in Doggett, *Man*, 180). In the light of such statements, the "retirement" should surely be read as merely the final act in a drama of Bowie's own design—the rise and fall of a rock star. As the perceptive Roy Hollingworth pointed out at the time: "It's just tactics. Remember just tactics" (qtd. in *History 1973*, 104).

In the summer of 1973, with *Melody Maker* in the UK and *Creem* and *Rock Scene* in the US busy obsessing over it, glam would hit its peak and enter an imperial phase that would last for at least another twelve months. In August, *Creem* ran a cover story entitled "The Androgyny Hall of Fame," which featured Bowie at its center with Bolan, Jagger, Iggy Pop, Alice Cooper, and Elvis Presley orbiting around him. Even in a more reluctant America, most urban areas would witness the rise of glam clubs playing host to both out-of-town and homegrown acts. A further measure of its commercial and cultural impact and reach could also been seen and heard in the glittery work of non-glam acts like Elton John, Wings, and even the Rolling Stones. Although Elton John had arguably flirted with it on the previous year's "Rocket Man," "Saturday Night's Alright for Fighting" (UK no. 7) represented an evidently less equivocal engagement with glam; while the glam ballad "Angie" (UK no. 5) was taken from the Stones' latest album *Goats Head Soup*, whose ubercamp cover featured a gauzy headshot of an androgynous Mick Jagger doing his best Isadora Duncan impression. So, the rock establishment was glamming up; and, if it was not altogether unsurprising that teeny-pop opportunists like the Osmonds should look to join the glitterati, this was a significant development that would take things to a different level.

That July, the Irish Republican Army (IRA) detonated twenty-one bombs in Belfast in a single day, leaving eleven dead and more than a hundred injured. Over the year, the IRA would also step up its bombing campaign on the British mainland. On December 18, bombs in London injured sixty. Such terrible events both contributed to, and were symptomatic of, a kind of national breakdown. In *Not ABBA*, Dave Haslam charts this "slide into instability," identifying it as signaling the arrival of what the historian Eric Hobsbawm called "the crisis decades." A state of high anxiety, then, was tangible in all walks of British life. No one was immune. At the vanguard of UK pop culture, it could of course be felt in glam. For this was the moment "when a post-war era of relentless economic growth, high employment and a massive rise in the ownership of material goods" appeared to come to a shuddering halt (Haslam 104–5). This was a grim state of internal affairs that would be compounded by global events. October's Yom Kippur war saw Israel engage the Syrians on the Golan Heights and the Egyptians at Suez, with Jordan and the Saudis quickly joining the Arab alliance. Middle Eastern oil producers OPEC then swiftly retaliated, cutting oil production by 5 percent and continuing to reduce its output by a similar amount every month until the Israelis withdrew. Eventually, the price of crude would quadruple. At the same time, both Saudi Arabia and Iran raised their prices. On November 11, Israel and Egypt struck a peace agreement, but the price of oil continued to rise. While no Western economy escaped, with two-thirds of its oil coming from the Middle East, the United Kingdom was particularly hard hit. Just forty-eight hours after that peace accord had been signed, with inflation now at over 20 percent, the British government declared a state of emergency. This was the fifth such declaration in three years. The year 1972, for example, had not gone well. An estimated twenty-four million working days had been lost to industrial action, in a year that had also begun with a mineworkers' strike that had only ended with the award of a 20 percent pay rise. However, this time the stakes appeared to be even higher. In October '73, the government had endeavored to check rampant inflation by imposing strict wage control. The powerful National Union of Mineworkers (NUM)—representing the interests of more than a quarter of a million workers—reacted to this by introducing an overtime ban. So, as Dave Haslam records, "These were, both literally and metaphorically, dark days, the lowest ebb Britain had reached since the Second World War." The oil shortage was "exacerbated by the decision of the NUM to stage an over-time ban, thus squeezing energy supplies still further" (122), while there was also the very real possibility of similar action by power workers and a rail strike. And, of course, as the state of emergency confirmed, there were to be implications for all, beyond television's mildly inconvenient 10:30 p.m. curfew and a 50 mph limit on the motorways. In the winter of 1973/1974,

> streetlighting was switched off, floodlit football matches cancelled, electric heating outlawed in offices and factories. In mid-December [Prime Minister Edward Heath] announced that British industry would be limited to a three-day week from January 1974. The word that appeared in news bulletins almost daily—"stoppage"—was all too apt. After a while it became hard to remember a time when there weren't blank television screens, electricity shortages or train cancellations. The nation was blocked, choked, paralysed, waiting for an end. (Wheen 7)

Even the music business was directly affected, as the weeklies got thinner and the oil crisis led to a shortage of vinyl that delayed releases and resulted in thinner discs. But what of the music itself? Was it simply the case that it offered "technicolor sounds in an overcast age" (Stanley 369)? Matters of sexuality and gender excepting, glam rockers were not usually given to making explicit political statements in either their work or interviews, but it was perhaps a measure of the extreme pressure exerted at this moment that many now would. "Who would have believed this country would get like this?" asked an uncharacteristically grounded Marc Bolan. "We've gone back to the Middle Ages in a week!" Mott the Hoople's Ian Hunter observed, "One minute it's 1973—now it's 1073" (qtd. in Turner, *Glam*, 113).

The historian Dominic Sandbrook has urged a little perspective here to actively counter stories "dominated by everything that went wrong—bombs, strikes, riots, disasters" by stressing "that for most people, those things happened off stage" (*State*, 31). After all, he has pointed out, one in three Brits polled at the end of '73 reported having enjoyed a meal out in the previous month; and "despite all the economic turmoil of the early 1970s, the strikes and inflation, the oil shock and power-cuts, most . . . remained far more prosperous than they could have expected twenty years before." Indeed, in 1973, there were more cars on the roads, "more products on the supermarket shelves, more color televisions in suburban homes, more planes taking off for the beaches of Spain." Yet, at the risk of contradicting himself, Sandbrook then goes on to acknowledge that for many—even the relatively prosperous, even presumably wealthy pop stars—this did not mean that it was not a "frightening world beset by inflation, terrorism, crime and delinquency." (Here, we should also not forget that there were still more than two million people in England and Wales living without either inside bathrooms or hot running water.) So, while Sandbrook is of course spot on when concluding "the point is not that Britain was a stagnant, or unchanging society, but that the overall picture was so messy, diverse and variegated that any generalisation is bound to be risky" (*State*, 20–30), he does not appear willing to apply his own conclusion to the popular cultural front line. Both young Britons and their music of choice—he has claimed—were largely untroubled by, supremely indifferent to, that "frightening world." Yet, even as a seven-year-old, I can confirm that it was most definitely not a case of noises off, that a palpable fear, anxiety, and nervous energy frequently stalked the pop charts and made for some striking musical interventions. David Essex, for instance, had announced his arrival as a glam-pop idol via one of the strangest singles ever to grace the upper reaches of the UK chart. Released in the late summer of '73, "Rock On" (UK no. 3) was a kind of "In Every Dream Home a Heartache" for the Top 40. Sparse and minimal, unafraid of space and silence, "Rock On" was—as its producer-arranger Jeff Wayne explained—"all about the hollows, absences and the mood." Percussion led to the extent that it often recalled Norman Whitfield's work with the Temptations on tracks like "Papa Was a Rolling Stone," the glam pedigree of "Rock On" was authenticated by the key contribution of Herbie Flowers, who was one of just three musicians used and whose double-tracked, delay-effected bass lines helped build its unusual polyrhythmic soundscape. Just as it had done on Lou Reed's "Walk on the Wild Side," Flowers's bass effectively supplied the song's lead riff. Complementing this sonic stretch, Essex's lyric was at once on point for glam in exploring the familiar territory of classic rock 'n' roll and 1950s Americana, but also undercut such potentially nostalgic referents by repeatedly dragging the listener back to a confusing present and asking the questions "And where do we go from here? Which is the way that's clear?" "Rock On" was hypnotic, angular, unsettling. Its follow-up single, "Lamplight," was nowhere near as sonically or lyrically adventurous. Neither, though, was it a conventional pop song. Top 10 at Christmas, "Lamplight" could be viewed as a "Time" for the Top 40, its Weimar vibe lending it a *Cabaret*-style theatricality that was perhaps only to be expected from an artist who had landed a lead part in the musical *Godspell* a few years earlier and who would "return" to the stage that December in a production of the rock opera *Tommy* at the Rainbow.

Bryan Ferry's solo album *These Foolish Things* (UK no. 5) would, however, appear to lend unequivocal support to the Sandbrook line. Its title could well be taken as an indication of its shameless desire to escape into the pop trivial. Perhaps anticipating critical disapproval and expecting reviewers in the rock weeklies not to like it, a nevertheless unrepentant Ferry had cheerfully admitted that the project was indeed an exercise in self-indulgence. "I hope the general point of it will be understood. It's amusement value, I think" (qtd. in vivaroxymusic.com). In this respect, it was also, of course, a highly glam exercise. Just like the first two Roxy albums, in fact, it too was full of pop joy, committed to collapsing boundaries, highly theatrical, irreverent, and so, to some, quite irritating. Its track sequencing alone created some interesting and bold (or annoying and sacrilegious) juxtapositions—"A Hard Rain's A-Gonna Fall" ran into "River of Salt," "Don't Worry Baby" immediately preceded a version of "Sympathy for the Devil," Dylan and the Stones cozied up to Ketty Lester and Lesley Gore. If anything, then, *These Foolish Things* was a more "peculiar" affair than David Bowie's own covers LP, *Pin Ups*—which had shared the same release date in early November, but which had at least been consistent in its mining of mid-'60s Brit-rock for its source material. In this, the Ferry record was also therefore a more obvious counter to classic rock, reaching back much further than Bowie had done. Written in the mid-1930s, "These Foolish

Things" had been made famous by Billie Holliday. Here, though, it represented not only a perfect fit for a world-weary Ferry, but for current times in which the narrator's expressions of loss and regret seemed entirely understandable. While "These Foolish Things" was played straight, Ferry's take on the Brill Building confection "It's My Party" is gloriously camp. Delivered from a young girl's perspective, there is a moment at exactly one minute in when Ferry's voice catches with faux emotion and he makes like he is just about to cry that captured the joyous humor of the whole project. This is humor that was by no means absent from a rip-roaring cover of Bob Dylan's "A Hard Rain's A-Gonna Fall" (UK no. 10), which, in true glam fashion, urged the listener to dance in the face of the impending apocalypse it documented. As with the cover of the Stones' "Sympathy for the Devil," our narrator delivers the news with theatrical abandon to the rich backing of instruments, voices, and effects; and as the end of both the song and "days" approaches, a fiddle plays a memorable, mad, dervish reel to accompany us to the other side.

On the evidence of *These Foolish Things*, Ferry would seem to be having even more fun than Bowie does on *Pin Ups*. He is more prolific than his rival too, as 1973 also sees the release of two Roxy Music LPs. Released just a month after his solo record, *Stranded* (UK no. 1) represented the band's first post-Eno vinyl work. Eno had quit the band in the summer, to be replaced by multi-instrumentalist Eddie Jobson (violin, keyboards, synths). Unlike his predecessor, however, Jobson would never be officially a member of the band, would receive no royalties, and would in fact be paid a weekly retainer. In a similar vein to "Virginia Plain" and "Do the Strand," album opener "Street Life" was upbeat and danceable. Perhaps because of this, it would give the band its third consecutive Top 10 hit single. "Street Life" helped *Stranded* become Roxy's first number one album, but the high-profile success of both—coupled with the knowledge of Brian Eno's departure—would subsequently lead some critics to argue that the band had become less musically adventurous as a result. At the time, though, *Stranded* did not appear to disappoint. Indeed, many reviewers—Eno somewhat mischievously included—maintained that Roxy Music got better when he left. "My favorite Roxy album is the third one, which I wasn't on," he said. However, he also noted that *Stranded* "contained the seeds of their destruction, because it was getting very polished by then and didn't really contain any new ideas" (qtd. in Stump 103). Roxy historian Paul Stump has identified a "discernible musical difference" between *For Your Pleasure* and *Stranded*, "largely concerning texture and composition," implying that Eno's departure resulted in the latter being less interesting and heralded the end of the "pleasant sense of flux and unpredictability" that he brought to the table. "Instruments begin to sound like ordinary rock instruments in an ordinary rock setting," with Roxy Music now "flying in conventional formation, with roles allotted according to rock convention" (102–3). Yet, on the evidence of a track like the sinewy, funky, futuristic "Amazona," with its squelchy midsong breakdown, this seems a little harsh if not downright inaccurate.

As its title infers, *Stranded* was as much a meditation on psychic disease as *Aladdin Sane* or even its predecessor *For Your Pleasure* had been. Indicating that, even if Eno's departure had ironed out some of the band's musical kinks and quirks to leave us with an ostensibly more conventional rock unit, it had done little to blunt Roxy's thematic edge. This should have come as no surprise, since lyrics were always Ferry's area. Here, it might be argued that "Street Life" sits rather uncomfortably on an album whose dominant tone is established by its closing trifecta—"A Song for Europe," "Mother of Pearl," and "Sunset." In its brooding rumination on love lost and loneliness, "A Song for Europe" brings to mind Piaf rather than Brecht—"Here I sit in this empty café, thinking of you." Tackling false promises and false hope, emptiness and bitter regret—"Though the world is my oyster, it's only a shell full of memories"—the song's descending chords offer up the faintest musical echoes of the Beatles' "While My Guitar Gently Weeps." However, while Ferry claimed it was a pun on the Eurovision Song Contest, its mournful sax and piano, French ("Jamais, jamais, jamais") and Latin words and phrases, and even the whistling at the close that recalls "These Foolish Things," all work to put genuine distance between "A Song for Europe" and the Anglo-American tradition. More Noel Coward than Noel Redding. For its first ninety seconds, "Mother of Pearl" does exhibit conventional rock stylings, even including a guitar solo. At this point, though, some things change—the pace slowing and the song becoming piano driven—while others stay the same. Indeed, with "every goddess a let-down," as Ferry points out, "it's the same old story / All love and glory . . . a pantomime." A recognition that even as we find ourselves on familiar lyrical ground, we are perhaps in musically unfamiliar territory. In this respect, "Sunset," featuring Ferry on piano with the accompaniment of an acoustic bass, offered an appropriate curtain call.

Becoming the singer's second number one of 1973 when it held the top spot for a month in November, Gary Glitter's doleful "I Love You Love Me Love" would also end up as the year's best-selling single. A tale of lovers grimly determined to stay a couple no matter what—"We're still together after all the things that we've been through"—it could hardly be classed as a celebration. Indeed, augmented by that by now familiar airless, supercompressed production, its glam-burlesque rhythm and pacing made it all rather cheerless—dead eyed, dirgey, funereal even. Its success is perhaps all the more surprising when—as Turner notes of this time—"the need for escapism, for some light relief, could hardly have been greater" (*Glam Rock*, 112). Or possibly not surprising, if one looks at pop hits like "Seasons in the Sun" and concludes that relatability operates on different levels. Sometimes the pop public prefers to stay put rather than run away, favors realism over "light relief." As the UK headed into the Christmas break, its singles chart stood as proof to this effect. It also demonstrated that one genre was particularly well suited to this multitasking. Eight of the Top 10 for the week ending December 22 could be classified as glam—Roxy Music's "Street Life" was at ten, Mott the Hoople's "Roll Away the Stone" at nine, David Essex's "Lamplight" was at eight, Pierrot-ed Leo Sayer was at number seven with his debut single "The Show Must Go On," Alvin Stardust's "My Coo-Ca-Choo" was at five, and Gary Glitter was still at number two. This Top 10 also featured not one but two glam Christmas singles—Wizzard's "I Wish It Could Be Christmas Every Day" and Slade's "Merry Xmas Everybody." While the former had settled into the number four position it would occupy for the next month, the latter held on to the number one position it had claimed in the first week of its release on the back of an unprecedented half a million advance orders and was already the fastest-selling 45 in British chart history.

"Merry Xmas Everybody" represented a conscious act of intervention. According to Noddy Holder, it had been conceived as "a real antidote to what was happening in the country at the time. We were right in the middle of a disastrous period politically. There were power-cuts every day and half the workforce seemed to be on strike" (qtd. in

Turner *Glam*, 113). So, by directly addressing this context, "Merry Xmas Everybody" would function as one of the least escapist novelty records ever. Its tableau vivant of a contemporary British working-class Christmas is very unsentimental, without a trace of religion or nostalgia. "Little Drummer Boy," it ain't. Again, as the song's lyricist Holder explained, this was no accident: "I knew exactly what I wanted in it. I didn't want a children's choir and sleigh bells" (qtd. in Harris, "Whatever," 54). "Merry Xmas Everybody" remains determinedly earthbound throughout—the fairies' job is to keep Santa sober, Granny may well be already drunk, there is no snow, and, stripping away the pretense that there is one true Santa, we are told that *"every* Santa has a ball." While its abbreviated title—it is pointedly "Xmas" not the fuller "Christmas"—indicates the breezy informality that lies within, the song's earthy snapshots border on the bawdy—"What will your daddy do, when he sees your mother kissing Santa Claus?" Then, toward the end, as the song builds to yet another boozy climax, Holder screams "It's Christmaaaaaaas!" for an ear-piercing five seconds—issuing an order rather than an invitation, in much the same way that "everybody's having fun" comes across as an offer we cannot refuse. Yet, though thoroughly grounded, the song is not without hope—"Look to the future now, it's only just begun." In this, as Holder explained,

> it fitted right with the political and social things going on at the time. It was very grim. . . . The whole country, just before the Christmas on '73, was in turmoil. That's why I came up with the line, "Look to the future now / It's only just begun." That's what everybody had to do. The country couldn't have been at a lower ebb. In times like that, people always turned to showbiz. (qtd. in Harris, "Whatever," 54)

Rather than being a song for Christmas '73, it was Roy Wood's intention that "I Wish It Could Be Christmas Every Day" should be added to the list of bona fide rock 'n' roll Christmas songs. Utilizing his take on that Spectoresque Wall of Sound heard previously on Wizzard's two number one singles—"See My Baby Jive" and "Angel Fingers"—"I Wish It Could Be Christmas Every Day" is a typically dessert-only confection—rich and sugary, (sleigh) bells and whistles, festive lyrical staples, brass, strings, and children's voices. In contrast to Slade's realism, Wizzard offered a kinder, gentler take on the holiday season, projecting a warm nostalgic vision that perpetuated seasonal myths—of folks with "rosy cheeks," for example, "skating in the park." Unlike Holder, Wood clearly had no qualms about deploying either sleigh bells or a children's choir. Indeed, a lengthy, half-minute-plus coda features just these two ingredients as kids' voices repeat the line "When the snowman brings the snow." By this time, Wood himself has already signed off with the instruction to "give your love for Christmas." Yet, the song is not pure-grade, 100 percent schmaltz. This is glam after all. Witness that raspberry blown at its start to the accompaniment of a ringing cash register, and Wood's barked order to the schoolkids— credited irreverently on the sleeve as "Miss Snob and Class C" and here addressed simply as "you lot"—to "take it!" Overall, though, the senti-mental does win out.

While Slade's "Merry Xmas Everybody" would emerge as the clear winner, the impressive chart performance of "I Wish It Could Be Christmas Every Day" would suggest that, when confronted with a choice, many record buyers simply purchased both singles. Though different in some respects, these songs communicated fun and joy, of-fered theatricality and spectacle, harnessed the unpretentious power of rock 'n' roll, and actively encouraged inclusivity. Britain was having a glam Christmas.

5

"TEENAGE RAMPAGE"

The first UK Top 10 singles chart of 1974 featured eight glam acts. Joining Slade and Wizzard were Alvin Stardust, Leo Sayer, Gary Glitter, David Essex, Mott the Hoople, and Roxy Music. The chart year would also be bookended by a couple of glam Christmas best-sellers—"Merry Xmas Everybody" and Mud's "Lonely This Christmas." And proving that it was not just for the festive season either, in the week ending February 23, three of Britain's four best-selling singles were glam—with Suzi Quatro at number one with "Devil Gate Drive" and Mud's "Tiger Feet" and Alvin Stardust's "Jealous Mind" tucked in just behind it. After a five-year absence, Lulu returned to the UK Top 10 in early '74 with a cover of the David Bowie song "The Man Who Sold the World" (UK no. 5). Recorded at Chateau d'Herouville during the *Pin Ups* sessions, Bowie produced, arranged, played, and sang on the track. It peaked at number three, two places higher than Bowie's latest single, "Rebel Rebel." Around the same time, Elton John took one of his most glam offerings, "Bennie and the Jets," to the top of the Billboard singles chart, while back in Britain, the Rubettes' "Sugar Baby Love" would eventually hit number one in the spring—having been forced to wait its turn by first Mud, then Suzi Quatro, and then Alvin Stardust. Such stories indicate the extent to which glam was the pop dominant. Glam-pop songwriter-producers Nicky Chinn and Mike Chapman—likened by Brian Eno to Phil Spector in a September *Melody Maker* inter-view—would be responsible for more singles sales in 1974 than the Beatles achieved in any single year of their illustrious chart career.

Nothing illustrated more graphically the extent to which glam had become front-page news than the media furor surrounding "Teenage Rampage" (UK no. 2)—a track mischievously described by its authors, Mike Chapman and Nicky Chinn, as a pop "Nuremberg rally" (qtd. in Thompson 268). Having already sought corporation bans on Alice Cooper's "School's Out" and Chuck Berry's "My Ding-a-Ling," Mary Whitehouse—founder/president of the National Viewers' and Listeners' Association—now directed her moral outrage toward Sweet's latest single. In a letter to the head of BBC Radio, she wrote:

> Dear Mr Trethowen. I am writing with regard to a "pop" record currently being played on the radio, namely, "TEENAGE RAMPAGE" sung by SWEET. The words include the following: "All over the land the kids are out to get the upper hand / They're out on the streets / to turn up the heat / And soon they'll be completely in command / Imagine the sensation at the teenage occupation / At thirteen they'll be learning / But at fourteen they'll be violent [sic— the actual lyric is "burning"] / Join the revolution NOW, NOW, NOW (crescendo) / Get yourself a constitution / Turn another page in the teenage rampage NOW, NOW, NOW." This record, thanks to the publicity given to it, is now No. 1 in the charts. Yesterday I rang your duty officer about the matter and asked that it should be brought to your attention immediately. I hope you will agree that the playing of such a record is wholly inadvisable in present circumstances and look forward to hearing that you have seen fit to ban any further transmission of this record. (Qtd. in Loui, n.p.)

Responding just a few days later, Trethowen wrote:

> Dear Mrs Whitehouse. Thank you for your letter of 13th January. Careful consideration has been given to "Teenage Rampage" but we have not felt that we would be justified in banning this record from the air. Nor do we feel that it would have been right for us to have excluded the recent recording from *Top of the Pops*. As you will know, we are not deterred from placing a ban on any record, however high it may be in the charts or however popular the group associated with it. Bans in the past have been placed on records by the Beatles and the Rolling Stones. However, in this case, although I doubt if anyone would think the lyrics particularly distinguished (and you know I am given to understatement), they do not identify any target for "the revolution" and we believe that young people, while

possibly enjoying the easy beat of the music, will be unaffected by the words, since they are totally empty of real content—like all too much pop music. This is by no means the first record of its kind and certainly past examples have proved harmless in their effect. Indeed, we believe that to ban this record would have the sole result of making young people feel it did have a significance, as well as a meaning, which, in my view, neither exists nor was intended. (Qtd. in Loui, n.p.)

So, hysterical overestimation was countered with contemptuous underestimation. Unsurprisingly, Mrs. Whitehouse took pop much more seriously than Trethowen, who manages to dismiss her, Sweet, and the band's fans in the space of a few patronizing lines. Charmingly, he thinks both the song and its young fans are stupid. Although he is right to note that "Teenage Rampage" did not "identify any target for 'the revolution,'" this does not of course make it "totally empty of real content." For, as with so much here-today-gone-tomorrow rock 'n' roll of the past, the value of "Teenage Rampage" surely lay in its status as a thrilling, inchoate war cry. After all, it did invite us, urge us, to "imagine the sensation."

When Gary Glitter opined that "rock really must have more to do with fantasy than reality" (qtd. in Turner, *Glam Rock*, 138), he was simply echoing "Starman's" call that "the children" should be allowed to "boogie." In its headlong rush into hedonism, that determined escape into pleasure and laughter, glam would often appear to be tapping into what Alwyn Turner identifies as "a long British tradition of amused detachment, fleeing from seriousness as well as from hard times" (*Glam Rock*, 16). "More champagne to lose this pain," as Ferry sang on *Country Life* ("If It Takes All Night"). Of course, this is a well-worn function of pop in any age, but one that had arguably much more riding on it in the unremittingly gloomy, doomy, deep funk of early 1974 when "there's something in the air / of which we all must be aware."

In his revisionist history *The Myth of Decline: The Rise of Britain Since 1945*, George Bernstein contends that "ordinary Britons and scholars alike, in focusing on Britain's economy and its role as a world power in the post-war era, have exaggerated the extent of [the nation's] decline." Too much attention, he argues, has been paid to "change that often was inevitable and so represents no failure on the part of the British people." Understandably, though, at the time, neither "ordinary" folk nor "scholars" could summon this kind of perspective (xiv). Instead, declinism ruled—the belief that Britain was in a state of terminal, irreversible decline being widely shared, and—as glam has demonstrated—frequently and forcibly expressed. Echoing Bernstein, Sandbrook claims that focusing on declinism risks obscuring "the fact that for most people, life was getting considerably better, not worse" (*State*, 59). Yet, as someone who lived through these times, it certainly did not *feel* like this. For us "ordinary Britons," the statistics simply did not lie, and their impact was keenly felt. By the mid-1970s, the UK's share of world trade had slumped from 25 percent in 1950 to less than 10 percent; and whereas the average annual growth rate for the national economy had been a record-high 2.8 percent between 1951 and 1973, the six-year period from '73 to '79 saw the rate slip by over half to 1.3 percent—the lowest average since records began. Furthermore, the UK's 16 percent average annual inflation rate between 1974 and 1981 was markedly higher—read, worse—than our benchmark economies (e.g., 8.4 percent in the US, 4.7 percent in West Germany, and 11 percent in France). In such a context, it should come as little surprise to anyone that declinism was "an established British state of mind" that "truly began to pervade the national consciousness," filling "doomy books aimed at the general reader," becoming "a melodramatic staple for newspapers, magazines, and television programmes," and pervading "the work of artists, novelists, dramatists, film-makers and pop musicians" (Beckett, *Lights*, 177). So it was that, in the case of the latter, the airwaves in the spring of '74 were filled with prime examples of declinism-on-45—as first Paper Lace's "Billy Don't Be a Hero" and then Terry Jacks's "Seasons in the Sun" made number one on the UK singles chart. In particular, Jacks's English-language version of a Jacques Brel lyric went beyond mere wistful—hearts were "skinned" as well as knees—in appearing to be, at best, an extended suicide note, at worst, a message from beyond the grave ("Bye bye papa / It's hard to die").

Events in the first half of 1974 undoubtedly contributed to the widespread and palpable sense of declinism that fueled British cultural life. Back in January, the so-called three-day week had been imposed by a British government desperately trying to combat the ill effects of a severe oil crisis exacerbated by homegrown labor unrest, such as the strike called by the National Union of Mineworkers that eventually began on February 4. To demonstrate that he had the country's backing, Prime Minister Edward Heath then called a snap general election for the end of that month. He lost. At the same time, the first few months of 1974 also witnessed a big increase in Irish Republican Army (IRA) activities on the UK mainland. In January there were two IRA bomb explosions in Birmingham and five in London; and in February, an IRA device would kill twelve on a bus traveling on the M62 highway that was carrying British army personnel and their families. Yet, Sandbrook argues that, while for most Britons "these things happened offstage" (*State*, 31); for "one social group,"

> the political and economic shocks of the seventies hardly registered even as a distant rumbling on the horizon. Unless their parents were unusually political, most children were barely affected by the major news stories of the day, which is perhaps one reason they later remembered the 1970s so fondly (*State*, 347).

This revisionism is, though, a little hard to swallow. Indeed, it is often the case that those who "remember" the early 1970s most "fondly" tend to be those who did not experience it firsthand. On the other hand, life on the ground could be tough for all. Indicatively, 1974 saw emigration rise sharply, and—"aided" by a fall in births—there followed three years in which the UK's population declined for the first time in its long history. The middle years of the decade also saw a noteworthy fall in average monthly disposable income from £202 in '74 to £187 three years later, prompting the *New Statesman* to declare that "living standards, for the first time in 40 years, are falling" (qtd. in Beckett, *Lights*, 176). As inflation spiraled, house prices fell too—by a hefty 13 percent in 1974 and an even chunkier 16 percent in the following year.

To assert that this had little, if any, impact on "ordinary" Britons, young or old, seems rather far-fetched. Particularly so when much of our cultural matter of choice did not let us forget it; particularly so since "it spoke ominously to audiences beyond the traditional constituencies of the elderly, the conservative and the instinctively pessimistic" (Beckett, *Lights*, 177). Towing a familiar critical line, Steve Millward has argued that by 1974 the "fervour had gone out of music and that what was left was sterile and going nowhere" (ix). Waiting impatiently for the arrival of punk, he has maintained that glam rock should be characterized by its "apolitical hedonism." Presumably with material like Bowie's *Diamond Dogs* in mind, Millward is at least ready to concede that it "had a darker side" (117). Glam's "darker" hue, though, was much in evidence right across the board in 1974. It might not have been *Walls and Bridges*, but a lot of it would undoubtedly channel the zeitgeist. Slade's uncharacteristically reflective, piano-led ballad "Everyday," for example, would peak at number three in the spring; Gary Glitter's positively funereal "Remember Me This Way" would achieve an identical chart placing; and the year was also noteworthy for several histrionic wide-screen glam elegies—Alice Cooper's "Teenage Lament" (UK no. 12), T. Rex's "Teenage Dream" (UK no. 13), and Mott the Hoople's "Saturday Gigs" (UK no. 41).

"Teenage Dream" worked on various levels. While 1973 had seen "20th Century Boy" and "The Groover" reach the Top Five, that year's T. Rex album *Tanx* had been a commercial disappointment, in failing to come close to matching the sales of its predecessors, *The Slider* (1972) and *Electric Warrior* (1971). Confirmation, if it were needed, that T. Rex was in decline came in March 1974 with the release of the *Zinc Alloy and the Hidden Riders of Tomorrow* LP. Credited to Marc Bolan and T. Rex, it could only limp to number twelve. It was hard, then, not to hear unalloyed regret, even self-pity on "Teenage Dream"—a track that as a single could not even make the Top 10. At over five minutes, "Teenage Dream" was a full-on pop melodrama featuring lush strings and swooning BVs. As Dave Thompson points out, "The plaintive chorus served up a slice of autobiographical pathos quite unlike the self-aggrandising of old" (274). As ever, it was all about Bolan. This time, though—as if perhaps to acknowledge that the game was up, the race run—that godlike self is vulnerable and "broken," living in "a rusty world" whose "prison bars are hard to clean." "Whatever happened to the teenage dream?" Bolan asks, before proceeding to answer his own question. In July, "Light of Love" would fail to make the Top 20. In November, "Zip Gun Boogie" stalled outside the Top 40.

Featuring ex-Spider Mick Ronson on lead guitar, Mott the Hoople's autobiographical "Saturday Gigs" recounted the band's history from 1969 to the present in typically droll fashion. Yet it also delivered the last rites. So, while '73 was a "jamboree" in which "the dudes were the news and the news was we," '74 was "a Broadway tour" and "we didn't much like dressing up anymore." Having apparently fallen out of love with glam—"Don't wanna be hip, but thanks for the trip"—and unable to see a future, the characteristic Hunter ad-libs in the track's fade-out urge us to never forget them because "we'll never forget you" to the backing of repeated "goodbyes." The valedictory message of "Saturday Gigs" should not, however, have come as a complete shock. The previous Mott single and final hit, "The Golden Age of Rock 'n' Roll," had still possessed at least something of the same melancholia in the midst of its celebration—"the golden age of rock 'n' roll will never die / as long as children feel the need to laugh and cry."

Two of its biggest acts might well have been down (T. Rex) and out (Mott the Hoople), but popular music abhors a vacuum. There were inevitably a host of newcomers eager to join the glam aristocracy. Appropriately enough, Queen released *Queen II* in March 1974. This album included the band's first hit single, "Seven Seas of Rhye" (UK no. 10), which featured a humorous music hall blast of "I Do Like to Be beside the Seaside" in its fade-out. In contrast to most of their peers, Queen openly professed a love for the 45. This could possibly have been a major contributing factor to what quickly became the music press's default critical position on the band. A position that, as Nick Kent's dismissal of the first LP as a "bucket of urine" had demonstrated, could be very hostile indeed. There were, though, a range of reasons for such disdain. Most, if not all, of which had been directed at glam acts for a few years now. (Ironically, even Roxy Music's drummer had accused Queen of being too contrived.) *Queen II* owed as much to Led Zeppelin and even progressive rock acts like Yes as it did to David Bowie or Roxy Music, and almost nothing to T. Rex. Yet Queen's sensibility was firmly—and literally—planted in the glam camp. "[Lead singer] Freddie Mercury's a pretty regular guy," wrote the *NME*'s Julie Webb in the opening lines to her interview with the band in March 1974, who "uses regular Biba black nail varnish, regular black eyeliner, and straightens his hair with regular electric tongs." Webb also informed her readers of Queen's ambition and drive. The band was "big business" with "an amazing amount of gear and a lighting system that Bowie would be jealous of," and "though you may hate them, they're gonna confound you by being huge" (qtd. in *History 1974*, 32). Typical of glam, Queen's close attention to "business" did not mean that the "show" was neglected. As Mercury explained, "You see, the thing is, we're on stage to entertain and it's no good saying, 'Look, we've got a new album and you are going to get a whole barrage of our new songs, whether you like it or not'" (qtd. in *History 1974*, 33). On their March tour, Queen duly closed every gig with "Jailhouse Rock," "Stupid Cupid," and the burlesque anthem "Big Spender." For the admiring Webb, Queen "have a flash way of putting it across that makes it with the audience." Putting it more colorfully, in the singer's own words, it was "just Freddie Mercury poncing on stage and having a good time" (qtd. in *History 1974*, 33). True to their word, Queen would continue to develop as a glam act—through the year and beyond. In July 1985, in front of a global audience of an estimated two billion, Queen would steal the show at Live Aid, performing a perfectly pitched, crowd-pleasing twenty-one-minute greatest hits medley that included sing-along sections of "Bohemian Rhapsody" and "Radio Ga Ga," the first verse of "We Will Rock You," and a rousing version of "We Are the Champions."

If Queen's brazen commitment to the cause of "show" presented a challenge to rock conservatives, then American ex-pats Sparks took that challenge to another level entirely. The punningly titled album *Kimono My House* had been recorded in London during the first few months of 1974, when sessions had been disrupted by power outages, and the record's proposed release date had been imperiled by a shortage of vinyl. A press handout in support of lead single "This Town Ain't Big Enough for Both of Us" had made the direct comparison with Roxy Music, in claiming that Sparks would "capture the imagination and affection of roughly the same audience sector." An uncredited review in *New Music Express* described the "rather charming" track as "totally bizarre" with "synthetic sounds—Mellotrons, Moogs and backward tapes—building from one delicious crescendo to another." It was, however, noted that this most idiosyncratic of singles was "not the sort of record you half-like," and that Sparks might well therefore "cause wars" (qtd. in *History 1974*, 58). One of presumably many—since the track went to number two in the UK singles chart—whose "imagination and affection" was captured was future Duran Duran bassist John Taylor. In fact, Taylor recalls Sparks having a similar audiovisual impact as Bolan, Bowie, and Roxy Music had before them:

> That period in pop was one of the most golden. Every week on *Top of the Pops* there was a treasure unveiled and Sparks were right in the middle of that with "This Town Ain't Big Enough For Both of Us." I saw the Mael brothers and thought I'd never seen anything like this in my life. You instantly knew that there was something about them that was very different. I was immediately fascinated

with that song. The arrangement is pretty extraordinary, the lyric surreal—unlike anything else out there at that time. The physical sound of it and the use of the gunshot, the guitar break, that voice! (Qtd. in Easlea, *Talent*, 75)

"This Town Ain't Big Enough for Both of Us" was unconventional, for sure. Noticeably lacking pop's standard structure. Ron Mael explained that he had been intrigued at the prospect of writing a song that was far from being a cliché but which used a clichéd line. Yet that cliché was a non sequitur—a payoff that simply did not follow on from verses that barely related to each other and which instead offered a series of apparently narrative-defying random images: "The mammals are your favorite type and you want her tonight / . . . / You hear the thunder of stampeding rhinos, elephants and tacky tigers." And what on earth was meant by lines such as "As 20 cannibals have hold of you / They need their protein just like you do"? It was as if a Captain Beefheart lyric had been wedded to a crazy disco beat. In *Melody Maker*, Geoff Brown declared that the band possessed "an immense sense of style":

> Because their style is real, not the tacky pizazz of the New York bands and not the vogueish calculatedness of the Britisher (excepting Mr Ferry). Though Americans, Ron and Russell [Mael] have more in common with *Paris Match* than with the *New York Times*; with the Champs Elysees than with Broadway; and, to cross the Channel, with the London Palladium than with Max's Kansas City. (Qtd. in *History 1974*, 68)

Sparks, then, was not remotely classic rock. Sparks was showbiz. Sparks was glam. "This Town Ain't Big Enough for Both of Us" was as cinematic as its movie-cliché title and gunshot effect suggested, as theatrical as Russell Mael's cabaret-castrato allowed, as odd as Ron Mael's lyrical and musical collages sanctioned. And Sparks was funny to boot. So, as countless teens—John Taylor and myself included—can confirm, Sparks were "the peacock people" who "enlivened and brightened" our mid-1970s lives, "who would appear in our homes once a week. Aspirational values, cheap tailoring and the bizarre mingled together" (Easlea, *Talent*, ix).

Whether well meant or not, the descriptors "clever" and "contrived" were also frequently ascribed to Cockney Rebel, whose leader, Steve

Harley, could match anyone in the pretention stakes. "At the time," he explained, "I was into Eliot, Wordsworth, Hemingway" (qtd. in Turner, *Glam Rock*, 115). Refusing to use electric guitar, Cockney Rebel's sound had been shaped by classically trained musicians on keyboard and violin. For Alwyn Turner, this "was a somewhat unexpected consequence of the way that glam had expanded the sound palette of rock music" (*Glam Rock*, 117)—an experimental drive that would eventually filter through to glam-pop. Witness Sailor's duo of campy, decidedly un-rock singles "Glass of Champagne" (UK no. 2) and "Girls Girls Girls" (UK no. 7) from the following year. Of course, Slade's classically trained Jimmy Lea had incorporated the violin into several of the band's biggest hit singles including "Coz I Luv You" (UK no. 1, 1971). Slade, though, had never declared in an interview, as Harley had done, that "the greatest works of contemporary song-writing were by Gershwin, Irving Berlin, Jerome Kern, and Cole Porter" (qtd. in *History 1974*, 9). Part of the reason, no doubt, why the following letter had appeared in *Melody Maker* in early '74:

> Who the hell does Steve Harley of Cockney Rebel think he is? In the *Melody Maker* you quoted him as saying "you've got no right to be on stage if you don't look a million dollars, not if you think you're in show business." So . . . good bands like Status Quo, Pink Floyd, Hawkwind etc have no right to be on stage because they wear jeans and T-shirts and look like they should be working for the council. Don't forget, Mr Harley, it's not eyelashes and glitter that make a good band, it's the music. (Qtd. in *History 1974*, 43)

Mr. Harley, though, was not listening. He appeared to take no notice of the classic rock ideologues lining up to criticize him for his showbiz allegiance. Indeed, "eyelashes" and "glitter" were precisely what the new Cockney Rebel single "Judy Teen" (UK no. 5) was all about. Whatever it was, it certainly was not Bad Company. Angular, with a near-tango rhythm and pace, "Judy Teen" showcased a more-mannered-than-Ferry vocal and with that most un-rock of instruments, the violin, very much to the fore. An unrepentant Harley then featured bare of torso, jazz of hands, and heavily made up with foundation, mascara, and lipstick on the cover of the band's *Psychomodo* LP. One might have concluded that he was looking for a reaction. Coproduced with Alan Parsons, a symphony orchestra and full choir were to be found within, along with explorations of melancholia, musings on alienation, and a range of nightmarish images. The title track, for example, had some familiar reference points—"I've seen 1984 in a terrible state" and "I'm so disillusioned / I'm on suicide street"—and its narrator talked of "losing a million brain cells every day." "Psychomodo" was very zeitgeisty and surprisingly punky—with its war cry of "destroy!" and the admission that "I'm so confused, I wish I could die, die, die, die!"

Reviewing the album in *New Musical Express*, Charles Shaar Murray semiconceded that there was "more to Harley and his gang of mincing Biba dummies than a fast mouth and a good costuming job." But, he then added, "not that much more." In Shaar Murray's opinion, "Most of *Psychomodo* [was] disposable, but three of the tracks on the first side work[ed] spectacularly well." One of these, "Mr. Soft" (UK no. 8) was released as a single and is described "a kind of modified Brechtian cabaret vamp of the kind that Bowie tackled on 'Time.'" Shaar Murray particularly liked what he described as the track's "'50s doo-wop bass backing vocal" (qtd. in *History 1974*, 58). It is, though, arguably more reminiscent of a sonorous Russian Orthodox male voice choir. In fact, "Mr. Soft" is a curious mélange a la Roxy Music's first two LPs, with its sawing, Romany fiddle, "quoting" of Czech composer Julius Fucik's "Entrance of the Gladiators," which traditionally accompanies the entrance of circus clowns, and frequent campy exclamations of "ooh la!"

Millward has written of "progressive glam"—a variant that, he suggests, "acknowledges the theatricality and commercial appeal of Queen but followed the more consciously arty approach pioneered by David Bowie" (135). This is presumably where we are encouraged to file bands like Sparks and Cockney Rebel. "Prog glam," though, was still overshadowed—blinded?—by the glam-pop that continued to thrive through the spring and summer of 1974. Mud, for example, followed up its number one single "Tiger Feet" with the near-identical, feline-referencing "The Cat Crept In" (UK no. 2). Suzi Quatro had a modest hit with "Too Big" (UK no. 14)—a rock 'n' roll revivalist workout reminiscent of Dion's "Runaround Sue." Speaking of revivalists, Showaddywaddy took its debut 45 "Hey Rock and Roll" to number two, while the Glitter Band scored a Top Five hit with "Angel Face" (UK no. 4) and American ex-pats the Arrows made the UK Top 10 with "Touch Too Much." All this despite a seven-week, high summer strike by BBC technicians that took *Top of the Pops* off-air and so threatened to cut off glam's (free-to-)air supply. Here, sales of Sparks' follow-up to "This Town Ain't Big Enough for Both of Us," "Amateur Hour," were believed to have suffered from this lack of all-important screen time, as it stalled just inside the Top 10.

Starving the *Top of the Pops'* unofficial house band of prime-time exposure, the strike could also help explain the comparatively poor performance of Sweet's next single. "The Six Teens" (UK no. 9) was, however, uncharacteristically reflective, marking a big step up from "Teenage Rampage" in both music and lyric. Like the latter, it was a glam anthem ("But life goes on, you know it ain't easy. . . . You just gotta be strong"); but now, instead of aiming at thirteen- and fourteen-year-olds, it was pitching a little higher—"You're all part of the six teens." In the song, Julie and Johnnie, Suzy and Davey, Bobby and Billy are all glam "children of the revolution," Bowie's "young dudes," kids who have grown up in the late '60s. The song asks, "Where were you in '68?" Yet, true to those who "never got it off on that revolution stuff," it does not appear to hanker after those days. In fact, we are told that Bobby and Billy "thought that '68 was out of date," and so "took the flowers from their hair" and "tried to make us all aware." The message, coming through loud and clear then, that it was "too bad, too late." If Chinn and Chapman had presented Sweet's audience with a more "mature" lyric, then this was accompanied by music that "could have been a Deep Purple B-side, or a new Queen anthem" (Thompson 312), as softer acoustic verses collided with heavier, harder, louder choruses. Presumably on the strength of "The Six Teens" and the key change it signaled, Sweet had been invited to support the Who at the latter's headline stadium gig at Charlton FC in June. Unfortunately, vocalist Brian Connolly's throat was damaged in a brawl, and so the band was forced to cancel. The next few years might have been very different for Sweet had this not happened.

Like "The Six Teens," as with so much glam work, David Bowie's *Diamond Dogs* (UK no. 1, US no. 5) was rooted in an avowedly antimythic attitude toward the late 1960s. Released three months ahead of the album, "Rebel Rebel" (UK no. 5) represented conclusive proof that Bowie was still glamming it up, still reaching out to his core constituency: "Your face is a mess, you're a juvenile success." Motored by a memorable, visceral riff, it explored familiar territory—"You got your mother in a whirl / She's not sure if you're a boy or a girl." According to Barry

Walters, "Rebel Rebel" was "Bowie's answer to all those deliciously dumb Sweet, Slade, Mud, Gary Glitter, Suzi Quatro and T. Rex hits he indirectly enabled" (n.p.). Related to this, it has also come to be viewed as his glam swan song. However, while it might well have been his last single in the glam-rock style, it was by no means his last glam single. That would be 2017's *No Plan* EP.

With that characteristic mix of modesty, diffidence, and sincerity, Bowie described *Diamond Dogs* as his "usual basket of apocalyptic visions, isolation, being terribly miserable." Declinism in the long-form format, then. On the album, he explained, "I'm saying the same thing a lot, which is about this sense of self-destruction. . . . There's a real nagging anxiety in there somewhere" (qtd. in Heylin, *Madmen*, 236). No longer working with the Spiders, Bowie himself played most of the guitar parts, in addition to playing keyboards, synths, and sax, and producing. He was also reunited with Tony Visconti, who arranged the strings. Bowie's guitar playing was not as polished as Mick Ronson's. However, these technical shortcomings undeniably contributed to the album's suitably feverish, fevered, on-the-edge quality. *Diamond Dogs* presented a sustained, overwrought, dystopian mix of dread and decadence, conceptually tighter than either of his two previous original works; Bowie grafted elements of George Orwell's *1984* to his own personal take on the apocalyptic times. Orwell's estate had refused him permission to transform *1984* into a stage musical. Therefore, material that he had been working on in the winter of 1973/1974, which he had hoped would form the basis of this production, was instead put to good use on *Diamond Dogs*—most evidently, on tracks like "1984" and "Big Brother."

If it was thematically consistent, the same could said for the album in terms of its music. Drawing upon Broadway, European cabaret, rock opera, and even blaxploitation, tracks ranged from up-tempo Stonesy rockers like "Rebel Rebel" to the jazzy "Sweet Thing" to the funky "1984." Furthermore, such eclecticism was well served by a "collection of songs that didn't resolve themselves but petered out in chaos, blended into the next track or were abruptly conjoined (Turner, *Glam Rock*, 135). For the *NME*'s Charles Shaar Murray, the album stood as nothing less than "the final nightmare of the glitter apocalypse" (qtd. in Hoskyns 98). Prefaced by a distorted howl, album-opener "Future Legend" features a synth- and guitar-backed, Richard Rodgers' "quoting" spoken intro of a little over a minute to supply a snapshot of postapocalyptic "Hunger City"—complete with "fleas the size of rats," "rats the size of cats," and mutant "peopleoids." It then segues straight into the title track "Diamond Dogs," which introduces listeners to Bowie's latest persona, "Halloween Jack," following the explosive declaration—"This ain't rock and roll / This is genocide!" Unsurprisingly given its length and more pointedly its subject matter, when released as a single, "Diamond Dogs" fell short of the UK Top 20—Bowie's first false move since "Changes" had failed to chart back in early 1972. Next up was the 8:50 song-suite "Sweet Thing / Candidate / Sweet Thing (reprise)," on which Mike Garson's jazzy piano work was much in evidence as it documented the hustler turning tricks, the politician "hustling" for votes, and the "sweet" narcotic relief of class A drugs. With its funky wah-wah rhythms, side two's "1984" was musically reminiscent of Isaac Hayes's "Shaft"—and the result, in large measure, of Bowie having apparently asked Visconti for what he described as "Barry White strings." Proceedings came to an unnerving—dramatic—close with the looped first syllable of the word "brother"—"bruh! bruh! bruh!"

Diamond Dogs was, according to Bowie, "my most political album . . . my protest" (qtd. in Millward 132). Yet, it never loses sight of that genre-defining communality, of glam's inclusive embrace. For at the heart of the album, aimed directly and sincerely at the fans, sat the soulful power ballad "Rock 'n' Roll with Me." In this song, Bowie declares himself to be "in tears," but these are surely "tears" of joy. So, while there is plenty of nightmarish hopelessness to be found on *Diamond Dogs*—more of it, in fact, than on any Bowie LP since *The Man Who Sold the World*—this is leavened by its unquenchable life force, its flashes of humor, and its sheer glamness, qualities that conspired to deliver what was believed at the time to be the costliest theatrical show rock had yet witnessed. In the wake of the album's release, Bowie toured North America for almost six months between June and December '74. *Melody Maker*'s Chris Charlesworth was in attendance at the opening night of the North American tour in Montreal. It was, he breathlessly reported, "a completely new concept in rock theatre" with "as much to do with rock 'n' roll as Bob Dylan has with Las Vegas." The ninety-minute, twenty-song show was a completely rehearsed and choreographed routine where every step and nuance has been perfected down to the last detail. There isn't one iota of spontaneity about the whole show. It's straight off a musical stage—a piece of theatre complete with extravagant mechanical sets, dancers and a band that stands reservedly to stage right and never receives a cursory acknowledgment, like an orchestra in the theatre pit. (Qtd. in *History 1974*, 76)

It was a show, Charlesworth concluded, that "belongs on Broadway or Shaftsbury Avenue rather than on the road"—

a Christmas pantomime would be an unfair parallel, but the ideas behind it were exactly the same. Bowie comes out of the show as some kind of magical being. A star above stars, as untouchable as the sky; not once does he address the audience, or even allude to their presence other than an odd grin. (Qtd. in *History 1974*, 76)

The set was "Hunger City." At the rear of the stage stood a twenty-foot-high bridge, built from span-girders and forming a catwalk that rose and fell at Bowie's command. Three lighting towers, disguised as toppling skyscrapers, beamed down on Bowie. Stage left was a phallic structure that would spurt blood. The musicians were positioned stage right. During the show, Bowie executed a series of well-rehearsed dance steps, acting out each song in character. As Charlesworth observed, the "expanse of unoccupied stage in the centre [was] ample for all manner of complex choreography involving chairs, ropes and sundry other props." For "Sweet Thing," for example, Bowie "appeared on the catwalk for the first time, dressed in a long trench coat and gazing down on the dancers below while singing and pointing"; for "Cracked Actor," "Hollywood-type movie cameras and spots were hastily set up around [Bowie] while a make-up man arrived to splash on face powder"; while for "Space Oddity,"

Bowie appeared to have left the arena, then a door atop one of the skyscrapers swung open to reveal him in a seat on a pole—actually a hydraulic boom extending from the base of the phallic [structure]. [Bowie] began the song perched up there, but as the verses progressed and [he] took on the identity of Major Tom, the boom moved forward and extended diagonally outwards so that he was projected somewhat precariously out above the front rows . . . Complete with flashing lights everywhere, the effect was nothing short of sensational. (Qtd. in *History 1974*, 77)

In Charlesworth's opinion, it was the "most original spectacle in 'rock' I've ever seen, a complete move forward in direction for both Bowie and pop in general," in which "the star comes out of it as an all-round actor/singer/dancer/entertainer, leaving behind his status as a simple singer-songwriter." The net effect, he concluded, was that "David Bowie in 1974 is not rock any more. He can only be described as an entertainer who looks further ahead than any other in rock" in offering "a combination of contemporary music and theatre that is several years ahead of its time" (qtd. in *History 1974*, 76–77).

However, such quintessential glamness appeared to be ruthlessly nipped in the bud midway through the tour, when Bowie scrapped both the lavish set and the show itself and started over. Foreshadowing the "plastic soul" of *Young Americans*, in September, the singer reemerged "as an anorexic matinee idol in tight-cut jacket and baggy trousers" (Hoskyns 98). For Clinton Heylin, this sudden reinvention was commercially motivated. David Bowie, he points out,

> had tried and failed to sell the States on a form of English rock as glam as "Get It On," and as camp as "Blockbuster," so it was time to come clean: he didn't have the patience (or the money) necessary to wait for middle America's mall-children to catch up. (*Madmen*, 290–91)

David Live—a double album featuring a cover of "Knock on Wood"— would reach the Billboard Top 10 in late '74. Mission accomplished? Was this, as many have suggested, Bowie's declaration of glam's demise? Perhaps, if we were to define it in purely sonic terms. However, it is evident that the glam *sensibility* would sustain him for the rest of his days.

Like David Bowie, Queen had already demonstrated that it was no stranger to variety. November's *Sheer Heart Attack*, though, would take this eclecticism to a new level. "I'd hate to just do hard rock all the time, dear," Freddie Mercury had told *New Musical Express* at the time of its release (qtd. in *History 1974*, 126). True to his words, lead single "Killer Queen" (UK no. 2, US no. 12) was described by one reviewer as "nothing like the noisy heavy metal sound to which we are accustomed . . . a mixture of Beach Boys, early Beatles and 1920s music hall. Quaite naice, actually" (qtd. in *History 1974*, 112). Conclusive proof that the band did indeed love the single, this tale of a high-class call girl with very expensive tastes could hardly have been more camp ("then again incidentally / if you're not that way inclined"), theatrical, and glam. With its reference to a decadent world of champagne, caviar, Parisian perfume, and "pretty cabinets," the song tapped into that by now familiar *Cabaret*-style Weimar vibe. As Mercury noted, "You almost expect Noel Coward to sing it." It was, he proudly declared, "one of those 'bowler hat, black suspender belt' numbers" (qtd. in *History 1974*, 112). Representing a departure from the heavier rock sound found on the band's previous two LPs, the pop chops of "Killer Queen" were nevertheless well served by trademark multitrack vocal harmonizing and distinctive Brian May guitar work. Yet, the versatility of *Sheer Heart Attack*—in part a product of the fact that all four band members wrote—would inevitably contribute to some less than positive, often po-faced reviews accusing Queen of purveying "supermarket rock." If, though, you could not love a track as joyfully daft as the banjo/ukulele-led Charleston "Bring Back Leroy Brown," then surely you needed to take a long, hard look for your heart.

Writing in the *NME*, Julie Webb remarked that Mercury was "very much hung up on maintaining the 'star' image" and that he "thinks he should dress accordingly." As the singer confirmed, "We're still as poncey as ever. We're still the dandies we started out to be" (qtd. in *History 1974*, 113). While a track like "Killer Queen" had demonstrated this was much in evidence audibly on the new album, it was also signaled visually. *Sheer Heart Attack*'s Mick Rock cover photo was the epitome of fully conscious playful camp, featuring all four band members in various states of Technicolor undress. Definitely not Roger Dean or Storm Thorgerson. As Rock, who had also shot the front cover of Lou Reed's *Transformer* LP, recalls:

> They came to me with a specific brief: "We wanted to look wasted and abandoned, like we've been marooned on a desert island." It was their concept. They brought their own clothes. I got in sprays, glycerine and Vaseline and we greased them up and spritzed them. (Qtd. in Hotten, web)

Reviewing a Queen gig for *Melody Maker* that November, Chris Welch reported that Mercury sported a succession of "stunning" costumes, that "Big Spender" was still in the set, and that the show's "mixture of heavy rock and glamorous display" served up "a healthy and encouraging spectacle" amid what he characterized as the "gloom" of the UK's rock scene (qtd. in *History 1974*, 131). This "gloom" was not confined to the world of rock. In October, Prime Minister Harold Wilson—who had been limping along with a minority government since February—called the year's second general election in the hope of securing a working majority. It worked. Just. Wilson would have a cigarette-paper-thin majority of three. In November, continuing political instability and economic woes were exacerbated by mainland terrorism, when the IRA killed twenty-one "civilians" in the Birmingham pub bombings. Another fall, another suitably crepuscular Roxy Music LP released into the gloaming. *Country Life* (UK no. 3, US no. 37)—whose opening couplet was "The sky is dark, the wind is cold"—had been preceded by the non-album single, "All I Want Is You" (UK no. 12). Not as obviously witty as previous 45s, it was ostensibly a conventional rock song—a sign, for some, that Roxy Music was well on the way to becoming "just another rock band" (Hoskyns 66). Yet, had Ferry's apparently uncontrollable urge to break into French—"l'amour, toujours l'amour"—been missed? And what lay behind his decision to sport a stained T-shirt on *Top of the Pops*? As *Country Life* would demonstrate, Roxy Music was not quite ready to join the rock mainstream just yet. For one thing, the LP's leadoff track "The Thrill of It All" represented either a brave or foolhardy—and certainly downright ornery—choice for a US single. (Needless to say, it bombed.) Similar in tempo to "Virginia Plain," "The Thrill of It All" displayed similar magpie tendencies—taking its title from a Doris Day movie while quoting directly from a Dorothy Parker poem called "Resume," with Ferry crying "Oy vey!" at one point. Posing the question "Do you wonder where you are going?" "The Thrill of It All" also explored familiar thematic territory—"You might as well know what is right for you and make the most of what you like to do"—and concluded that "all the pleasure that's surrounding you should compensate for all you are going through." So, stylish hedonism—"high life ecstasy"—is mobilized to counter the heavy, saturating sense of decline—"Let your senses skip / Stay hip, keep cool." Advocating decadent living, "A Really Good Time" offered the same advice—"Listen to me, I'm not finished yet." "Bitter Sweet" shared its title with a Noel Coward operetta, but was arguably more Brechtian in form and theme with its oompah rhythm, oboe solo, and Ferry's Sprechgesang sections in which he talk-sings of being "stranded between life and art." The Tudor stylings of "Triptych" provided a sharp contrast with the boogie-woogie of "If It Takes All Night." In *Stranded*, Greil Marcus writes of Roxy Music "emerging in the wake of David Bowie but outclassing him in imagination and humor" (290). If true, such qualities—which, of course, made the band simultaneously inter-esting and important—were the very things that made commercial suc-cess in the States, at best, tricky, and, at worst, unlikely. This was a terrain where rigid radio formats and equally inflexible music business practice made life difficult for such an uncategorizable, shape-shifting act. These were qualities that were neither valued nor deemed neces-sary in rock.

Perhaps mishearing *Country Life*, Alwyn Turner contends that "the celebration of decadence had lost its appeal" by the end of the year (*Crisis?*, 103). Yet, if this was the case, then what was disco all about? During the British high summer of '74, disco enjoyed its mainstream breakthrough with three number one singles—George McCrea's "Rock Your Baby," the Three Degrees' Gamble-and-Huff-produced "When Will I See You Again," and Carl Douglas's disco-novelty "Kung Fu Fighting." Having had his first UK hit in the fall, Barry White made number one in December with "You're My First, My Last, My Every-thing." In addition, KC and the Sunshine Band had success with "Queen of Clubs" (UK no. 7) and "Sound Your Funky Horn" (UK no. 17), while Kenny's "The Bump" (UK no. 3)—a hit in early 1975—would perhaps represent one of the first glam-disco hybrids.

Released as a single in the fall, Bowie's live version of "Knock on Wood" (UK no. 10) has been widely interpreted as proof of glam's demise. It had, of course, emerged from a tour that had morphed into a soul revue. In October, *Melody Maker* reported that Bowie had stopped off in Philadelphia to "change sound and record a new album":

> Blue-eyed soul! This is David Bowie in Philadelphia's Sigma Sound studios—home of the hottest soul producers in the world, Gamble and Huff. . . . And the result is his first soul album, provisionally called *Someone Up There Likes Me*, out in the New Year. . . . The Philadelphia album, produced by Tony Visconti, features a vocal

back-up chorus, led by Ava Cherry. . . . Bowie originally wanted to use MFSB, the Gamble and Huff house band . . . but they had other commitments at that time, so Bowie settled for a band which included Carlos Alomar (guitar), Willie Weeks (bass guitar), Andy Newmark (drums), Larry Washington (congas), David Sanborn (saxophone), Mike Garson (piano) [and] Luther Vandross (BVs). (Qtd. in *History 1974*, 112)

Sweet's latest and *last* Chinn-Chapman confection, "Turn It Down" (UK no. 41), was released in the same month. Unlike "Teenage Rampage" back at the beginning of the year, this time a Sweet single *was* subject to a BBC ban for lyrics that featured a reference to "degenerate bums" and used the mild cuss words "godawful" and "for god's sake." Even more so than its predecessor "The Six Teens," the harder rock sound of "Turn It Down" would illustrate the band's concerted attempt to "change sound" and so reach out to an older demographic. These two tracks also appeared on *Desolation Boulevard*, which was released in the UK in November and which included five self-compositions, a cover of the Who's "My Generation," and an eight-and-a-half-minute version of Bernstein's "The Man with the Golden Arm." Although it has subsequently come to be viewed as a lost classic, it met with low sales and critical indifference at the time. Perhaps this indicated that Sweet was trying too hard to distance itself from the teen fan base that had made it. Or perhaps it signaled, as it did with Slade, that the changes being made were being undertaken a little too rapidly to bring those fans along for the ride. "Far Far Away" (UK no. 2) was the first single to be lifted from *Slade in Flame*, OST (original soundtrack) to the band's first movie. A contemplative ballad-as-travelogue, "Far Far Away" was a suitable musical hors d'oeuvre for a gritty and sometimes genuinely dark tale of the rise and fall of a fictional '60s group called Flame that was clearly based on the band's own dealings with the music business. So, as the year ended, had that business had its fill of glam too? Was the industry about to kill the thing that it once loved? Although the feeling was mutual, Nicky Chinn and Mike Chapman had distanced themselves from Sweet to focus their songwriting and production energies on cracking the North American market via a comparatively new (and presumably more pliable) act called Smokie.

The year 1974 had begun with Slade's ubercheerful, rabble-rousing "Merry Xmas Everybody" at number one on the UK singles chart. Rather indicatively, it would end with a four-week run as the nation's best-seller for Mud's maudlin "Lonely This Christmas." In the intervening months, there had been number one singles for Mud ("Tiger Feet"), Suzi Quatro ("Devil Gate Drive"), Alvin Stardust ("Jealous Mind"), the Rubettes ("Sugar Baby Love"), Gary Glitter ("Always Yours"), and David Essex ("Gonna Make You a Star"). In total, twenty weeks of glittery chart toppers. Eight weeks less than in the previous year. Not a bad year by any means, but not as stellar as '73, making it difficult to take issue with Brian Eno, who observed that "glam sort of faded out, didn't it?" (qtd. in Hoskyns 103). Yet Eno also noted of glam that it "wasn't about glamour so much as the idea of changing identity or thinking up your own identity" (qtd. in Hoskyns 8). Something that David Bowie, Bryan Ferry, Sweet, and Slade were either already engaged with or, at very least, seriously contemplating as '75 dawned.

6

"GOT TO LEAVE YOU ALL BEHIND AND FACE THE TRUTH"

In 1975, glam albums could only manage to top the UK chart for a not-so-grand total of four weeks—down six on the previous year, and so representing the genre's poorest return since its emergence in 1971. Of course, it could be argued that it was never really "about" the long-form format. Yet, this is a stat that might still be read as symptomatic of glam's decline. Besides which, there was plenty of evidence pointing to a serious downturn in fortune in the singles market too. By the band's high standards, Slade—glam's most successful singles act—would experience an underwhelming '75, with just a couple of rather modest successes. "How Does It Feel?" was the second single to be taken from the OST of the *Slade in Flame* movie, which had gone on general release in January. A piano- and brass-led ballad that had been written by Jimmy Lea back in 1969, "How Does It Feel?" stalled at number fifteen—making it (un)comfortably Slade's worst chart showing since "Get Down and Get with It" and breaking a run of twelve Top Five singles. This relatively poor performance might well have simply reflected the fact that those who had bought *Slade in Flame* already possessed the track. It was, though, perhaps not the Slade the fans either wanted or expected—a lengthy, rather downbeat, uncharacteristically wistful song that was unlikely to appeal to those who had not bought the album.

"At its peak," Alwyn Turner notes, "glam had kept the nation's youth supplied with brevity and danger, fantasy and fun."

But its time had passed. The charts were now full of American disco and of British groups recreating the high school pop of the Kennedy years . . . where glam had used early rock and roll as a launch pad into the unknown, this was unthreatening revivalism. (*Glam Rock*, 145)

Having had the previous year's best-selling single with the gloriously silly "Tiger Feet," Mud made number one in the spring of '75 with a rather pedestrian, desultory cover of "Oh Boy." While such continued commercial success might have suggested that it was a case of business as usual, the evident contrast between these two tracks could well be taken as a sign that glam was ossifying. "Oh Boy" was blank revivalism, lacking the inventiveness, wit, and emotional investment of a Roy Wood homage or even a 10cc pastiche. Although more lively and likable, "unthreatening revivalism" was a category into which one could also place the bedraped and becreped Showaddywaddy's cover of Eddie Cochran's "Three Steps to Heaven" (UK no. 2) and even the Bay City Rollers' version of the Four Seasons' "Bye Bye Baby." Certainly, neither of these constituted a "launch pad into the unknown." Thanks largely to the six-week residency of "Bye Bye Baby" at the top of the singles chart, the Bay City Rollers would be crowned the UK's biggest pop act of '75 as the nation's media talked up "Rollermania."

While Sweet's hard-fought, hard rock reinvention had seen the proto-glam-metal "Turn It Down" stall just outside the Top 40, Queen's "Now I'm Here" had followed swiftly on the high heels of "Killer Queen" in peaking at number eleven in the early weeks of 1975. Though often dismissed as an ersatz Zeppelin, *Sheer Heart Attack* (UK no. 2, US no. 12) demonstrated that the band had found its sound and, in the process, established its identity. Coming from a diametrical point on the rock-pop spectrum, this was something that Sweet would have a much harder time achieving. Given the band's well-documented bubblegum beginnings and its apparent reliance on Nicky Chinn and Mike Chapman, it was always likely to be a much tougher journey than it had been for Queen. Having now focused all their attention and energy on writing soft rock material for a new band called Smokie, Chinn and Chapman did not have a new single for Sweet. Were it not for the fact that it had been looking to sever ties with the songwriting team, the group might well have felt abandoned. Instead, though, Sweet felt liberated. As drummer Mick Tucker explained, "It was as though a light bulb had been switched on. For the first time, we could see what Sweet should sound like and why we never had in the past. It was amazing" (qtd. in Thompson 367). For Bob Stanley, this was the moment at which Sweet "decided to be a second-rate Led Zep instead of a first-rate Sweet" (338). Such a judgment, however, seems neither fair nor true. The self-penned "Fox on the Run" was a great, possibly the finest, Sweet single—a stomping anthem making up-front use of synths but which was still full of pop hooks and so fully glam. "Fox on the Run" would reach number two in the UK—matching the success of "Ballroom Blitz," "Hellraiser," and "Teenage Rampage"—and, more importantly for the band, number five in the US. Reputedly the fourth-biggest-selling single *on the planet* in 1975, it appeared to vindicate Sweet's decision to take control of its musical destiny.

As the strenuous efforts made by Sweet, David Bowie, and even Chinn and Chapman demonstrated, having reached saturation point at home, success in the States was perhaps a prerequisite for glam's continuation. This, though, would not be easily achieved. While ex-pat American acts such as Sparks, the Arrows ("My Last Night with You") and Suzi Quatro were lucratively plying their glam trade in the UK, comparable levels of homeland success had thus far eluded them all. Meanwhile, across the Atlantic, the New York Dolls, who had once been supported by Quatro, "represented America's most committed response to the British glam rock movement—not least because they owed their fashion sense to the same west London stores and stalls that were frequented by Bowie and Bolan" (Doggett, *Man*, 162). Having given their first live performance on Christmas Eve 1971 at New York City's Endicott hostel, the Dolls' garagey debut LP finally came out in the summer of 1973 with a cover that could hardly have been more glam. Beneath the band's name scrawled in garish red lipstick, there slouched the draggy Dolls—all makeup, a mélange of male and female thrift-store clothes, vertiginous stacked heels, and big hair. In an end-of-year poll, *Creem* readers would vote the New York Dolls both the "Best" and "Worst" new band of '73. Though championed by some—Ellen Willis and Robert Christgau, for example—and despite touring with Mott the Hoople, the band's North American appeal would remain largely confined to the boroughs. Consequently, US sales of *New York Dolls* were low, at around the one hundred thousand mark. Unsurprisingly, while not translating directly into chart success, the UK would

prove more receptive. In fact, October '72 had seen the Dolls supporting the Faces at the latter's Empire Pool, Wembley, gig, almost a full
year before the debut record's release. Around the same time, *Melody
Maker's* Roy Hollingworth—who had championed several homegrown
glam acts—appeared more than willing to do the same for the Dolls,
introducing the band to his readers as "no lazy, bored 30-year olds in
jeans, picking notes and their noses, but kids having a great time. Playing heavy rock like it had just been discovered." (This was, of course,
the gist of what British rock journalists would say about the Sex Pistols
and the Clash just a few years later.) "Not for them any boring, endless
singer-songwriters; not for them any polite sobering up in the quality of
rock . . . not for them any attention to what old men are flogging off as
hip." Instead, he proposed that the New York Dolls would "crush the
languid cloud of nothingness that rolls out from the rock establishment,
and falls like endless drizzle on the ears," with music that "may sound
like drivel" but at least it is "alive" (qtd. in *History 1973*, 96). "Sure we
have a few technicalities about our music," admitted the band's suitably
glam-monikered lead guitarist Johnny Thunders,

> but, my god, we have feel. We don't attempt to be a type of Segovia
> with guitar work, but when we play, everyone casts their shackles
> aside and dances. We're playthings; kids want to have us. (Qtd. in
> *History 1973*, 97)

As lead vocalist David Johansen confirmed, the Dolls were (self-)con-
sciously plugged into the glam sensibility: "The thing about rock today
is that you have to impress somebody. . . . It lost a lot when it became
just like that. They forgot that you also have to entertain people" (qtd.
in *History 1973*, 97). Representing the orthodoxy's line, presenter and
DJ Bob Harris had declared the Dolls to be purveyors of "mock rock" in
his sniggering outro to a performance on the BBC's late-night rock
showcase *The Old Grey Whistle Test*. Yet it was evident to all who were
prepared to see and *listen* that the band could "walk the walk." Produced by Todd Rundgren—who had flirted with glam on his solo LP *A
Wizard: A True Star* and had even had a US hit single with the very on-
point "Hello, It's Me"—and recorded swiftly and cheaply, *New York
Dolls* radiated an unpolished, nervous energy and excitement, its songs
always seemingly on the verge of collapsing in on themselves. Recycling
familiar rock 'n' roll riffs, it was—as the best glam tended to be—

colorful, cartoonish, campy, and avowedly teen focused. Original songs like "Personality Crisis" and "Trash" pushed all the right buttons, contained all the right reference points. "Jet Boy," for instance, appeared to be built around gender confusion—"Flying around New York city so high / *Like he was my baby*." The ubercamp "Looking for a Kiss" kicked off with Johansen "quoting" directly from the Shangri-Las' 1964 track "Give Him a Great Big Kiss"—"You'd best believe I'm in love L-U-V!"—and concluded with the singer's ostentatious schmatz, while the album's only cover was a version of rock 'n' roll originator Bo Diddley's "Pills" (1963).

Prior to reinventing himself as Jobriath, Bruce Wayne Campbell had appeared in both Los Angeles and New York productions of *Hair* and had featured on a folk-rock album as part of a group called Pidgeon. His debut solo album was backed by a high-profile marketing campaign, which saw a billboard in Times Square; ads in *Vogue*, *Penthouse*, and *Rolling Stone*; and his striking image on 250 New York buses. His manager, Jerry Brandt, invariably spoke for his charge—deeming the artist "too big to do it himself." Brandt was a huckster in the Colonel Parker mold, who claimed to have worked with Muhammad Ali and declared that Jobriath would be "the biggest artist in the world," a "singer, dancer, woman, man," with the "glamour of Garbo." He also very publicly, very loudly, and at every opportunity, referred to his client as a "true fairy" (qtd. in highsnobiety.com).

A two-album deal with Elektra had come with a sizable advance, reputed to be worth $500,000. Whatever the exact amount, it was a deal that label boss and founder Jac Holzman would soon come to regret. "I made two errors of judgement in my days at Elektra," he said, "and Jobriath was one of them." Released in late '73, Jobriath's eponymous debut was, in Holzman's opinion, "an awful album" (qtd. in Cochrane 69). The critics, however, disagreed. In fact, even in the less glam-friendly States, the reviews were generally favorable. *Cashbox* declared the record to be "one of the most interesting debut albums of the year," *Rolling Stone* noted of Jobriath that he had "talent to burn," and *Record World* went as far as to predict a "tremendous following" (qtd. in Hoskyns 90). Clearly influenced by Bowie, the work of Elton John, and producer Bob Ezrin's liaison with Alice Cooper, Jobriath's rock credentials were further boosted by the backing he would receive from well-respected musicians, including Peter Frampton and Led Zeppelin bass man John Paul Jones. *Jobriath* was still, though, a heavy glam affair. This was evident for all to hear right from the start. The gospel BVs, crunching guitars, and barroom piano of the histrionic "Take Me I'm Yours"—track one, side one, and lead single to boot—carried the unmistakably powerful whiff of musical theater and the kind of rock operatics that, just a few years later, would be so successfully channeled by Jim Steinman. Lyrically, it was arguably more sexually outré than either Bowie's "Moonage Daydream" or Reed's "Walk on the Wild Side"— "I'd do anything for you or to you / . . . / I would love you to use me, abuse me." In "Take Me I'm Yours," Jobriath offered himself up as a "slave" to "perversity," someone willing to be "chained" or tied. Elsewhere on the album, to the musical accompaniment of harpsichord and synths, the narcissistic "I'm a Man" combined a proud statement of sexuality ("I am what I am") with a plea for acceptance and understanding ("I'm a fragile man . . . soft of touch, a gentle man"). Featuring just piano and voice, with its Broadway vibe and references to Ginger Rogers, Busby Berkeley, Betty Grable, and the Ziegfeld Follies, the ultracamp "Movie Queen" bore a similarity to the kind of material Steve Harley was producing with Cockney Rebel, as Jobriath declared that he had "always wanted a movie queen to call [his] very own." "Space Clown," a wide-screen ballad reminiscent of a Bowie track like "Lady Grinning Soul," managed to heroically introduce two glam staples into a single track by mixing Pierrots with sci-fi.

In the UK, where the album's release was delayed by several months, the critics were notably less forgiving than their American counterparts. After a clip of him performing had been screened on *The Old Grey Whistle Test*, serial glam denier Bob Harris had dismissed Jobriath as a Bowie wannabe, while the *New Musical Express* viewed the LP as symptomatic of glam rock's dog days, "a brilliantly conceived and designed package built around a run-of-the-mill talented young New York queen." "You will soon be told," wrote Ian MacDonald,

> that this cat is going to be the big breeze in 1974. Receive this piece of information with sceptical, though polite, curiosity, weigh it carefully, and then watch it crumble and trickle through your fingers. (Qtd. in *History 1974*, 31)

In the States—where *Esquire* had come to a similar conclusion in pronouncing the singer to be the "hype of the year"—Jerry Brandt's huckstering would backfire disastrously. Jobriath came to be increasingly and widely perceived as a novelty in a market that traditionally despised such things. Billing Jobriath as "the true fairy of rock 'n' roll" was always likely to make securing bookings quite tricky. However, laying the blame fully with Brandt risks overlooking the extent to which Jobriath's sexuality was simply too open and too frankly expressed for the homophobic times. As band keyboardist Hayden White confirmed:

> The damage from that alone prevented us from performing in certain cities because of the fear that the band would get physically harmed. As it was, we were booed off the stage at the Nassau Coliseum for "being faggots"—and that's New York. (Qtd. in Cochrane 70)

By the beginning of 1975, both Jobriath and the New York Dolls had been dropped by their record companies.

If glam was to succeed in the States, then, perhaps it would have to do so by harnessing some of its elements to a more conventional rock style. Glam by stealth. A process that was already well under way, but which was much more audible and visible in '75, when one of the year's biggest box office draws was a showman like Elton John. Of homegrown acts, Aerosmith's lead vocalist Steve Tyler confessed to an admiration for the New York Dolls, noting that his partnership with lead guitarist Joe Perry owed as much to Johansen and Thunders as it did to Jagger and Richards. Indeed, Columbia Records had been persuaded to sign Aerosmith on the strength of the band's showcase gig at Max's Kansas City, a venue that had become something of a New York base for glam and where the Dolls would regularly perform. Although quickly morphing into something akin to the schlock rock of Alice Cooper, KISS had in fact started out as an approximation of the New York Dolls; and, as Gene Simmons admitted, of all the glam acts, "Slade were certainly our greatest influence, not only in the drafting of rock songs, but also as performers" (qtd. in Turner, *Glam Rock*, 138). From February 1974, when the band's eponymous debut LP was released, KISS would ruthlessly sell its own variant of glam to millions of American fans. Yet, Stateside success would continue to elude the band KISS happily acknowledged as its role model. In fact, Slade's concerted but ultimately doomed efforts to crack the US market would prove nothing short of disastrous, resulting in commercial marginalization at home. According to Dave Thompson, glam's failure to fly in America "was simple, Americans hate having fun" (278). On one level, of course, this is a ridiculous generalization. Yet there could well have been a kernel of truth in it insofar as their rock music culture was concerned. After all, the fall of 1975 witnessed the solemn canonization of Bruce Springsteen as the real rock deal, when, having been declared in all seriousness to be the "future of rock 'n' roll," he appeared as a *Time* magazine cover star and was touted as "rock's new sensation." There was little that was solemn or serious about avowedly pop glam. This meant that while its practitioners did make LPs, it was at heart "a singles-oriented phenomenon"—a modus operandi ill suited to American FM radio and now even to AM radio, which was busy forging an alliance with soft rock. However, from the fans at least, there was clearly still a demand for dressing up and putting on a show. Hence, a phenomenon like KISS, whose cartoonish, comic-book shtick made their brand of glam unlike like that of Sweet, let alone of David Bowie or Roxy Music. Lumpy hard rock tracks like "Strutter" and "Rock and Roll All Nite" were long on familiar heterobanalities and short on campy humor; but rockets were fired from guitars, the bass player breathed fire, the drummer levitated, and all members of the band wore towering heels, acres of spandex, and face paint that they were never seen without in public.

In her review of David Bowie's Carnegie Hall show back in September 1972, Ellen Willis had complained of feeling "unsatisfied" and even "the slightest bit conned." Coming across as "more like an aesthete using stardom as a metaphor," Bowie-as-Ziggy did not look or sound right "in the American context" (qtd. in Doggett, *Man*, 160). This was a similar conclusion arrived at by *Rolling Stone*'s Jann Wenner, who also believed that very different contexts had played a defining role in determining Bowie's success or otherwise, since the singer "had a very campy, gay sensibility which has always been part of the English popular culture, and not so here, not as ingrained." Perhaps Bowie—and by extension glam—was simply "a little too precious for the American audience" (qtd. in Sounes 256)? If so, this would mean that it would have to find another way in. On the Rolling Stones' '72 tour, Mick Jagger had worn a Ziggy-style one-piece. Yet, this was not the conclusive proof of bandwagonism, some spangly flag of cynical convenience, that it was sometimes taken for. For the Stones were arguably glam before glam, theirs by no means a sudden embrace of narcissism, camp theatrics, and rampant hedonism. The band would often be credited with playing a major role in shaping what the '60s had come to mean, but its sensibility and practice could be said to have marked it as a '70s outfit even before that decade had begun. Then, when it did arrive, it was clear that the Rolling Stones were neither hairy-assed, plod rockers nor plaid-clad troubadours. Leaving no one in any doubt, that 1972 North American tour was "bigger, louder and more extravagantly visual than anything staged by contemporary American bands" (Sounes 140). There was fire-breathing dragon artwork and a sixteen-foot-by-forty-foot mirror onto which six spotlights shone and reflected light onto the stage and into the crowd. Jagger wore the aforementioned Ossie Clark–designed jumpsuit perforated with eyelets and lashed together with cord—a costume accessorized with bangles, bracelets, a cross on a chain, and a pink sash that he would undo, burlesque-style, as the show progressed. *Très* Mercury, darling. (But *pre*-Freddie, of course.) Immediately after completing these US dates, Jagger flew back to London to catch David Bowie's triumphant Ziggy show at the Rainbow—where he would, of course, witness a similarly attired performer.

In contrast to its gritty, ramshackle predecessor *Exile on Main Street*, 1973's *Goats Head Soup* had apparently signaled the band's glam embrace on vinyl too, particularly on tracks like the shimmering ballad "Angie" and the louche and supersleazy "Star Star." Further proof, if any were needed, was supplied by the gauzy portrait of a bescarfed, androgynous Jagger on the album's cover, which could not have been more on message. It was, however, the Stones' next record—1974's *It's Only Rock and Roll*—that would unequivocally confirm that the band was now in full glam effect. Something that did not go unnoticed by the critics, who predictably charged the Stones with shameless bandwagoneering and regarded the album as an all-inclusive affront—from its very title to its cover to what lay within—to their firmly held belief in rock music as "transcendence not just cheap thrills" (Appleford 140). The album's artwork by the Belgian Guy Peellaert—the same artist kindred spirit Bowie had commissioned for *Diamond Dogs*—figured a sort of glam Nuremberg rally that would remarkably succeed in outcamping the cover of its predecessor, and in so doing contributed greatly to the rapidly hardening critical consensus that viewed this as the moment when the Stones irreversibly tipped headlong into self-parody. However, what really sealed the deal lay "within." As an apparently brazen act of gormless self-mythologizing, title track "It's Only Rock and Roll" was taken by the band's growing army of critics as damning evidence of the Stones' wholesale defection to glam. After all, what could be less "classic rock" than celebrating the function of music as simple palliative to "ease the pain, ease your brain"? As has been demonstrated, though, uberglam texts like *Ziggy Stardust*, *Aladdin Sane*, and *Diamond Dogs* had all "dramatized some of the darker obsessions of the early 1970s—apocalypse, angst, insanity and suicide" (Haslam 116). Declinism made vinyl. In fact, get past all the gloss and glitter, and one can find some pretty dark stuff in a lot of glam. "Is there a heaven?" Ferry had asked in the doomy "In Every Dream Home a Heartache." With echoes of Bowie's "Rock 'n' Roll Suicide" and "Ziggy Stardust," "It's Only Rock and Roll" kicked off with the singer asking whether his audience would be satisfied "if [he] could stick [his] hand in [his] heart and spill it all over the stage." Throughout, Jagger sounded "both in command and truly spooked as he contemplates the entertainment value of self-mutilation and public suicide. Perhaps real tears and insanity would also be amusing." These, then, represented "heavy questions." Even if—in typical Stones and typical glam fashion—Jagger appeared to be "playing them for laughs" (Appleford 139). Was he interrogating the destructive consequences of a wholesale commitment to rockism? If so, then "It's Only Rock and Roll" was hardly the vacuous call of the self-obsessing glam rocker.

The Stones' North American tour in the summer of 1975 would deliver even more glam bang for its nine bucks. This comparatively steep ticket price helped finance a highly theatrical show that had cost an estimated $1.6 million. "A lotus-shaped stage with moving petals and the first fully-suspended lights-and-P.A. rig, allowing an unobstructed view from every seat" provided the suitably glitzy backdrop to a performance in which "the corn came thick and fast: Jagger riding that inflatable white penis; a dragon's head spitting confetti" (Fricke 68). The fans loved it. The tour was a rip-roaring success. Stones albums continued to sell in their millions. Yet, through most of the 1970s, the band was subjected to an evaluative double whammy—one that saw it persistently graded against its '60s "self" and judged by criteria that were clearly shaped by that classic rock ideology to which virtually all rock journos subscribed. Similar to other glam acts, this would mean that the Stones were constantly being measured against something they never were or ever claimed to be. Perhaps the real failure lay with disapproving critics spooked by the unruly character of popular music in the 1970s. Like glam, the Stones embodied the decade's "ability to provide for an experimentation with self and with the borders between genres and forms, eras and periods" (Waldrep 5). Something that presented a challenge to those wedded to a very different model of rock practice and performance.

Notwithstanding the Stateside success of the likes of the Stones, KISS, and Elton John, it often seemed that while glam loved America, America was less inclined to return that affection. It might not have meant less than zero in the US, but its appeal was undoubtedly limited—typically confined to the coastal fringes and one or two big cities in between. Indeed, in glam's annus mirabilis, 1973, it appeared that the two countries "were as far apart as they'd ever be in the modern pop era." In this year, there had been an impressive total of ten glam number one singles in the UK. Over in the States—where it seemed that music fans "were still pretending the Beatles hadn't split"—there were none (Stanley 339–40). Two years later, and not one of Billboard's thirty-five number one singles achieved a similar feat in the UK. This suggests that the two nations continued to run on divergent pop rails, as does the fact that none of the UK's seven glam best-sellers came anywhere close to topping the US chart. The difference was perhaps understandably less marked in terms of albums, where, for instance, three LPs—*Elton John's Greatest Hits*, Wings' *Venus and Mars*, and Led Zeppelin's *Physical Graffiti*—were all transatlantic number ones in 1975. It is nevertheless telling that while the last of these would enjoy six weeks at the top of Billboard, it managed just a solitary week as the UK's best-seller.

Although not in agreement on glam, both nations did, however, share a mutual enthusiasm for disco. In 1974, disco's breakthrough year, George McCrae's "Rock Your Baby" and Carl Douglas's "Kung Fu Fighting" had been number ones in the US and the UK. Disco could be said to have developed as a response to the failures of rock. It "shared with glam a taste for hedonism, for escapism in the face of economic crisis, as well as a rejection of blues-rock jamming and its acceptance of homosexuality and of those marginalised by society" (Turner, *Glam Rock*, 144). The disco sensibility, then—in common with glam's—was characterized by a "determination to laugh, dance, and copulate in the face of the apocalypse," and so what was often missed about both was their "sensitivity to fragmentation and decay" (Philo, "Sucking," 296–97). Instead, of course, both genres were routinely dismissed as glib and self-centered by a rock mainstream—and in particular its scribes—disinclined to positively survey the field of '70s pop music, minded to take a dim view of its apparent lack of purpose and engagement, and unwilling, it seemed, to embrace anything different or new. Glam *and* disco boldly renounced rock's core values and eschewed its general direction of travel. To their many critics, then, both were proof that the 1970s could never be a match for the already fabled 1960s. Indeed, by the mid-'70s, the current decade had already become a "forgettable" one—a "forgettability" that owed almost everything to the sixties, "the outsize decade that dwarves all others in recent memory." So that, "by contrast," as Alice Echols notes,

> the Seventies seemed the decade when nothing, or nothing good, happened—an era memorable for [America's] hapless Presidents, declining prestige, bad fashions, ludicrous music, and such over-the-top narcissism that Tom Wolfe dubbed it the "Me Decade." Before the decade was out, this narrative of decline had become routine. (xv–xvi)

You gotta problem with disco (or glam, for that matter), then, clearly, you gotta problem with the seventies. For the latter, as represented by the former, was effectively figured as a betrayal of the beloved sixties—symptomatic of its status as "a trashy postscript" (James Wolcott qtd. in Schulman 145). Glam and disco would often meet with fiercest resistance from those who believed that the music could offer little or nothing of the weighty naturalism, sincerity, and authenticity that orthodox, '60s-stamped rock delivered. Disco—just like glam—was routinely condemned for witlessly channeling the zeitgeist, for bottling that "me decade," for soundtracking an "era of narcissism, selfishness, personal rather than political awareness" (Schulman 145). Yet, critics of both genres were surely missing the beat. Glam and disco would self-consciously deploy narcissism as a weapon, just as they would harness the cultural-political firepower supplied by and through the practice and celebration of hedonism. In this way, both were rather decadent, potentially subversive, fin de siècle propositions, sharing in an often desperate desire to dance in the face of the impending meltdown—seeking an "escape, an ultimately unreachable exit from a bleak world of stifling families, pinched circumstances, and decaying neighborhoods" (Schulman 144). In May 1975, CBS News reported that "Britain is drifting towards a position of ungovernability." In July, UK inflation stood at 26 percent and unemployment had risen by 250,000 in the space of just six months, and was fast approaching the one million mark. Disco was born of a similar context. Like glam, it was a "tale played out against a recession":

> The 70s [was] not . . . a particularly affluent decade. The oil crisis had sent domestic prices in America rocketing, and the knocks to the national confidence had led to a period of inflation. Discos suddenly became a more affordable alternative to going out to a gig. (Easlea, *Dance*, 66)

As with glam, disco was routinely condemned as contrived, mercenary, and fake; the pair was dismissed as shallow, insubstantial, and inauthentic. Yet, of course, both forms were playing by an entirely different set of rules. This made for a mutuality that helped "explain" Bowie's *Young Americans*, T. Rex's notably soulful *Zinc Alloy and the Easy Riders of Tomorrow*, and Roxy Music's "Love Is the Drug." Just as glam's embrace of dance music might be seen and heard to have been reciprocated by disco's embrace of glam, in the form of LaBelle Epoque, Funkadelic, and Chic.

In Bob Stanley's view, "like rock 'n' roll, and rave to come, glam's lack of a manifesto allowed all kinds of oddballs a stab at glory" (343). It is perhaps inaccurate to claim that glam lacked a "manifesto," but the fact that it was not beholden to one musical style undoubtedly meant that the more creative glamsters—those who were always pretty "fluid" anyway—continued to demonstrate that there was some mileage left. In the early spring of '75, "Make Me Smile (Come Up and See Me)" made it to the very top of the UK singles chart. Less angular than either "Mr. Soft" or "Judy Teen," it represented Cockney Rebel at its most pop, yet without sacrificing any of the cockeyed wit that had characterized those ostensibly less commercial offerings. In fact, "Make Me Smile (Come Up and See Me)" was arch, mannered, and allusive. Something that could also be said of Sparks' singles in 1975. As "This Town Ain't Big Enough for Both of Us" had demonstrated, looking for a plan or "manifesto" as far as Sparks was concerned was always likely to be a source of major frustration. However, the band's progressively more outré three single releases in 1975 did at least appear to be (sort of) linked. Reminiscent of "This Town," January's "Something for the Girl with Everything" was perhaps the most conventionally pop of the trio of 45s. With its Weimar vibe and cry of "All for one and one for all!," July's "Get in the Swing" featured a tuba, a French horn, a violin, and a dialogue with God. "Looks Looks Looks"—which just made the UK Top 30 in the fall—had apparently attempted to recreate a pre–World War II big band sound, in part, by employing former members of the Ted Heath Orchestra. With BVs inspired by Sinatra records, it made for an unlikely single. Nevertheless, it was very glam in its balmy eclecticism, humorous wordplay ("You've got a built-in seat that makes you look effete") and camp puns ("A face can launch a thousand hips").

Through the year, less fleet-of-foot glam acts were navigating the changing pop landscape in more prosaic fashion with mixed results. Mud, for example, continued to enjoy chart success as a fully fledged rock 'n' roll revival act ("Oh Boy" and "One Night"); Suzi Quatro's "Your Mama Won't Like Me" (UK no. 31) represented an ill-starred, ill-advised, and ill-conceived flirtation with disco; and November's lame cover of "Papa Oom Mow Mow" (UK no. 38) demonstrated little more than the fact that Gary Glitter had run out of gas. In May, Slade's "Thanks for the Memory (Wham Bam Thank You Mam)" had climbed into the UK Top 10. In doing so, it would at least outperform the previous single, "How Does It Feel?" Yet, the chart gain was marginal and, ultimately, could not disguise the undeniable fact of the band's declining commercial fortunes. (There would, in fact, be a near-six-year hiatus before Slade revisited the UK Top 10.) Although "Thanks for the Memory" featured both trademark humor ("an onion keeps everyone away") and ribaldry ("love-smell on your sheets"), it was still hard not to interpret this subdued single as a farewell ("thanks for the ball"), particularly as the band had now very publicly declared its intention to relocate to the States in the hope of achieving success in a market that had, thus far, resisted its charms. As it looked to complete its transformation into a hard rock outfit, this was also a move made by glam rivals Sweet. Sweet's second self-penned single, the hubristic "Action" (UK no. 15)—complete with cash-till sound effect—had launched a bitter, ballsy attack on those the band believed had either tried to block or exploit its success: "So you think you'll take another piece of me to satisfy your intellectual need." As contemporaneous interviews often bore out, Sweet's "enemies" included now-former songwriter-production duo Chinn and Chapman, and, on occasion, even Queen, whose "Bohemian Rhapsody" did bear a resemblance to the highly compressed, multi-tracked sections of "Action." In early '76, the synthy, operatic single "Lies In Your Eyes" (UK no. 35) would carry on communicating this burning sense of being slighted—this time none too deeply buried in its familiar lover spurned narrative. By this point, however, as Brian Connolly explained:

> Everything we did from then on was geared completely towards America. We didn't care about the UK anymore, we didn't care about *Top of the Pops*, [BBC DJ] Tony Blackburn and *Melody Maker*. If we could have upped sticks and emigrated, become American citizens and wiped out the past five years, just been a brand new band making the music we were making, we would have. . . . We knew exactly what we were doing. (Qtd. in Thompson 426)

While both Slade and Sweet envisioned success in America arising from their muscular embrace of a less glitzy, more prosaic form of hard rock, David Bowie appeared to see things very differently. "But now I'm all through with rock and roll. Finished. I've rocked my roll. It was great fun while it lasted, but I won't do it again" (qtd. in Heylin, *Madmen*, 287). Musically, he did seem to be distancing himself from orthodox rock. March 1975's *Young Americans* LP was clearly a long way from contemporaneous rock albums like Bad Company's *Straight Shooter*, the Eagles' *One of These Nights*, and Led Zeppelin's *Physical Graffiti*. It also seemed to be a long way from *Ziggy Stardust*, *Aladdin Sane*, and *Diamond Dogs*. Yet, as one of glam's principal architects, even those more recognizably rock albums that had preceded *Young Americans* had been motored by a conscious antirock sensibility. They were all also driven by a modus operandi fueled by reinvention and transformation. Clinton Heylin, though, has called it differently. In his view, Bowie simply opted for soul in one final, desperate bid for US success:

> He had tried and failed to sell the States on a form of English rock as glam as "Get It On," and as camp as "Blockbuster," so it was time to come clean: he didn't have the patience (or the money) necessary to

wait for middle America's mall-children to catch up. (*Madmen*, 290–91)

But why go for an African American popular music form to reach white middle America? Surely a less risky move would have been to get Mick Ronson back on board and make more straightforward rock? Still, whatever drove Bowie's decision, it undoubtedly paid off. *David Live*—a recording of a show from the latter part of the *Diamond Dogs* tour when it had morphed into a soul revue—had made the Top 10 on both sides of the Atlantic in late '74. *Young Americans* would put in a similar performance, its title track supplying him with his first Billboard Top 10. Greater chart success then followed in the summer, when the seriously funky "Fame," the second single to be taken from the album, would see Bowie claim his first US number one. In early '76, in the first of three shows at the venue that kicked off his North American tour, David Bowie would perform to seventeen thousand fans at LA's Forum. Dressed in a white shirt, black pants, and a waistcoat, his copper-red hair swept back, he opened the set with "Station to Station"—the title track from his latest album that would go on to peak at number three on Billboard and so become his most commercially successful LP in the US to date. Closer to disco than even than its predecessor "Fame," a new single, "Golden Years," had given Bowie yet another transatlantic Top 10 and earned him a *Rolling Stone* cover. According to Howard Sounes, the secret of Bowie's American success was no secret at all. It was down to the fact that he "persisted"—he "toured, he did call-in shows, and appeared on American television, promoting himself tirelessly" (256). This work ethic, though, hardly set him apart from less successful glam peers like Slade and Sweet, for whom success in the States would not be earned by simply laboring long and hard.

Early '76 saw Roxy Music achieve its one and only Billboard Top 30 hit with "Love Is the Drug." Up to this point, one might well have concluded that American audiences had been baffled by a band whose shape-shifting tendency played out very poorly indeed in the home of rock naturalism. Perhaps more than any single act, Roxy Music's lack of US success—the pursuit of which has been memorably described by Dylan Jones as "like trying to catch a fly with chopsticks" (43–44)—highlighted the significant transatlantic divide in both taste and practice that would come to characterize much of the decade. For one thing,

Roxy's "air of sexual ambivalence . . . was enough to complete their demonization in a male dominated rock culture still caught up in the denim-clad tailwinds of hippiedom" (Rigby 53). Indeed, the band had been subjected to homophobic abuse from the outset. This made it all the more ironic that when American chart success finally arrived, it should ostensibly be delivered via disco—a style subject to similarly sourced rockist-fueled condemnation as effeminate and fake. Opening with the scene-setting crunch of gravel, the slam of a car door, the turning of ignition, and an engine's throaty roar, the highly cinematic audioscape of "Love Is the Drug" was very glam in construction. With typical Roxy acidity, the sleazy lyric that followed had absolutely nothing to do with "love." Instead, it was about cruising—"I troll down town, the red-light place" and "parked my car, staked my place in the singles bar." Sex, then, is the real "drug" here. "I suppose it's a sort of disco record," confessed Bryan Ferry, before adding that "new customers [were] always welcome" (qtd. in Rigby 148). Yet, the track also retained much of Roxy's, and glam's, characteristic tongue-in-cheek humor—as when, for instance, "the lights go down, you can guess the rest."

In peaking at number two on the UK singles chart, "Love Is the Drug" became the band's most successful 45 to date in its own backyard too. (It would, in fact, take another "disco record," 1979's "Dance Away," to match this performance. Indicatively, "Dance Away" was also the only Roxy Music single to get close to "Love Is the Drug" on Billboard, reaching number forty-four.) "Love Is the Drug" had been kept from hitting the top spot in Britain by a reissue of David Bowie's "Space Oddity." Backed with "Changes" and "Velvet Goldmine," it is tempting to view Bowie's first UK number one as a fitting bookend to a glam era that had begun almost exactly five years earlier with the release of T. Rex's "Ride a White Swan." Certainly, from an industry perspective at least, it might have seemed as if every last ounce had now been squeezed out of the genre. Yet, it was not *quite* done. Sailor's high-camp "Glass of Champagne" would reach number two in early '76, while Slik's gumbo of classical references, melodrama ("ashes to ashes, dust to dust, will love last forever? / I know that it must, my love"), and a rousing teen-pop chorus would ensure that "Forever and Ever" went one better.

If these represented glam's death rattle, then it was clear that it had no intention of going out with a whimper. No single track encapsulated glam's unwillingness to go quietly more effectively than "Bohemian Rhapsody." "No! No! No! No!" "Bohemian Rhapsody" was enjoyably, knowingly over the top. It was an apposite, (unwittingly?) meta, curtain call for the glam years—"Goodbye everybody, I've got to go / Got to leave you all behind and face the truth." At nearly six minutes long but never outstaying its welcome, "Bohemian Rhapsody" stood as a symphonic endgame that simultaneously demonstrated the pleasures of the genre and the fact that it could possibly go no further. At a time when most of rock's main protagonists appeared to have stopped smiling, it had humor and joy in spades. Undeniably overwrought ("spare him his life from this monstrosity"), full of "Bismillahs" and "Beelzebubs," "Gallileos" and "Figaros," it was never pretentious or portentous, due, in large measure, to the fact that it was so funny and so much fun— "Thunderbolt of lightning, very, very frightening." Brought to a fitting close with the clash of a gong, here be glam in excelsis. If this was the end, then "Bohemian Rhapsody" would take glam out as it came in. Both ends burning. "Hot Love" had been at the top for six weeks. "Bohemian Rhapsody" would be the UK's number one for a staggering nine. Elsewhere on the Mercuryal, generically on-point *A Night at the Opera* (UK no. 1, US no. 4), "Seaside Rendezvous" was perhaps this LP's equivalent of "Bring Back Leroy Brown." In a vampy, vaudeville, end-of-the-pier, music hall style, it featured Mercury on the upright piano, accompanied by kazoos and a duck whistle, belting out a super-camp lyric—"What a damn jolly good idea," "so tres charmant, my dear," and "get a new facial / start a sensation"—that climaxed with him asking his audience to "give us a kiss." For Peter Doggett, tracks like "Seaside Rendezvous" and "Bohemian Rhapsody" channeled "a sense of joy that was entirely self-generated," creating music "that was about nothing more weighty than the pleasure of its own existence" (*Shock*, 455). Although not necessarily intended as a criticism (and indeed possessing a good deal of truth), this suggests that glam could be a rather onanistic affair—one offering its practitioners plenty of "jollification" ("Seaside Rendezvous") but "no escape from reality" ("Bohemian Rhapsody"). Yet if it really was that solipsistic, against what exactly should it be measured? How is mid-decade rock any more engaged or outward looking? One of 1975's most commercially successful LPs, Bad Company's *Straight Shooter* (US and UK no. 3) included such tracks as "Feel Like Makin' Love," "Good Lovin' Gone Bad" and "Wild Fire Woman."

One would be hard pressed to find more solipsistic fare than these tired, misogynistic odes to liaisons de la route.

Back in January, in a piece entitled "Kiss It Goodbye," *Creem* had filed a report on a "Death of Glam" event that had been held at Los Angeles's Palladium in late '74. This eulogy had been rather hasty. At this point, at least in the UK, glam still had a good twelve months more to run. With differing levels of artistic and commercial success, 1975 did, though, undoubtedly witness various and varied attempts at negotiating the inevitable "end of days" that pretty much everyone knew would surely arrive. Most of its players knew that it was "only rock and roll," that it was joyously ephemeral pop stuff. Yet, there would be an afterlife.

7

"WHO CAN I BE NOW?"

So, was there a pop vacuum that needed urgent filling in 1976? Glam may have appeared to have expired along with the final, sustained chord of Freddie's grand piano. However, as the varieties of rock and pop that followed confirm, reports of its death were greatly exaggerated. For, in their musical practice and performance, punk and post-punk, New Romanticism and New Pop, and—more obviously—glam-metal, were all indelibly glitter stained. With punk, then, it is too simplistic to argue that it enthusiastically nailed down glam's coffin lid. Although punk apparently reveled in its aggressive commitment to that great big glam no-no, authenticity, it also clearly adopted and/or adapted several of the latter's key ingredients. Indicatively, David Bowie and Roxy Music were often the only pre-punk role models British punk allowed itself. "Without Roxy," declared Adam Ant, "there'd have been no punk" (qtd. in Doyle 45); and, indeed, it is widely recognized that—particularly in the time before the movement had recorded music to call its own—tracks like "Editions of You" (1973) would function as a soundtrack staple at many a punk gathering. Pete Shelley had even covered the song in his pre-Buzzcocks band, Jets of Air. So, as Alwyn Turner has pointed out, UK punk was "largely populated by those who had grown up on glam, whether as musicians . . . or fans," noting that the "vast majority of British punks had grown up with T. Rex, the Spiders from Mars and Mott the Hoople, and [that] most were quick to claim the Stooges and the New York Dolls as well." He also persuasively triangulates, in proposing that despite the superficial differences, punk—like disco—had much in common with glam: there were art school backgrounds, references to Weimar and science fiction, a love of the seven-inch single and of invented names, a taste for provocation and for excessive dressing up. (*Glam Rock*, 146)

Many punks, then, concurred with the Specials' Jerry Dammers, who viewed it "as a piss-take of rock music, as rock music committing suicide, and it was great and it was really funny" (qtd. in Maconie 223). Iconoclastic, humorous, determinedly antirock, and avowedly teen-centric, punk was the work of the *children* of the children of the revolution. Yet, in comparing it unfavorably with punk, Dick Hebdige has looked to highlight glam's dereliction of duty. Punk is lionized for eschewing what he identifies as glam's "meta-message" of "escape—from class, from sex, from personality, from obvious commitment" (66). This is, though, a surprisingly one-dimensional assessment that arguably misreads both styles in underestimating the latter while romantically overestimating the former.

Less contentiously, glam was more audibly and visibly present in New Romantic's DNA. Found, for example, in Duran Duran's highly self-conscious mash-up of Bowie, Roxy, the Sex Pistols, and Chic; and, specifically, on tracks like "Careless Memories" (1981)—with its campy, cinematic lyrical references to "gun-smoke drifting in an empty room"—and the stompy, Glitteresque glory that was "Friends of Mine" (1981). Of course, *that was then*; but how did established glam acts fare in the immediate wake of its apparent demise? As has already been noted, while most could see it coming, their survival strategies were many and varied—ranging from pure, bloody-minded denial to wholesale willingness to "let go" and move on. Like Sweet, Mud had severed links with Chinn and Chapman. The band was also on a new label, Private Stock, having left RAK. These changes presaged a move away from glam-pop, and, particularly, the Elvis pastiches that had characterized its more recent output. A change in musical direction had, in fact, been evident on late 1975's "Show Me You're a Woman" (UK no. 8), which had seen Mud come over like a male Three Degrees on what was a somewhat rough approximation of the then-voguish Philly Soul. Summer of 1976's "Shake It Down" (UK no. 12) was an out-and-out, if unconvincing, cash-in on disco's continuing appeal, while "Lean on Me," an uninspiring cover of the Bill Withers soul classic, had made the

Top 10 in December. It would be the last time the band troubled the UK chart. This was a fate that did not befall Showaddywaddy. Persisting with the rock 'n' roll revivalism that had served it so well thus far, the band would be rewarded with its first UK best-seller, when "Under the Moon of Love" made number one in late '76. Six further Top 10 singles followed up to the end of 1978, by which time Showaddywaddy had been joined by another revival act, Darts, whose double A-side single "Daddy Cool / The Girl Can't Help It" had been the first of seven consecutive UK Top 20 hits the band enjoyed between fall of 1977 and the summer of 1979.

In February 1976, Slade's characteristically self-effacing valedictory single "Let's Call It Quits" (UK no. 11) had stalled just outside the Top 10. By now, all the band's energy was devoted to cracking the North American market. Britain, it would appear, had been given its notice to "quit." Like Slade, Sweet's response to glam's demise had been to focus its attention on building what it hoped would be a lengthy and lucrative career as a hard rock act in North America. This had also been driven by the band's long-standing desire to take control of its own artistic destiny. However, 1976 kicked off even less successfully than it did for rival Slade. "Lies in Your Eyes" could only limp to number thirty-five, while March's *Give Us a Wink*—the band's first self-produced and self-written album—failed to chart in the UK. *Give Us a Wink* did, though, perform better in the US, where it reached the Top 30, and so perhaps validated the band's now pretty much wholesale commitment to pursuing North American success. Through '76, Sweet would play a string of headlining shows in the States, but the following year would see no activity either live or on vinyl anywhere in the world. In fact, Sweet would not chart again until early 1978, when—helped by its inclusion on the soundtrack of the Jackie Collins soft-porn movie *The Stud*— "Love Is Like Oxygen" made the Top 10 on both sides of the Atlantic. After this, unlike a resurgent Slade in the early '80s, Sweet would never again be a commercial force to reckon with.

This, of course, was not to be David Bowie's fate. Preceded by the transatlantic Top 10 single "Golden Years," January 1976's *Station to Station* (UK no. 5, US no. 3) had been the first Bowie album to perform better in the States than in his homeland. The more challenging spring release "TVC15" (backed with "We Are the Dead") did, however, prove less palatable to both markets. It peaked in the midsixties on Billboard, and, in only just reaching the Top 40, broke a run of fifteen consecutive UK Top 30 hits that had begun with "Starman" back in the summer of 1972. In hindsight, "TVC15" could be considered an aperitif for what would become known as Bowie's "Berlin Trilogy"—three albums that either derived directly from or, as with the last of them, were influenced by his time living and working in the German city. The first of these was January 1977's *Low* (UK no. 2, US no. 11), which had included the single "Sound + Vision" (UK no. 3, US no. 69). Backed by another album track, the autobiographical (?) "A New Career in a New Town," "Sound + Vision" appeared to lend weight to a hardening critical consensus that viewed glam as a stage or phase in Bowie's "career." As an illustration of his ability and willingness to keep moving, it was, though, simply another expression of that very glam sensibility that had lain behind each transformation. Extracted from an album Bob Stanley has described as the "blankest, loneliest record in all pop" (333), it should come as no great surprise to learn that June's "Be My Wife" fared even worse commercially, in failing to chart in either Britain or the US.

Undeterred, in a prolific year, October 1977 saw the release of *Heroes*, which featured King Crimson's Robert Fripp and ex-Roxy synth man Brian Eno. Once again, while Bowie's superloyal fan base ensured that it would be another Top Five album in the UK, its Billboard chart peak of just thirty-five signaled a precipitous decline in his commercial fortunes in North America—one given further confirmation when its rousing title track failed to even make the Hot 100. September 1978's live double *Stage* (UK no. 5, US no. 44)—which had included versions of "Ziggy Stardust," "Hang On to Yourself," "Soul Love," "Five Years," and "Star," alongside tracks from *Station to Station*, *Low*, and *Heroes*—steadied the commercial ship a bit in the States; but the final part of the trilogy, 1979's *Lodger*, would continue the uncompromising musical journey Bowie now appeared to be on. Although *Lodger* (UK no. 4, US no. 20) did return him to the Billboard Top 20, it noticeably failed to supply any hit singles of even the minor, let alone major, variety.

Roxy Music's fifth album *Siren* had performed as expected in the UK; but, given the success of "Love Is the Drug," its chart peak of just fifty in the States was the source of some disappointment. In a presumably connected development, the band had called it quits in the middle of 1976. Bryan Ferry's third solo LP, *Let's Stick Together*, was released

that summer and spawned two UK Top 10 singles, including the title
track with its memorable video promo featuring a superlouche, pencil-
mustachioed Ferry and then girlfriend, model Jerry Hall, in a tiger-
print dress complete with tail. In very glam fashion, *Let's Stick Together*
also featured several "covers" of Roxy Music originals—"Sea Breezes,"
"2HB," "Chance Meeting," and "Remake Remodel" from the band's
first album, and "Casanova" from *Country Life*. Pop will eat itself. By
the time *In Your Mind* (UK no. 5) came out in February 1977, though,
Ferry's critical stock had hit rock bottom. While David Bowie had, by
and large, escaped the critics' opprobrium, this was not the case for
Ferry, who was subjected to sustained attacks, often bordering on outright abuse, from the British "inkies." At the mild end of the spectrum,
Charles Shaar Murray would write in October 1977 that Roxy Music
had been rapidly sidetracked/soundtracked into a

> chintzy evocation of Thirties/Forties movie star Gatsby and cocktail
> eleganza that had flat-out nothing to do with rock and roll at all,
> simply being an extension of the vapid croonerama that made the
> invention of rock and roll necessary in the first place. (*Shots*, 223)

Ferry's solo work, then, might have taken the "faux-matinee idol image
to its logical conclusion" (Hoskyns 64). Yet, it is too simplistic to simply
fix him as a kind of McCartney to Eno's Lennon, as the UK press
seemed keen to do at the time. Although the band's trademark wit and
camp might not be immediately apparent in Ferry's solo LPs, the Roxy
MO was still surely in evidence. Recasting those five Roxy Music songs,
for instance, was very postmodern and so very Roxy Music. As Ferry
explained, "It was weird 'cos in a way it was like I was covering myself
and trying to do them in a different way" (qtd. in Doyle 49).

It had not helped, however, that Ferry had relocated to California in
1977. At almost the exact moment David Bowie had made his "interesting" and so, in the eyes of the rock press, credible move east to Berlin—
where he would team up with the man they continued to see as Roxy's
true artistic heartbeat—Bryan Ferry had headed west, to the very epi-
center, the dark heart, of the showbiz mainstream. For a time, Ferry
has admitted, he rather enjoyed mixing it with movie stars, while also
recognizing that

> LA was very conservative in those days, there was nowhere to go,
> there weren't any cool restaurants. It was very old-fashioned in that
> sense. . . . There was no kind of street life. After a while it seemed
> rather empty and barren. (Qtd. in Doyle 49)

Punk was, of course, a major contributing factor to the mistreatment of
Bryan Ferry. Barney Hoskyns has proposed that punk "was glam ripping itself apart," drawing directly from the work of Dick Hebdige in
seeing and hearing it as a conscious "addendum to the 'text' of glam
rock—an addendum designed to puncture [its] extravagantly ornate
style" (95). In January 1978, *Harper's* magazine had identified the
"fragmentation and paranoia" as the "real keynotes" of the seventies
(qtd. in Beckett, *Lights*, 178). For many, then, punk "was the most
famous cultural significance of this mid-70s unease and volatility" (178).
Yet surely it was the undeniably more visible and audible glam that—at
the very least—got there first in registering such "unease and volatility"? At the time, with punk right in front of them, the critics simply
could not see or hear this. Writing in the *New Musical Express* in
October 1977, Charles Shaar Murray noted that glam had now "re-
ceded, leaving nothing but a sequinned scum over some of the rock that
it touched." While Shaar Murray clearly shared in that palpable sigh of
relief emanating from the massed ranks of the UK's music journos who
were simply glad to see the back of it, he was forced to concede that
"there was room for an awful lot of enigma-variation in the glitter universe." Above all, he appreciated that

> what it meant was that what the world needed less of was some guy
> in a beard standing with his back to the audience playing an organ
> solo for twenty-five minutes, and what it needed more of was short,
> sharp attractive-sounding records performed by interesting-looking,
> visually flamboyant geezers with a different attitude.

In this way, glam constituted the very essence of pop life. It was

> about posters on the wall, singles on the jukebox. That satin top in
> the window that would, please god, still be there come Friday when
> the pay packet / pocket money arrived so it could be worn to the
> Bowie / T Rex / Roxy Music concert on Saturday.

Plus, like all significant youth music movements, "it was a great parent shocker" (*Shots*, 223–26). In the same month as Shaar Murray's funeral address, a double A-side single of Roxy Music's "Virginia Plain" and "Pyjamarama" had been released. Designed to boost sales of a greatest hits package, it reached number eleven on the UK chart, where it found itself alongside the Sex Pistols' "Holidays in the Sun," Elvis Costello's "Watching the Detectives," the Boomtown Rats' "Mary of the Fourth Form," and the Stranglers' "No More Heroes." It did not seem out of place in such punky company. Neither had Marc Bolan. A little over two years earlier—in the summer of 1975—T. Rex had released the finest glam single of 1975. Spacey synths prominent at the start could do nothing to disguise the trademark boogie-shuffle and amiably bonkers lyric of "New York City" (UK no. 15) featuring a woman with a frog in her hand. With Flo and Eddie's distinctive banshee BVs, its single verse of just two lines, and chorus of three repeated lines with a fourth as payoff, it had all the ingredients of a classic T. Rex track. In this respect, it could easily be viewed as a retread, as proof of Bolan standing still. Of all the glam acts, then, T. Rex seemed to be the least mobile. Yet, this would not spell the end for Bolan. In the summer of 1976, "I Love to Boogie" (UK no. 13) represented the band's first single release of the post-glam era. Simple and repetitive, brief and shorn of hippy-dippy lyrical references, it was an expression of glorious denial and a willful refusal that aligned it with punk. In 1977 Marc Bolan would find his open embrace of punk reciprocated, as he took the Damned on tour and introduced the Jam and Generation X as musical guests to millions of viewers of his children's TV show, *Marc*. T. Rex and the Damned might have seemed unlikely allies. Bolan's most recent album, *Dandy in the Underworld* (UK no. 26), had, though, been a pretty lo-fi affair; and, in practice and sensibility, like the two genres they represented, they were not so different. Sex Pistols vocalist John Lydon and guitarist Steve Jones were self-confessed glam fans. Something that could be heard on the band's surprisingly rich, glossy even, debut album *Never Mind the Bollocks, Here's the Sex Pistols* (UK no. 1), which had come out in the fall of '77. As many punks did, the band also revered Iggy Pop, and Lydon had, in fact, auditioned with a version of Alice Cooper's "Eighteen," while the Banshees and the Skids would cover "20th Century Boy" and "All the Young Dudes," respectively. The punks themselves were often prepared to acknowledge a kinship. The rock scribes less so. On the very cusp of a comeback, Marc Bolan was killed in a car crash in September 1977. *Record Mirror* ran with the headline "Glam Rock Is Dead."

In early 1979 a reformed Roxy Music returned with a new album. *Manifesto* was the first of what would eventually be a trio in the band's Mk II era (1979–1982), in what are sometimes disparagingly referred to as the band's "disco years," a time during which there would be some notable US successes—for example, "Dance Away" is only bettered in its Billboard showing by "Love Is the Drug," while no Roxy LP will beat *Manifesto*'s peak position of number twenty-three—and, rather predictably, plenty of critical opprobrium. Embracing synth-pop and dance will also line up Roxy Music with the New Romantics, on whom, together with David Bowie, the band would have a profound influence in terms of both sound and (out)look, as pop culture—initially in the UK, but eventually in the States too—shifts in a "neo-glam direction" (Reynolds, *Rip*, 336).

Manifesto featured an "east" and "west" side, reflecting its collision of New Wave/post-punk and disco/dance. (In the case of the latter, did the presence of Luther Vandross on BVs and Marotta and Ferrone on percussion, and the fact that some tracks had been mixed at Atlantic's studio in New York, codify Ferry's still-burning desire to crack the States?) As it limped to number forty, the first single to be taken from the album, "Trash," hardly marked an auspicious return to the UK chart. It was, however, noteworthy for its adoption as a ready-made anthem for a new, still at this point nameless, subcultural scene then emerging from selected West End clubs that would subsequently come to be known as New Romantic. More successful second single "Dance Away" (UK no. 2, US no. 44) combined a by now familiar desperate desire to escape with a debilitating ennui. This, of course, made it very on message, linking it with earlier songs like "Love Is the Drug" and future Roxy tracks like "Same Old Scene" (1980) and "Avalon" (1982). For Gary Mulholland, "Dance Away" lacked "any of the pop-art edge and threatening ambiguity that made" Roxy Music Mk I "so extraordinary." Yet, he is still forced to concede that "although essentially a goodbye to the essence of Roxy Music, it was a fond farewell":

> It begins with Ferry lighting a [cigarette] and sighing, before that familiar vibrato leer sums up his entire "alone at the cocktail party"

schtick: "loneliness is a crowded room," and of course, the spectacular "she's dressed to kill / and guess who's dying?"

Ultimately, Mulholland has argued that "Dance Away" witnessed
"lounge-rock" giving way to "old-folk's disco" (86), an uncharitable assessment that was widely shared. Reviewing *Manifesto*, *Trouser Press*
charged Roxy Music with a "lack of adventurousness," for "pandering"
and so "conceding" to the "dreaded disco," and made a telling distinc-
tion between the album and "human music" (qtd. in Rigby 199). Writing in *Rolling Stone*, Greil Marcus dismissed the record as a "lovely
footnote" that led "nowhere" (*Manifesto*, web). Yet, as if to demonstrate
that they were more than a footnote, the band toured Europe with
twitchy post-punk art-rockers Wire, and hardly anyone appeared to
notice that the album's opener and title track featured a full two minutes of angular music-as-noise prior to Ferry's vocals crashing in—"I'm
for life around the corner that takes you by surprise / That comes leaves
all the need and more besides." As a comeback, it was neither humble
nor apologetic—boldly declaring "I am for the revolution's coming,"
urging us to "hold out" when "in doubt," and to "question what [we]
see." Once the lyric was done, it proceeded to serve up the kind of noise
then being made by John Lydon's post-Pistols outfit, Public Image Limited. By this time, Roxy Music had also recruited a new bass player—
the former Vibrator, Gary Tibbs, who would go on to play with Adam
and the Ants.

As a fourteen-year-old budding New Romantic, I had first become
aware of Roxy Music in the autumn of 1980, when, on the strength of
the modish hit single "Over You" (UK no. 5, US no. 80), I had purchased a cassette of the band's seventh studio album, *Flesh + Blood*.
Normally, there would be a battle to gain control of the communal
stereo we were fortunate enough to have access to in our school rec
room—a struggle that, in this Darwinian bear pit where seniority was
everything and I was currently at the very bottom of the heap, I would
invariably lose. However, attempts at playing *Flesh + Blood* proved
surprisingly successful. It was clear that Roxy Music—even a Mark II
version supposedly flirting dangerously with disco—was still a palatable
proposition to pop kids of all ages. To those eighteen-year-olds with a
taste for Crimson and Floyd, to the sixteen-year-olds "into" their punk
and New Wave, and of course to my own peers, desperately casting

around for a pop music style to call our own. It was perhaps for this reason that *Flesh + Blood* (UK no. 1, US no. 35) would prove to be even more commercially successful than *Manifesto*. There were, in fact, only five LPs that would better it for UK sales in 1980. Predictably, though, it also proved even less appealing to the rock authenticity lobby than its immediate predecessor. *Rolling Stone*, for example, declared it to be "shockingly bad." With its creation of a sonic landscape that will prove instantly influential, this is the album where and when Ferry's search for studio perfection really kick in. Yet the undeniably glossy end product is never cold to the touch. It could, in fact, be deemed warmer, more "human," than any predecessor. In the UK singles chart at the same time as Bowie's "Ashes to Ashes," "Oh Yeah (On the Radio)" (UK no. 5) combined a great hook with plenty of savvy references to the "radio." It was straightforwardly inclusive in a most un-Roxy way. Indeed, Rigby has rightly described it as "unashamedly sentimental," its lyric "drawing for a change—straightforwardly, sincerely—on common currency" and so "trad[ing] cheerfully in outright cliché—cars, radios, movie shows, 'our song'" (226). In contrast, "Same Old Scene" (UK no. 12)—the second single to be taken from *Flesh + Blood*—mined classic Roxy Mk I territory. Similar to "Love Is the Drug," it was motored by world-weariness, ennui, cynicism, and not a little self-loathing, depicting "a nocturnal existence devoted to non-stop clubbing and younger partners as a decadent vacuum" (Rigby 227). "Nothing lasts forever," we are repeatedly told. "Our lighter moments" are "precious few," the world being marked by the "heavy weather, we're going through." Dismissed by *Melody Maker* as "empty, disco-oriented pap," the "infectious rhythmic pulse" of "Same Old Scene" would prove highly influential. Indeed, it has been suggested that Duran Duran constructed "Planet Earth" and "then a career" on it (Rigby 227).

Whether true or not, it would appear Roxy Music might just have beaten David Bowie to the New Romantic punch. *Lodger* (1979), Bowie's last album of the '70s, had included the track "Boys Keep Swinging." When released as a single, it reached the UK Top 10. However, perhaps it was its androgyny and ubercampness—visually reinforced by a promo film featuring a cross-dressing Bowie—that was just too rich, *too glam*, for the States, where RCA released "Look Back in Anger" instead. The video had been directed by David Mallett. From a conventional beginning featuring the besuited singer miming to the song, Bowie then proceeded to appear as a trio of drag queens, from vamp to aging actress. Due to the very shifts Bowie himself had been instrumental in effecting, the impact of this video when screened on *Top of the Pops* in the summer of '79 was not as game changing as his performance of "Starman" had been on the same show seven years earlier. It did, though, demonstrate that here was an artist-musician still pushing. "Boys Keep Swinging" (UK no. 7), on which Brian Eno received a cowriter credit, had been produced by its musicians swapping "their" instruments, so that guitarist Carlos Alomar played drums, while drummer Dennis Davis played bass. According to Gary Mulholland, the end result was Bowie's "last great Berlin-era single" and "one of [his] funniest":

> With a glam-stomp compressed into a jangling ragged polyphony, it exhibits the first signs of the self-parody that would come to dominate Bowie's future. . . . But the pompous, pom-titty-pom voice he chooses here is perfect for the two levels of piss-take. Firstly, there's the whole homo-erotic undertone, all that swinging and other boys checking you out. But, more pointedly, "Boys Keep Swinging" baldly states that which was patently untrue . . . that young men still ruled the world. (86)

As Bowie himself confessed, "the effect is somewhat histrionic" (qtd. in Doggett, *Man*, 304).

"Ashes to Ashes," the lead single from 1980's *Scary Monsters and Super Creeps* (UK no. 1, US no. 12), has sometimes been viewed as evidence of Bowie's rather opportunistic reinvention as a New Romantic. Much of this is arguably down to its promo video, which featured Bowie in a Pierrot suit being accompanied on a Sussex beach by a bulldozer and several New Romantic scenesters recruited from Convent Garden's Blitz club. Of course, with the vision threatening to relegate the sound to a distant second, it was all very glam. "Ashes to Ashes" brought back the character of Major Tom, and further suggested that here was a sequel to "Space Oddity" by using characters and key themes from Bowie's earlier work: the Pierrot leading space cadets through an alien landscape; the madman in his padded cell; Major Tom, the now-spaced-out junkie with a bulldozer on his trail. "For me, it's a story of corruption," Bowie explained at the time, admitting that the song's "most anguished section—in which he effectively demolished his past as being neither good, bad nor spontaneous" was a confession—with those "three lines represent[ing] a continuing, returning feeling of inadequacy over what I've done, in as much as I don't feel much of it has any import at all" (qtd. in Doggett, *Man*, 315). As Peter Doggett notes, the song "was certainly a confrontation with the past, a confession about the present, and a sense of misgiving about the future" (*Man*, 316). "Ashes to Ashes," then, would not have been out of place on *Aladdin Sane*.

Bowie would help "make" New Romanticism, and not vice versa. For the so-called Blitz kids, he and other glam acts were the movement's "absent saints." Blitz "faces" like Boy George and Steve Strange were self-confessed Bowie, Bolan, and Roxy Music fans for whom "style was as crucial and defining as music" (Doggett, *Shock*, 508). "Surrounded on all sides by a casual array of slightly askew cinematic stereotypes in a self-consciously down-at-heel club in Covent Garden," Rosetta Brooks had described the Blitz in the very first issue of *ZG* magazine as looking something like the cantina scene in *Star Wars*:

> Tuesday night is the focal point at which these self-consciously styled individualists are brought into contact with one another. The setting is the ground against which these ironic self-images stand or fall within the microcosmic star system that posing represents. (537)

Here were the Blitz kids, aka the futurists, aka the New Romantics— members of the same scene Robert Elms had christened "The Cult with No Name" in a piece in the *Face* that had been subtitled "Nightclubbing and the Quest for a Life of Style." It had all started back in the fall of 1978, when Tuesday night was "Bowie Night" down at Billy's on Wardour Street—"a subterranean otherworld of diamante and occasional drag, where sharp dress meant everything and to be out was literally outside" and ex–Rich Kid Rusty Egan deejayed with the "turntables dominated by the Thin White Duke and the air was thick with an atmosphere of stylish and extravagant sleaze." According to Elms, it was Egan's idea "to transform a chance gathering of fashionable young things into an evening specially set aside for those with an abiding interest in all things Bowie and beautiful." As a result,

> Tuesday night became the night to look right as the still dominant black leather of the post-punk depression was rejected in favour of

gold braid and pill-box hats. It was toy soldiers, Cossacks and queens to the outsider, an odd fantasy world down the stairs; to the participants it was a mutual admiration society for budding narcissists, a creative and competitive environment where individualism was stressed and change was vital.

Billy's, noted Elms, "wasn't a place for those who dressed up for the occasion but for those who dressed up as a way of life"—at this point, "those" numbering no more than a few hundred. In February 1979, "Bowie Night" *decamped* to the Blitz in Covent Garden. Yet, it was still "a very small, closed world of some 300 devotees, among them clothes designers, artists, hairdressers and musicians" whose "looks . . . ranged from shoulder-padded futurism to fringed outlaw revivalism," and who "were revelling in the belief that they were all special, every one a star in their own right." *Très* glam, with a playlist that had by now expanded to include Iggy Pop, Kraftwerk, the electro-work of Giorgio Moroder, homegrown synth acts like Human League, and even—for a time in the winter of '79—an "immaculate version of Berlin in the Thirties" (15–17). Signing off his piece, Elms reported that

> outside of London the story is just starting. You might think this kind of thing couldn't happen in your town but you'd be wrong. The idea of commandeering a local club for one night of fashion and fun has already spread to Cardiff (The Tanschan) and Birmingham (at the Rum Runner). Embryonic scenes are also happening in Liverpool and Southend. (17)

And, as the *Face*'s Mick Middlehurst would confirm, in Manchester too. Interestingly, it was during one of his interviews with provincial New Romantics that he was told that Britain was "wide open for a huge pop hero at the moment. Sooner or later someone is going to take the teen market by storm, it must happen" (qtd. in Middlehurst 20). It did happen, and "sooner" than anyone—barring possibly the new "pop hero" himself—could have predicted.

In October 1978, Adam and the Ants had released "Young Parisians," a rather quirky piece reminiscent of Cockney Rebel, Sparks, or even Mk I Roxy Music—"Young Parisians are so French—they love Patti Smith." It demonstrated that, while nominally a punk, Adam was glam at heart. However, "Young Parisians," like his other late '70s single releases—"Deutscher Girls," "Zerox," "Car Trouble"—failed to chart. So, openly craving commercial success, Adam had paid former Sex Pistols manager Malcolm McLaren £1,000 for advice that he hoped would make him a pop star. Shrewdly betting on a post-punk return to glamour and heroic imagery, McLaren offered several ideas—including pirates, Native Americans, eighteenth-century fashions, and African rhythms—and urged his "client" to "wear gold and look like you don't need a job" (qtd. in Reynolds, *Rip*, 310). Unfortunately, Adam could only watch as, encouraged by his mentor, his band proceeded to desert him for a band McLaren himself was then in the process of putting together. (Fronted by the fifteen-year-old Annabel Lewin, Bow Wow Wow would also put some of McLaren's suggestions into practice and go on to enjoy limited commercial success.) For Adam, this was a set-back, but one that "did not soften his resolve" because he wanted to be a pop star so badly "with a single-mindedness bordering on obsession" (Rimmer 541). "I want success," Adam openly admitted in 1981. "Cult is just a safe word meaning 'loser.'" In Gary Mulholland's view, "no one, perhaps in Britpop history, ached to be a star as much as Adam Ant" (134). This had, of course, been said about Marc Bolan back in 1970. What was indisputable, though, was that Adam Ant would become the UK's biggest pop sensation since T. Rex.

Teaming up with former Banshees guitarist Marco Pirroni, he proceeded to put McLaren's seemingly random, possibly even madcap, ideas into highly glam practice—making use of Burundi rhythms delivered by a twin-drum attack last heard powering the Glitter Band guitars and "spaghetti western vocal chants to do nothing else but big himself up and make us dance" (Mulholland 130). In April 1981, as Ant-mania kicked in, Paolo Hewitt wrote in *Melody Maker*:

> All the time I spend with Adam Ant, I had a recurring feeling: déjà vu. At first, I thought it was a dream I'd had and left it at that. But the feeling persisted. So much so, in fact, that it was only on the train coming back [from an Ants gig in Newcastle] that I suddenly realised what it was. Then *I knew that I had been here before. Ten years ago, in fact, when Marc Bolan, David Bowie, Slade and Gary Glitter started inciting the kind of fan worship that Adam Ant is presently experiencing.* (Qtd. in *History 1981*, 48, my italics)

And Hewitt went on to note that

> the faces on the audience, the dressing up, the screaming, biting, and pinching, the devotions, and the worship, reminded me of when I first fell in love with music. Bolan was my first hero, Bowie my second. I was a fan then and so was Adam Ant. Only now he has five singles in the charts. (48)

Just like Bolan, Adam Ant would sell an "unmistakable 'look' (as he always put it) and an unmistakable 'sound' (ditto), but also a half-baked set of theories and attitudes that pinned the two together" (Rimmer 541). As Adam stressed, "The look has got to be as good as the sound." He also readily admitted that he "hadn't got an original thought. The originality comes in how I clash the ideas together and present them. That's all it ever is" (qtd. in *History 1981* 51, 49). This was all very glam, of course. As was the fact that, as with the glam stars of the early 1970s, he "understood that the formats and possibilities of mainstream broadcasting, from *Top of the Pops* to [teen-pop magazine] *Smash Hits*, were not only available but wide open, and had huge and thrilling expressive potential" (Stanley 529). This focus was also evidence of the strongly held (and frequently expressed) belief that what he was "doing" was show business. "I am more involved in showbiz than rock 'n' roll. I don't think rock 'n' roll is showbiz. I think rock 'n' roll is rock 'n' roll and showbiz is showbiz" (qtd. in *History 1981*, 50). A host of memorable videos bordering on pantomime and the band's "Prince Charming Revue" tour in late '81 would, then, effectively action the words and deeds of Bolan, Bowie, and a host of glam forebears, while simultaneously playing a lead role in British pop's glossy turn. As Kureishi and Savage point out, "the early eighties were a time of pop unleashed" and "the New Pop aesthetic was playful, referential, at times even academic, and wore its calculation on its sleeve" (535). Rather like Roxy Music then? "To be honest," Adam told Paolo Hewitt,

> the least influential music I've listened to is rock 'n' roll really. The most influential when I was at [art] college were Roxy. I was really into Roxy and that's when I wrote a letter to Ferry. (Qtd. in *History 1981*, 49)

Dave Rimmer famously said, in direct reference to New Pop, that it was "like punk never happened." He was wrong. For New Pop was as determinedly antirock as punk. It was also as determinedly antirock as glam.

Adam and the Ants' *Kings of the Wild Frontier* (UK no. 1, US no. 41) had been released in November 1980 and would go on to become the UK's best-selling album of 1981. On "Dog Eat Dog" (UK no. 4), Adam had extended an inclusive message reminiscent of "Starman," telling his rapidly growing army of followers that "it makes me proud to smile at you / and see innocence shining through." In the spring of '81, "Stand and Deliver," with the nation's teens gripped by Ant-mania, had entered the UK singles chart at number one, only the third single to do so since the glory days of glam back in 1974. Expressing New Pop / New Romantic values, it was, of course, also highly representative of a glam sensibility. Not least in its direct referencing of the dandy: "I'm the dandy highwayman / . . . / I spend my cash on looking flash and grabbing your attention." Of the accompanying promo film, Adam explained that it was "an Errol Flynn video," intended to look "like a three-minute Hollywood movie" (qtd. in *History 1981*, 51). If anything, follow-up single "Prince Charming" (UK no. 1) succeeded in being more brazenly showbiz, more camp, and more glam than its immediate predecessor— encouraging us not to "stop being dandy," reminding us that "ridicule [was] nothing to be scared of," and supplying us with another glossy promo video that featured a now-gone-to-seed former Brit-movie starlet Diana Dors as Fairy Godmother and synchronized dance moves that would make Mud proud.

Adam's tenure as the UK's biggest pop star was nearing its end by the spring of 1982. However, not before his first solo single, "Goody Two Shoes," made number one. A song about fame, "Goody Two Shoes" also included that most glam of ingredients, the direct reference to classic rock 'n' roll, in "quoting" the iconic rhythmic riff of "Jailhouse Rock" as it came to its theatrical conclusion. One of the acts lining up to replace Adam Ant in teen hearts was Duran Duran—a Birmingham band in whom the glam force would remain very strong. (As it would also prove to be in the band's two mid-1980s side projects—Arcadia and Power Station. Most obviously, perhaps, in the latter's cover of "Get It On," which went one place higher on Billboard than the T. Rex original in the summer of 1985.) Duran Duran were provincial New Romantics, whose first single, "Planet Earth" (UK no. 12) had been reminiscent of the upbeat apocalyptic glam-pop of Sweet's "Hellraiser" or even Bowie's "Diamond Dogs." In a patronizing 1982 piece on the band, Paul Morley described Duran Duran as "lightweight poseurs," "gummed-up glammed-over techno-rock twits," who have "blinded [him] by their bounce" (551, 555). The band members themselves, however, are as unrepentant as their glam idols in being fully (self-)conscious of what they are "about" and who they are "for." "It's coming back to what it was like before punk," they tell Morley. "During punk and just after there were no bands like us or Adam [and the Ants] playing Odeons that any age could go and see" (qtd. in Morley 553). Furthermore, as bass player John Taylor explains, "we were just never really into that grey, small-time independent thing. Our heart was in the early '70s" (qtd. in Morley 556). Paul Morley, though, is having none of it. He has clearly come to bury Duran Duran—"Duran Suave are committed to dragging glamour and fun and games into pop music: simplistically and selfishly, [like the] Bay City Rollers"—and concludes that the band "are heroes of the movement away from reading the self-important words to looking at the pictures" (553, 556). Like Duran Duran's eponymous debut LP, 1982's *Rio* (UK no. 2) would belatedly make the Billboard Top 10 in the wake of the band's successful MTV-motored US "invasion" in the following year. (In 1983, UK synth-pop acts would claim an estimated third share in both the Billboard singles and albums charts.) Via graphics and art-work, accompanying promo videos, and, of course, what lay musically within, *Rio* constituted the ultimate New Romantic pop package, the apotheosis of the post-punk glam aesthetic. Not so much the sons of Margaret Thatcher that the self-righteous likes of Morley et al. fre-quently pegged them as, as the sons of—often similarly reviled—glam fathers, for whom "recessions and economic insecurity" had also "pro-vide[d] fertile ground for fantasy" (Turner, *Glam Rock*, 148).

A lot of early '80s music might have been largely shorn of first-wave glam's latent dread; but there was still plenty of irony, camp, and, cer-tainly, no shortage of pop joy and glamour. It was also hard to miss the "dread" in the work some of the "Bowie-Roxy kids" were now produc-ing. In the summer of 1979, Tubeway Army, featuring Gary Numan, had had an unlikely UK number one single with the chilly electro-pop of "Are 'Friends' Electric?" from the equally bleak best-selling album *Replicas*. Although starting out as a punk outfit, Numan's inspiration and idol was David Bowie. This influence would be more in evidence on his first solo LP, *The Pleasure Principle* (UK no. 1), as well as in some of the things Numan would say in the many interviews he was now subjected to as a bona fide pop star. Stage shows would include stunning lighting, extravagant set design, and even robots. It was, as Numan explained to *Melody Maker*, "showbiz for showbiz's sake more than anything. I think I'm just taking it back to cabaret" (qtd. in Reynolds, *Rip*, 324). Japan's David Sylvian—who had taken his stage name from the New York Dolls' Syl Sylvain—was consciously rebelling against the mundane realities of urban Britain in the 1970s. In true glam fashion, Sylvian has spoken of his persona as functioning like a mask behind which to hide; key to his desire to be anyone but himself. The band's *Quiet Life* LP had made little impact when first released in January 1980. It would, however, reach number thirteen in the spring of 1982 as Japan hits its commercial peak. Though the single "Life in Tokyo" had failed to chart on its initial release in May 1979, a Giorgio Moroder remix would see it make the UK Top 30 in the fall of '82. Sylvian's affected, mannered vocals drew frequent and justifiable comparison with Bryan Ferry's idiosyncratic, un-rock-like vibrato-croon. There was also a familiar Weimar fixation to be heard on tracks like "Night Porter," "Suburban Berlin," and, particularly, "Ghosts" (UK no. 5)—the band's biggest hit and one that would arguably signal its most direct lineage with glam. No great surprise here, perhaps, given Japan had started out as New York Dolls wannabes with a Bowie/Roxy fixation.

"Blitz kids" Spandau Ballet's debut album *Journey to Glory* (UK no. 5) featured a title, artwork, and sleeve notes that combined to create a similar Teutonic vibe, a "Nietzschean tone of beauty-as-cruelty" (Reynolds, *Rip*, 327):

> Picture angular glimpses of sharp youth cutting strident shapes through the curling grey of 3 A.M. Hear the soaring joy of immaculate rhythms, the sublime glow of music for heroes driving straight to the heart of dance. Follow the stirring vision and the rousing sound on the path towards journeys to glory. (Qtd. in Reynolds, *Rip*, 327)

The band's first appearance on *Top of The Pops* in December 1980, performing its debut single "To Cut a Long Story Short" (UK no. 5), had given the nation's youth its first sighting of the New Romantics—"They wore spats and sashes, capes and neckerchiefs. Tweed jackets, even" (Beckett, *Promised*, 197)—while the third single taken from the album, "Musclebound" (UK no. 10) was a kind of New Romantic "Rock and Roll, Part 2." Ridiculous but fun. The Human League did not bother with such approximations. Its precommercial breakthrough mash-up of Gary Glitter's "Rock and Roll" and Iggy Pop's "Nite Clubbing" (UK no. 56) was indicative of the band's glam antecedents. Chart success would only come, though, after vocalist Phil Oakey had recruited two new band members—Joanne Catherall and Susanne Sulley—whom he had spotted dancing at "Futurist Night" in Sheffield's Crazy Daisy nightclub. According to Simon Reynolds, the album that immediately followed this change in personnel, *Dare* (UK no. 1),

> could only have been made by a group who knew about Roxy, Iggy
> and Kraftwerk, but their music was inviting and accessible enough to
> win over the great unhip masses—mums and dads, teenage girls,
> children, grannies. (Reynolds, *Rip*, 333)

As *Dare* was climbing to the top of the UK album chart, another Sheffield band, ABC, had made its *Top of the Pops* debut. Coming on like Roxy Music, lead singer Martin Fry led knowingly from the front in "white evening shirt with a dark but spangly suit—again the feel was traditional glamour in quotation marks—and danced in a cautious, heavy-shouldered way" (Beckett, *Promised*, 188). The message was very New Pop, very New Romantic, very glam—*anyone can be a star*. As Fry explained, "We wanted to look like we came from Vegas, so we went to Carnaby Street and hired this very camp tailor who used to make clothes for Marc Bolan" (qtd. in Reynolds, *Rip*, 379–80). ABC had evolved from a post-punk, Joy Divisionesque band called Vice Versa. The change in name was accompanied by a radical change in outlook. "Words like 'artistic integrity' are meaningless these days. It's got to be color, dance, excitement." The journey from Vice Versa to ABC was, for Fry, like going "from matt to gloss" (qtd. in Beckett, *Miracle*, 186), and nothing captured this better than the kitschy, campy, cartoonish, carnival promo video to "The Look of Love" (UK no. 4).

Powered by New Romanticism, New Pop reached its zenith in 1982. Described by the duo's vocalist Billy MacKenzie as sounding like "Abba on acid" (qtd. in Reynolds, *Rip*, 406), that summer saw the Associates' marvelously overwrought *Sulk* (UK no. 10) deliver three sizable hit singles: "Party Fears Two" (UK no. 9), "Club Country" (UK no. 13), and "18 Carat Love Affair" (UK no. 23). MacKenzie and fellow bandmate Alan Rankine loved, and evidently channeled, the glam work of Bowie (a cover of "Boys Keep Swinging" had been their debut single), Roxy

Music, and Sparks. Like their glam heroes, they too would draw on interwar torch songs, Sinatraesque ballads, disco, movie scores, and even postwar musicals. As Rankine, perhaps unnecessarily, pointed out, there was also "a hell of a Germanic thing going on in our music" (qtd. in Reynolds, *Rip*, 356). Elsewhere, though, in the gauzy gossamer-thin New Romantic years, glam dread was either missing or buried beneath a layer of heavily stylized pomp and pretense—as with Ultravox's rather silly but always enjoyable Weimar pantomime "Vienna" (UK no. 2). It would, however, find a more willing carrier in the form of goth rock. The Banshees had reportedly first met at a Roxy Music gig at Wembley; and, together with bands like the Cure and the Sisters of Mercy, owed a clear debt to glam in both sound and vision. As Banshee bass man Steve Severin confirmed, "That's what appealed about the intelligent side of glam—the fact that there was some kind of theatre going on, a drama was being presented" (qtd. in Reynolds, *Rip*, 404). Fueled by glam and rockabilly, goth rock would emerge from its spiritual home in Soho's Batcave over the winter of 1982–1983, offering an apparently real alternative to the then-dominant sounds of synthy dance pop. In the case of glam, the most obvious family resemblance could be found in arch-goth band Bauhaus, whose coverage of not one but two glam classics— "Telegram Sam" (UK dnc) and "Ziggy Stardust" (UK no. 15)—made it an easy spot. While the latter was noteworthy for being particularly reverential, much of the band's self-penned material such as April 1983's "She's in Parties" (UK no. 26) could be just as glam soaked— "Learning lines in the rain, special effects by Loonatik and Drinks / The graveyard scene, the *golden years*."

As had been the case with glam, there was much suspicion and often open contempt for this music in the UK's rock press. New Pop or New Romanticism (or whatever it was called) was antirock. Predictably, "attitudes to synths were even more polarised" over in the States, where "for many metal fans, keyboards were innately queer, their presence immediately signifying the ruination of 'real' metal." Indeed, "since Bowie," what had developed was "a real sense in which England . . . connoted 'gay' in the American rock imagination"—a perception often motored by the "over-bearing heterosexism of mainstream American rock" (Reynolds, *Rip*, 335). Yet, as it had done since its inception, glam would continue to find a way around this. In February 1978, Van Halen released its eponymous debut LP, and, lo, glam-metal was born. The band's cover of the Kinks' garage classic "You Really Got Me" was a Billboard hit and helped propel the album into the US Top 20. Van Halen was fronted by the flamboyant David Lee Roth, whose theatricality and showmanship supplied the band with most of its glam chops. Yet, as with Alice Cooper and Kiss, it was all still pretty testosterone-fueled stuff, with Roth playing the dandy in the Stones' heteronormative mold. The album *1984* included Van Halen's first US number one single, the hook-filled and synthy "Jump." Afterward, Roth departed to focus on a solo career of diminishing commercial returns, which was notable for a rather Ferryesque, campy, novelty medley of pre–rock 'n' roll songs, "I Ain't Got Nobody / Just a Gigolo" (US no. 12).

Other high-charting covers in the early '80s that indicated a disproportionate presence in the mix of more glam than metal included ex-Runaways Joan Jett's versions of the Arrows' "I Love Rock and Roll" (US no. 1, UK no. 4) and Gary Glitter's "Do You Wanna Touch Me?" (US no. 20) and Quiet Riot's cover of Slade's "Cum On Feel the Noize" (US no. 5). Sheffield's Def Leppard was more successful in the States, where "Photograph" (US no. 12) had been the band's breakthrough hit in 1983 and contributed to *Pyromania* peaking at number two on the Billboard album chart. Its follow-up, 1987's *Hysteria*, would go one place higher, with its hit singles "Animal" (US no. 19), "Pour Some Sugar on Me" (US no. 2), and "Love Bites" (US no. 1) all betraying the influence of Queen, Mott the Hoople, Slade, and Mick Ronson. Subsequent covers of Sweet's "Action" and Alice Cooper's "Elected" merely confirmed Def Leppard's glam credentials. The mid- to late 1980s also witnessed glam-metal's high-water mark, as the success of acts like Mötley Crüe—*Theatre of Pain* (US no. 6) and *Girls, Girls, Girls* (US no. 2)—and Poison—*Look What the Cat Dragged In* (US no. 3) and *Open Up and Say . . . Ahh!* (US no. 2)—confirmed. However, the genre made very little impression in the UK, where, in a period dominated by the Stone Roses, the Happy Mondays, rave culture, and indie "shoegazers," a band like the Manic Street Preachers would keep the glam fires burning on May 1992's "Motorcycle Emptiness" (UK no. 17) and July 1993's "La Tristess Durera" (UK no. 22). Cross-dressing and androgyny were most frequently delivered via two of its members, Nicky Wire and Richey Edwards, who wore T-shirts emblazoned with the slogan "All rock and roll is homosexual." Although sometimes identified as the instigators of Brit-pop (1993–1997), none of the acts associated with this genre were as self-consciously and recognizably as glam as Suede. Lead singer and principal lyricist Brett Anderson's mannered vocals, self-confessed admiration for Marc Bolan, and Bowie-like pronouncements—"I see myself as a bisexual man who's never had a homosexual experience. I've never seen myself as overtly heterosexual, but then, I don't see myself as gay. I sort of saw myself as some kind of sexual being that was floating somewhere" (qtd. in Maconie 275)—were accompanied by guitarist Bernard Butler's decidedly Ronsonesque licks on darkly decadent, melodramatic tracks like "Metal Mickey" (UK no. 17) and "Animal Nitrate" (UK no. 7) that would not have been out of place on *Aladdin Sane* or *Diamond Dogs*.

In the late 1990s, American ex-pats Placebo would find a more receptive audience and considerable commercial success in the UK. "Nancy Boy" would reach number four in Britain in the spring of 1997, with two more Top 10 singles—"Pure Morning" and "You Don't Care about Us"—to follow. Placebo would also record a cover of T. Rex's "20th Century Boy" for the Tod Haynes movie *Velvet Goldmine* (1998), which told the story of bisexual glam rock star Brian Slade—a fictional character heavily influenced in the creation by David Bowie, Marc Bolan, and Jobriath.

January 2018. "There is Old Wave. There is New Wave," ran a famous record company ad in the late '70s. "And there is David Bowie." Yet, Bowie is "for life," not just for a specific decade or era. As one of Anglo-American popular music's most influential artists, he has demonstrated that glam can be a rich and nourishing resource—"a velvet goldmine"—rather than a time-limited, rigid musical style or practice. For this reason, it is possible to identify its presence in some unexpected, possibly even unlikely, late twentieth- and early twenty-first-century places. In grunge, for example, where there was a kinship belying its spiky conscious counter to "hair metal," a real anxiety of influence could be found in, say, Nirvana's raw cover of Bowie's "The Man Who Sold the World" (1994). There was an easier spot, of course, with Brit-pop. Here, glam's sensibility was even on occasion tied to something musically familiar—on Oasis's Gary Glitter–referencing "Hello" (1995) or on Supergrass's buoyant and cocksure "Alright" (1995). And what are changelings Marilyn Manson—the self-styled "Pale Emperor"—and Lady Gaga, if not glam-franked superstars for the twenty-first century, continuing to practice transformation and reinvention in direct response to the challenge Bowie set? In the words of the Starman himself, "Who can I be now?"

FURTHER READING

Appleford, Steve. *The Rolling Stones: It's Only Rock and Roll; Song by Song.* New York: Schirmer Books, 1997.

Auslander, Philip. *Performing Glam Rock: Gender and Theatricality in Popular Music.* Ann Arbor: University of Michigan Press, 2009. Excellent, academic study that comes at glam from an illuminating angle.

Barker, Hugh, and Yuval Taylor. *Faking It: The Quest for Authenticity in Popular Music.* London: Faber and Faber, 2007.

Bayles, Martha. *Hole in Our Soul: The Loss of Beauty and Meaning in American Popular Music.* Chicago: University of Chicago Press, 1996.

Beckett, Andy. *Promised You a Miracle: UK 80–82.* London: Allen Lane, 2015.

———. *When the Lights Went Out: What Really Happened to Britain in the Seventies.* London: Faber and Faber, 2010.

Berkowitz, Edward. *Something Happened: A Political and Cultural Overview of the Seventies.* New York: Columbia University Press.

Bernstein, George. *The Myth of Decline: The Rise of Britain Since 1945.* London: Pimlico, 2004.

Blake, Andrew. *The Land without Music: Music, Culture and Society in Twentieth-Century Britain.* Manchester, UK: Manchester University Press, 1997.

Boucher, Caroline. "Roxy: Glamourous Paupers." *Disc,* September 16, 1972, web.

"BowieNet Live Chat Transcription—4/6/01 with David Bowie." www.bowiewonderworld.com/chats/dbchat0601.htm. Retrieved June 21, 2018.

Bracewell, Michael . *Re-make/Re-model: Art, Pop, Fashion and the Making of Roxy Music, 1953–1972.* London: Faber and Faber, 2007.

Brooks, Rosetta. "1980: Blitz Culture." In *The Faber Book of Pop,* edited by Hanif Kureishi and Jon Savage, 537–39. London: Faber and Faber, 1995.

Browne, David. *Fire and Rain: The Beatles, Simon and Garfunkel, James Taylor, Crosby, Stills, Nash and Young and the Lost Story of 1970.* Cambridge, MA: Da Capo, 2011.

Buckley, David. "On 'Time.'" *Mojo* no. 255 (February 2015): 54.

———. "Station to Station—the 100 Greatest David Bowie Songs." *Mojo* no. 255 (February 2015): 54.

———. *The Thrill of It All: The Story of Bryan Ferry and Roxy Music.* Kindle edition, 2013.

Cagle, Van. *Reconstructing Pop/Subculture: Art, Rock and Andy Warhol.* Thousand Oaks, CA: Sage, 1995. Outlines a persuasive case for Bowie as cultural politician, but arguably overplays the influence of Warhol et al. Perhaps understandable, given the rather US-centric nature of the study.

Chambers, Iain. *Urban Rhythms: Pop Music and Popular Culture*. London: Macmillan, 1986.

Chapman, Rob. "They Came From Planet Bacofoil." *Mojo*, December 1995, web.

———. "The Waiting Game." *Mojo* no. 106 (September 2002): 44–50.

Cochrane, Rob. "I'm Ready for My Close-Up Now." *Mojo* no. 60 (November 1998): 68–70.

Cohn, Nik. "On the Pop Song." *Daily Telegraph Review*, January 23, 2016, 4–6.

Collins, Andrew. "Sweet's Blockbuster." *Circles of Life* (blog). February 7, 2017. https://circlesoflife143.wordpress.com/2017/02/07/the-sweet-blockbuster-1973/.

Contributor in Music (Anon). "The Unbelievably True Story of Jobriath, Music's First Openly Gay Rock Star." https://www.highsnobiety.com/2017/04/25/jobriath-gay-rock-icon/. Retrieved June 21, 2018.

Doggett, Peter. *Electric Shock: From the Gramophone to the iPhone—125 Years of Pop Music*. London: Bodley Head, 2015.

———. *The Man Who Sold the World: David Bowie and the 1970s*. London: Bodley Head, 2011. Song-by-song analysis that does for Bowie what Ian MacDonald did in *A Revolution in the Head* for the Beatles.

Doyle, Tom. "On Roxy Music." *Mojo* no. 252 (November 2014): 44–49.

Du Noyer, Paul. "Bowie on Bowie." *Mojo* no. 268 (March 2016): 72–78.

Dyer, Richard. "In Defence of Disco." In *On Record: Rock, Pop and the Written Word*, edited by Simon Frith and Andrew Goodwin, 410–18. London: Routledge, 1990.

Easlea, Daryl. *Everybody Dance: Chic and the Politics of Disco*. London: Helter Skelter, 2004.

———. *Talent Is an Asset: The Story of Sparks*. London: Omnibus, 2009.

Echols, Alice. *Hot Stuff: Disco and the Remaking of American Culture*. New York: Norton, 2010.

Egan, Sean, ed. *The Mammoth Book of the Rolling Stones*. London: Robinson, 2013.

Elms, Robert. "The Cult with No Name." In *Night Fever: Club Writing in the Face 1980–1997*, edited by Richard Benson, 15–17. London: Boxtree, 1997.

Ennis, Philip. *The Seventh Stream: The Emergence of Rock 'n' Roll in American Music*. Hanover, NH: University Press of New England, 1992.

Fricke, David. *Mojo* no. 236 (July 2013): 68.

Frith, Simon. "1973: A Year in Singles." In *Penguin Book of Rock and Roll Writing*, edited by Clinton Heylin, 486–95. London: Penguin, 1993.

Gahan, Dave. "What an Amazing Legacy." *Mojo* no. 268 (March 2016): 88.

Gilbert, Pat. "On 'The Jean Genie.'" *Mojo* no. 255 (February 2015): 60.

Gillett, Charlie. *The Sound of the City: The Rise of Rock and Roll*. Rev. ed. London: Souvenir, 1983.

Harris, John. *Guardian*, January 12, 2016, 33.

———. "Whatever Happened to the Likely Lads?" *Mojo* no. 156 (November 2006): 48–56.

Haslam, Dave. *Not ABBA: The Real Story of the 1970s*. London: Fourth Estate, 2005.

Hawkins, Stan. *The British Pop Dandy: Masculinity, Popular Music and Culture: Male Identity, Music and Culture*. Aldershot, UK: Ashgate, 2009.

Hebdige, Dick. *Subculture: The Meaning of Style*. London: Routledge, 1993.

Hepworth, Dave. *1971: Never a Dull Moment*. London: Bantam, 2016. By the author's admission, it's all about "rock" and mostly about albums. Perhaps why, though setting out to challenge "the cliché that the early 70s were a mere lull" before punk hit hard, glam's significance is rather downplayed. Almost dismissive of Marc Bolan, 1971's biggest "thing."

Heylin, Clinton. *All the Madmen: Barrett, Bowie, Drake, Pink Floyd, the Kinks, the Who and a Journey to the Dark Side of British Rock*. London: Constable, 2012.

———. *The Act You've Known All These Years: The Life, and Afterlife, of Sgt. Pepper*. Edinburgh: Canongate, 2007.

———. *From the Velvets to the Voidoids: A Pre-punk History for a Post-punk World*. London: Penguin, 1993.

History of Rock 1972. London: Time, 2016.

History of Rock 1973. London: Time, 2016.

History of Rock 1974. London: Time, 2016.

History of Rock 1975. London: Time, 2016.

History of Rock 1981. London: Time, 2017.

Holdship, Bill. *Mojo* no. 236 (July 2013): 68.

Hoskyns, Barney. *Glam! Bowie, Bolan and the Glitter Rock Revolution.* London: Faber and Faber, 1998. As its title suggests, this brief and largely Bowie-Bolan-Roxy-focused study persuasively documents glam's rock revolt.

Hotten, Jon. "One Vision: The Unseen Queen, As Photographed by Mick Rock." https://www.loudersound.com/features/one-vision-the-unseen-queen-as-photographed-by-mick-rock. Retrieved June 21, 2018.

Inglis, Ian. "Synergies and Reciprocities: The Dynamics of Musical and Professional Interaction between the Beatles and Bob Dylan." *Popular Music and Society* 20, no. 4 (1996): 53–79.

Jackson, Andrew Grant. *1965: The Most Revolutionary Year in Music.* New York: Thomas Dunne, 2015.

Jones, Dylan. *iPod, Therefore I Am: A Personal Journey through Music.* London: Weidenfeld and Nicolson, 2005.

Kaufman, Will. *American Culture in the 1970s.* Edinburgh: Edinburgh University Press, 2009.

Kureishi, Hanif. "The Bromley Contingent." *Guardian Review*, August 12, 2017, 2–4.

Kureishi, Hanif and Jon Savage, eds. *The Faber Book of Pop.* London: Faber and Faber, 1995.

Loui. Post under "Teenage Rampage: Mary Whitehouse, the BBC and Sweet." The Sweet Glam Forum. August 26, 2016. http://www.tapatalk.com/groups/thesweetglamforum/mary-whitehouse-teenage-rampage-the-bbc-and-sweet-t9846.html. Retrieved August 16, 2017.

Maconie, Stuart. *The People's Songs: The Story of Modern Britain in 50 Records.* London: Ebury, 2013.

Marcus, Greil. "Roxy Music: Manifesto." https://www.rollingstone.com/music/albumreviews/manifesto-20021018. Retrieved June 21, 2018.

———. *Stranded: Rock and Roll for a Desert Island.* Cambridge, MA: Da Capo, 2007.

Marr, Johnny. "What an Amazing Legacy." *Mojo* no. 268 (March 2016): 87.

Marsh, Dave. *The Heart of Rock and Soul: The 1001 Greatest Singles Ever Made.* London: Penguin, 1989.

McCormick, Thomas. *America's Half-Century.* Baltimore: Johns Hopkins University Press, 1989.

McKay, Alastair. "The Rise and Fall of Ziggy Stardust." In *Uncut Ultimate Music Guide: David Bowie*, 28–29. London: Time, 2015.

Melly, Jim. *"Last Orders, Please": Rod Stewart, the Faces and the Britain We Forgot.* London: Ebury, 2003.

Middlehurst, Mick. "Bringing on the Clones." In *Night Fever: Club Writing in the Face 1980–1997*, edited by Richard Benson, 18–21. London: Boxtree, 1997.

Miller, James. *Almost Grown: The Rise of Rock.* London: William Heinemann, 1999.

Millward, Steve. *Fast Forward: Music and Politics in 1974.* Kibworth Beauchamp, UK: Matador, 2016.

Moore, Suzanne. "We Wanted to Know What He Knew." *Guardian*, January 12, 2016, 33.

Morley, Paul. "1982: A Salmon Screams." In *The Faber Book of Pop*, edited by Hanif Kureishi and Jon Savage, 551–59. London: Faber and Faber, 1995.

Mueller, Andrew. *"Pin Ups." Uncut: The Ultimate Music Guide: David Bowie.* June 2015, 38–39.

Mulholland, Gary. *This Is Uncool: The 500 Greatest Singles Since Punk and Disco.* London: Cassell Illustrated, 2002.

Palmer, Tony. *All You Need Is Love: The Story of Popular Music.* London: Futura, 1977.

Paytress, Mark. *Bolan: The Rise and Fall of a Twentieth Century Superstar.* London: Omnibus, 2002. Definitive biography.

———. "Yeah, I Want That Sound." *Mojo* no. 138 (May 2005): 72–88.

Peacock, Steve. "The Case of the Vanishing Image." *Sounds*, July 1972, web.

Penman, Ian. "Wham Bang, Tea-Time." *London Review of Books*, January 5, 2017, 21–26.

Philo, Simon. *British Invasion: The Crosscurrents of Musical Influence*. Lanham, MD: Rowman & Littlefield, 2014.

———. "Not Sucking in the Seventies: The Rolling Stones and the Myth of Decline." *Rock Music Studies* 2, no. 3 (2015): 295–314.

Reynolds, Simon. "Is Politics the New Glam Rock?" *Guardian Review*, October 15, 2016, 14.

———. *Retromania: Pop Culture's Addiction to Its Own Past*. London: Faber and Faber, 2011.

———. *Rip It Up and Start Again: Postpunk 1978–1984*. London: Faber and Faber, 2005.

———. *Shock and Awe: Glam Rock and Its Legacy from the Seventies to the Twenty-First Century*. London: Faber and Faber, 2016.

Reynolds, Simon, and Joy Press. *The Sex Revolts: Gender, Rebellion and Rock 'n' Roll*. London: Serpent's Tail, 1995.

Rigby, Jonathan. *Roxy Music: Both Ends Burning*. London: Reynolds & Hearn, 2008.

Rimmer, Dave. "1981: The Birth of the New Pop." In *The Faber Book of Pop*, edited by Hanif Kureishi and Jon Savage, 539–42. London: Faber and Faber, 1995.

Rogan, Johnny. *Roxy Music: Style with Substance—Roxy's First Ten Years*. London: Star, 1982.

Sandbrook, Dominic. *Seasons in the Sun: The Battle for Britain, 1974–1979*. London: Penguin, 2013.

———. *State of Emergency: The Way We Were; Britain 1970–1974*. London: Penguin, 2011. Perhaps surprisingly, doesn't really "get" glam. What he does "get," however, is the context out of which it grew and to which it responded. As ever, a story told with clarity and élan.

Savage, Jon. *England's Dreaming: Sex Pistols and Punk Rock*. London: Faber and Faber, 1991.

———. "Kiss and Tell." *Mojo* no. 60 (November 1998): 82–84.

———. *1966: The Year the Decade Exploded*. London: Faber and Faber, 2015.

———. "A Work of Art." *Mojo* no. 268 (March 2016): 84–85.

Schulman, Bruce. *The Seventies: The Great Shift in American Culture, Society and Politics*. Cambridge, MA: Da Capo, 2002.

Shaar Murray, Charles. *Shots from the Hip*. London: Penguin, 1991.

———. "The View from Seat T39." In *The Faber Book of Pop*, edited by Hanif Kureishi and Jon Savage, 406–10. London: Faber and Faber, 1995.

Shapiro, Peter. *Turn the Beat Around: The Secret History of Disco*. London: Faber and Faber, 2005.

Shuker, Roy. *Key Concepts in Popular Music*. London: Routledge, 1998.

Sioux, Siouxsie. "What an Amazing Legacy." *Mojo* no. 268 (March 2016): 84.

Sounes, Howard. *Seventies: The Sights, Sounds and Ideas of a Brilliant Decade*. London: Simon & Schuster, 2006. Offers buzzy, wide-ranging snapshots in myth-busting defense of "brilliant" 1970s.

Stanford, Peter. "Queen: Their Finest Moment at Live Aid." *Daily Telegraph*, September 24, 2011. telegraph.co.uk. Retrieved December 17, 2017.

Stanley, Bob. *Yeah Yeah Yeah: The Story of Modern Pop*. London: Faber and Faber, 2013.

Strong, M. C. *The Wee Rock Discography*. Edinburgh: Canongate, 1996.

Stump, Paul. *Unknown Pleasures: A Cultural Biography of Roxy Music*. London: Quartet, 1998.

Thompson, Dave. *Children of the Revolution: The Glam Rock Story 1970–75*. London: Cherry Red, 2010. Sparky, blow-by-blow account of the peak glam years.

Trynka, Paul. "Man and Spiderman." *Mojo* no. 255 (February 2015): 62–67.

Turner, Alwyn. *Crisis? What Crisis? Britain in the 1970s*. London: Aurum, 2008.

———. *Glam Rock: Dandies in the Underworld*. London: V&A, 2013.

Visconti, Tony. "Hype Man Cometh." *Mojo* no. 255 (February 2015): 65.

———. "We All Thought He Had More Time." *Mojo* no. 268 (March 2016): 86–87.

VivaRoxyMusic. www.vivaroxymusic.com/articles_189.php. Retrieved June 21, 2018.

Waldrep, Shelton. "Introducing the Seventies." In *The Seventies: The Age of Glitter in Popular Culture*, edited by Shelton Waldrep, 1–15. New York: Routledge, 2000. Revisionist challenge to the crowded anti-'70s lobby.

Walters, Barry. "David Bowie, Diamond Dogs." Pitchfork.com, January 16, 2016. Retrieved December 15, 2017.

Whatley, Francis, dir. *David Bowie: The Last Five Years*. BBC2, January 7, 2017.

Wheen, Francis. *Strange Days Indeed: The Golden Age of Paranoia*. London: Fourth Estate, 2010.

Wyn Jones, Carys. *The Rock Canon: Canonical Values in the Reception of Rock Albums*. Aldershot, UK: Ashgate, 2008.

FURTHER LISTENING

Arranged chronologically to capture the "glam years." UK record labels unless otherwise stated.

1966–1970, "Children of the Revolution"

"Have You Seen Your Mother Baby, Standing in the Shadow?" the Rolling Stones (September 1966), Single, Decca. And have *you* seen the promo video?

"We Love You," the Rolling Stones (August 1967), Single, Decca. More cross-dressing in the Oscar Wilde–referencing promo.

"Debora," Tyrannosaurus Rex (April 1968), Single, Regal Zono. Minor UK hit for Bolan.

"Jumping Jack Flash," the Rolling Stones (May 1968), Single, Decca. "It's a gas, gas, gas."

"Yummy Yummy Yummy," Ohio Express (May 1968), Single, Pye. Bubblegum.

"One Inch Rock," Tyrannosaurus Rex (August 1968), Single, Regal Zono. Bolan reached the UK Top 30 with this single.

Unicorn, Tyrannosaurus Rex (May 1969), Album, Regal Zono. Peaked at no. 12 in the UK.

"Space Oddity," David Bowie (July 1969), Single, Philips. Early Bowie foray into space dread. UK no. 5.

"Sugar, Sugar," the Archies (September 1969), Single, RCA. More bubblegum. Biggest-selling single in the US in 1969.

"Lola," the Kinks (June 1970), Single, Pye. No. 2 in UK; Top 10 in US.

"Ride a White Swan," T. Rex (October 1970), Single, EMI. Peaked at no. 2 in January 1971. Glam's breakthrough single.

"I Hear You Knocking," Dave Edmunds Rockpile (November 1970), Single, MAM. UK best-seller for six weeks.

T. Rex, T. Rex (December 1970), Album, EMI. Now "abbreviated" and mean serious glam business.

1971, "Get It On"

The Man Who Sold the World, David Bowie (January 1971), Album, Mercury. Did Not Chart (DNC). Pre-glam; but check out Bowie in a dress on the UK cover.

"Funny Funny," Sweet (January 1971), Single, RCA. Sweet's first Chinn-and-Chapman-written-and-produced hit.

"Hot Love," T. Rex (February 1971), Single, EMI. Six weeks at no. 1 in UK.

"Eighteen," Alice Cooper (February 1971), Single, Warner Bros. Top 30 in the US.

"Co-Co," Sweet (May 1971), Single, RCA. No. 2 in the UK. No. 93 in the US. Still in bubblegum mode. Still not playing own instruments!

"Get Down and Get with It," Slade (June 1971), Single, Polydor. Slade's first hit 45.

"Get It On," T. Rex (July 1971), Single, EMI. Four weeks at no. 1 in the UK. Billboard Top 10 in early '72.

Electric Warrior, T. Rex (September 1971), Album, EMI. A total of eight weeks at no. 1 in the UK, and the year's best-selling LP. Peaked at no. 32 in the States.

"Coz I Luv You," Slade (October 1971), Single, Polydor. Four weeks at no. 1 in UK.

"Alexander Graham Bell," Sweet (October 1971), Single, RCA. Disappointingly stalled outside the UK Top 30.

"Jeepster," T. Rex (November 1971), Single, EMI. UK no. 2; DNC in the USA.

Hunky Dory, David Bowie (December 1971), Album, RCA. DNC on initial release, but would peak at no. 3 in September 1972. Featured some glam songs ("Queen Bitch" and "Changes," for example) while covering some key glam subject matter (space travel and gender-bending).

Killer, Alice Cooper (December 1971), Album, Warner Bros. Top 30 on both sides of the Atlantic.

1972, "Hang On to Yourself"

"Telegram Sam," T. Rex (January 1972), Single, EMI. Two weeks at no. 1 in UK. No surprise. It's the height of Trexstasy, and this is quintessential glitter rock.

"Look Wot You Dun," Slade (February 1972), Single, Polydor. UK no. 4.

"Rock and Roll (Parts 1 & 2)," Gary Glitter (March 1972), Single, Bell. Eventually climbed to no. 2 in UK, thanks to the dance hall/disco appeal of "Part 2."

"Back Off Boogaloo," Ringo Starr (March 1972), Single, Apple. Starr directed Bolan's movie *Born to Boogie* and released this glam-inspired single that reached both the UK and US Top 10s.

Slade Alive!, Slade (April 1972), Album, Polydor. UK no. 2.

"Starman," David Bowie (April 1972), Single, RCA. Bowie's first UK Top 10 since "Space Oddity." Jet-propelled by a memorable TV performance on *Top of the Pops*. Only reached no. 65 in the US.

"Rocket Man," Elton John (April 1972), Single, DJM. Excluding duet with Kiki Dee, highest-charting UK single of the decade (no. 2). Top 10 in the US.

"Metal Guru," T. Rex (May 1972), Single, EMI. Back-to-back UK no. 1s for Bolan.

The Rise and Fall of Ziggy Stardust and the Spiders from Mars, David Bowie (June 1972), Album, RCA. Peaking at no. 5, represented Bowie's first genuine long-form best-seller. Only reached no. 75 on Billboard.

Roxy Music, Roxy Music (June 1972), Album, Island. UK Top 10 for RM's impressive debut LP.

"Little Willy," Sweet (June 1972), Single, RCA. Another UK hit single.

"Take Me Bak 'Ome," Slade (June 1972), Single, Polydor. Slade's second UK no. 1.

"All the Young Dudes," Mott the Hoople (July 1972), Single, CBS. UK no. 3; US no. 37. Bowie-penned, T. Rex name-checking, glam anthem/manifesto. LP of same name would also include a cover of Velvet Underground's "Sweet Jane."

"School's Out," Alice Cooper (July 1972), Single, Warner Bros. A UK no. 1 for three weeks. Top 10 in the States. Worth noting that it isn't college that is "out."

The Slider, T. Rex (July 1972), Album, EMI. UK no. 4; US no. 17.

"Virginia Plain," Roxy Music (August 1972), Single, Island. Like "Hot Love" and "Starman" before it, this one gets a boost from a memorable performance on *Top of the Pops*. Peaks at no. 4 in the UK.

"Mama Weer All Crazee Now," Slade (August 1972), Single, Polydor. Yet another no. 1 for Slade.

"Children of the Revolution," T. Rex (September 1972), Single, EMI. No. 2 in UK.

"John, I'm Only Dancing," David Bowie (September 1972), Single, RCA. Queerer and queerer.

"Wig Wam Bam," Sweet (September 1972), Single, RCA. Top 10 UK. Noticeably harder, rockier sound. First 45 on which the band played its own instruments.

"I Didn't Know I Loved You (Till I Saw You Rock and Roll)," Gary Glitter (September 1972), Single, Bell. UK Top 5.

"Crazy Horses," the Osmonds (October 1972), Single, MGM. UK no. 2. A cash-in maybe; glammest Osmonds' single, no question.

"Elected," Alice Cooper (October 1972), Single, Warner Bros. UK no. 4; just no. 26 in the US.

Transformer, Lou Reed (November 1972), Album, RCA. Bowie-produced LP that reached UK Top 20 and US Top 30.

"Walk on the Wild Side," Lou Reed (November 1972), Single, RCA. UK Top 10; Billboard Top 20.

"The Jean Genie," David Bowie (November 1972), Single, RCA. UK no. 2; just no. 71 in US.

"Gudbuy T'Jane," Slade (November 1972), Single, Polydor.

Slayed?, Slade (December 1972), Album, Polydor. Second glam LP to reach no. 1 in the UK.

"Solid Gold, Easy Action," T. Rex (December 1972), Single, EMI. Another no. 2.

"Blockbuster," Sweet (December 1972), Single, RCA. Spent five weeks at no. 1 in early '73.

"Ball Park Incident," Wizzard (December 1972), Single, Harvest. UK Top 10.

1973, "Cum On Feel the Noize"

"Do You Want to Touch Me?" Gary Glitter (January 1973), Single, Bell. Yet another UK no. 2.

"Cum On Feel the Noize," Slade (February 1973), Single, Polydor. Fourth UK best-seller.

"Pyjamarama," Roxy Music (March 1973), Single, Island. Non-album single.

For Your Pleasure, Roxy Music (March 1973), Album, Island. Top 5 in UK; peaked at no. 193 in US.

Billion Dollar Babies, Alice Cooper (March 1973), Album, Warner Bros. Three weeks at no. 1 in the UK, where it registered glam's third long-form best-seller. No. 1 on Billboard too.

"20th Century Boy," T. Rex (March 1973), Single, EMI. Peaked at no. 3 in the UK.

"Hello Hello I'm Back Again," Gary Glitter (March 1973), Single, Bell. No. 2 (again).

Tanx, T. Rex (March 1973), Album, EMI. "Only" reached no. 4 on the UK album chart.

"See My Baby Jive," Wizzard (March 1973), Single, Harvest. Spent a month at no. 1 in the UK.

Aladdin Sane, David Bowie (April 1973), Album, RCA. Five weeks as UK's best-seller, to become glam's fourth no. 1 LP. Billboard Top 20 too.

"Drive-In Saturday," David Bowie (April 1973), Single, RCA. Peaked at no. 3 in the UK.

"Hellraiser," Sweet (April 1973), Single, RCA. Follow-up to "Blockbuster," makes no. 2.

"Can the Can," Suzi Quatro (April 1973), Single, RAK. Three weeks as UK's best-selling single.

"Skweeze Me Pleeze Me," Slade (June 1973), Single, Polydor. Another no. 1.

"The Groover," T. Rex (June 1973), Single, EMI. UK no. 4 "only."

"Live and Let Die," Wings (June 1973), Single, Apple. McCartney goes glam. UK Top 10; US no. 2.

"I'm the Leader of the Gang (I Am)," Gary Glitter (July 1973), Single, Bell. A four-week run at no. 1 in the UK.

"48 Crash," Suzi Quatro (July 1973), Single, RAK. UK no. 3.

"Do the Strand," Roxy Music (July 1973), Single, Island. US-only single, where—unsurprisingly—it failed to chart.

"Rock On," David Essex (August 1973), Single, CBS. UK no. 3.

New York Dolls, New York Dolls (August 1973), Album, Mercury. DNC in the UK. Scrapped in Top 200 in the band's native US.

Mott, Mott the Hoople (August 1973), Album, CBS. UK Top 10.

"Angel Fingers (A Teen Ballad)," Wizzard (August 1973), Single, Harvest. Back-to-back UK no. 1s for Roy Wood.

"Ballroom Blitz," Sweet (September 1973), Single, RCA. Peaked at no. 2 in the UK.

Sladest, Slade (September 1973), Album, Polydor. Four weeks as the UK's best-selling LP for the UK's biggest pop act of the day.

Goats Head Soup, the Rolling Stones (September 1973), Album, Rolling Stones. Complete with ubercamp, very glam cover shot of Mick Jagger giving it the full Isadora Duncan.

Pin Ups, David Bowie (October 1973), Album, RCA. Five weeks at no. 1 for Bowie's covers album. Billboard Top 30 too.

"Sorrow," David Bowie (October 1973), Single, RCA. UK no. 3.

These Foolish Things, Bryan Ferry (October 1973), Album, Island. Covers album included credible if rather irreverent version of "A Hard Rain's Gonna Fall."

"My Friend Stan," Slade (October 1973), Single, Polydor. UK no. 2.

"Dyna-Mite," Mud (October 1973), Single, RAK.

"Daytona Demon," Suzi Quatro (October 1973), Single, RAK. UK Top Five.

Stranded, Roxy Music (November 1973), Album, Island. UK no. 1 for a week.

"Streetlife," Roxy Music (November 1973), Single, Island. A UK Top 10.

"Truck On (Tyke)," T. Rex (November 1973), Single, EMI. Stalled at no. 12.

"Roll Away the Stone," Mott the Hoople (November 1973), Single, CBS. Top 10 for Christmas.

"I Love You Love Me Love," Gary Glitter (November 1973), Single, Bell. Four weeks at no. 1 for this rather funereal single.

Band on the Run, Paul McCartney & Wings (December 1973), Album, Apple. No. 1 on both sides of the Atlantic for McCartney's most glam LP.

"The Show Must Go On," Leo Sayer (December 1973), Single, Chrysalis. UK no. 2 for debut single.

"Merry Xmas Everybody," Slade (December 1973), Single, Polydor. Five weeks at no. 1 and the last in a run of six UK best-sellers in just two years.

"I Wish It Could Be Christmas Every Day," Wizzard (December 1973), Single, Harvest. UK no. 4. Were it not for Slade's Xmas single—see above—this would surely have made no. 1.

1974, "Teenage Rampage"

"Teenage Rampage," Sweet (January 1974), Single, RCA. UK no. 2 (and the first single I ever bought).

"Tiger Feet," Mud (January 1974), Single, RAK. No. 1 for four weeks, the biggest-selling single of the year (and the first single purchased by my younger brother).

"The Man Who Sold the World," Lulu (January 1974), Single Polydor. Bowie written, produced, and arranged track gives Lulu her first UK hit in five years when it peaks at no. 3.

"Sugar Baby Love," the Rubettes (January 1974), Single, Polydor. Four weeks at no. 1 in the spring.

Muscle of Love, Alice Cooper (January 1974), Album, Warner Bros. US Top 10; just Top 40 in UK.

"Teenage Lament," Alice Cooper (January 1974), Single, Warner Bros. A UK no. 12.

Here Come the Warm Jets, Brian Eno (January 1974), Album, Island. Eno's solo debut reaches the UK Top 30.

Silverbird, Leo Sayer (January 1974), Album, Chrysalis. UK no. 2.

Old, New, Borrowed, and Blue, Slade (February 1974), Album, Polydor. Another UK no. 1.

"Rebel Rebel," David Bowie (February 1974), Single, RCA. UK Top Five; Billboard no. 64. Conclusive proof that Bowie was still glamming it up—"Your face is a mess / You're a juvenile success."

"Devilgate Drive," Suzi Quatro (February 1974), Single, RAK. Two weeks at UK no. 1.

"Bennie and the Jets," Elton John (February 1974), Single, DJM. A UK B-side but a US no. 1.

Kiss, KISS (February 1974), Album, Casablanca. DNC in UK; peaked at no. 87 in the US.

"Seven Seas of Rhye," Queen (February 1974), Single, EMI. First Top 10 single, featured music-hall-style chorus of "I Do Like to Be beside the Seaside" in the fade-out.

Queen II, Queen (March 1974), Album. EMI.

Zinc Alloy and the Easy Riders of Tomorrow, T. Rex (March 1974), Album, EMI. Would only reach no. 12, with the majestic "Teenage Dream"—on which it was hard not to hear self-pity—peaking at no. 13 on the UK singles chart.

"Every Day," Slade (March 1974), Single, Polydor. Wistful, most un-Slade-like ballad reaches no. 3 in the UK.

"Judy Teen," Cockney Rebel (March 1974), Single, EMI. Angular glam peaks at UK no. 5.

"Remember Me This Way," Gary Glitter (March 1974), Single, Bell.

"Angel Face," the Glitter Band (March 1974), Single, Bell. UK no. 4.

"Golden Age of Rock 'n' Roll," Mott the Hoople (March 1974), Single, CBS. The band's last UK Top 20 hit.

"The Cat Crept In," Mud (April 1974), Single, RAK. Follow-up to "Tiger Feet" reaches no. 2 in UK.

"Shang-A-Lang," Bay City Rollers (April 1974), Single, Bell. UK no. 2.

"This Town Ain't Big Enough," Sparks (April 1974), Single, Island. Unlikely UK no. 2 hit.

"Touch Too Much," Arrows (May 1974), Single, RAK. UK Top 10 for Anglo-American outfit.

Diamond Dogs, David Bowie (May 1974), Album, RCA. UK no. 1; US no. 5. Check out the album's cover art by glam's go-to artist Guy Peellaert.

Kimono My House, Sparks (May 1974), Album, Island. UK no. 4.

"Hey Rock and Roll," Showaddywaddy (May 1974), Single, Bell. First UK hit for rock 'n' roll revivalists.

Axe Victim, Be Bop Deluxe (June 1974), Album, Harvest. DNC. Includes "Adventures in a Yorkshire Landscape," which—though rather "proggy"—is also glam. Hence close links with Cockney Rebel, whom the band supported.

The Psychomodo, Cockney Rebel (June 1974), Album, EMI. Debut LP makes the UK Top 10.

"The Bangin' Man," Slade (July 1974), Single, Polydor. Another big UK hit, no. 3.

"Light of Love," T. Rex (July 1974), Single, EMI. Only manages to reach no. 22 in the UK.

"Mr. Soft," Cockney Rebel (July 1974) Single, EMI. Second UK Top 10.

"The Sixteens," Sweet (July 1974), Single, RCA. Epic glam anthem somewhat limps into UK Top 10.

"Amateur Hour," Sparks (July 1974), Single, Island. UK Top 10 for follow-up to "This Town Ain't Big Enough for Both of Us."

"Knock on Wood," David Bowie (September 1974), Single, RCA. Live cover version of soul classic made the UK Top 10.

It's Only Rock 'n' Roll, the Rolling Stones (October 1974), Album, Rolling Stones. Here the Stones are at their most glam, especially on the title track (and in its camp promo video). Cover also by Peellaert.

Eldorado—A Symphony by the Electric Light Orchestra, Electric Light Orchestra (October 1974), Album, Warner Bros. Check out those *Oz*-inspired sparkly shoes on the cover!

"Killer Queen," Queen (October 1974), Single, EMI. No. 2 in UK; no. 12 in US. Campy tale of a high-class call girl with expensive tastes.

"All I Want Is You," Roxy Music (October 1974), Single, Island.

"Far Far Away," Slade (October 1974), Single, Polydor. UK no. 2 for first single taken from *Slade in Flame* OST.

"Tell Him," Hello (October 1974), Single, Bell. Top 10 UK hit for glam-disco hybrid.

"Let's Get Together Again," the Glitter Band (October 1974), Single, Bell. UK no. 8.

"Never Turn Your Back on Mother Nature," Sparks (October 1974), Single, Island. UK Top 20.

Rollin', Bay City Rollers (October 1974), Album, Bell. Four weeks as UK's best-seller.

Country Life, Roxy Music (November 1974), Album, Island. No. 3 in the UK; Billboard Top 40.

Sheer Heart Attack, Queen (November 1974), Album, EMI. UK no. 2; US no. 12.

David Live, David Bowie (November 1974), Album, RCA. Live set from US tour; reaches no. 2 in the UK, and peaks at no. 8 in the States.

Desolation Boulevard, Sweet (November 1974), Album, RCA. First "proper" LP, featured "The Six Teens," "Turn It Down," and "Fox on the Run." DNC in the UK; but US no. 25.

"Lucy in the Sky with Diamonds," Elton John (November 1974), Single, DJM. A US no. 1 for this glam-soaked cover.

"The Wild One," Suzi Quatro (November 1974), Single, RAK. UK no. 7.

"Zip Gun Boogie," T. Rex (November 1974), Single, EMI. T. Rex single fails to reach UK Top 40.

"Turn It Down," Sweet (November 1974), Single, RCA. Subject to a TV ban and "heavier" in all departments, this final Chinn-and-Chapman-written-and-produced single fails to make the UK Top 40.

"Saturday Gigs," Mott the Hoople (November 1974), Single, CBS. Aka "Saturday Kids." "In '74 was the Broadway tour, we didn't much like dressing up any more," "goodbye," and "don't you ever forget us." UK no. 41.

"Lonely This Christmas," Mud (November 1974), Single, RAK. Four weeks at no. 1.

"The Bump," Kenny (December 1974), Single, RAK. More glam-disco. Originally recorded by the Bay City Rollers, would peak at no. 3 in the UK in early '75.

Slade in Flame, Slade (December 1974), Album, Polydor. OST to uncharacteristically downbeat Slade movie peaks at "just" no. 6.

1975, "Got to Leave You All Behind and Face the Truth"

"Now I'm Here," Queen (January 1975), Single, EMI. Peaks at no. 11 in the UK. More high campery that—like "Get It On"—fades out with a reference to rock 'n' roll classic "Little Queenie" for good glam measure.

"Something for the Girl with Everything," Sparks (January 1975), Single, Island. Another UK Top 20.

"Make Me Smile (Come Up and See Me)," Cockney Rebel (February 1975), Single, EMI. UK no. 1 for two weeks.

"How Does It Feel?," Slade (February 1975), Single, Polydor. Only reaches UK no. 15 and so represents Slade's poorest chart return since "Get Down and Get With It."

Bolan's Zip Gun, T. Rex (February 1975), Album, EMI. Fails to chart in the UK.

"Young Americans," David Bowie (February 1975), Single, RCA. Brits apparently not as enamored as Americans. Only reaches no. 18 in the UK; but gives Bowie his biggest US hit single (no. 28).

"Fox on the Run," Sweet (March 1975), Single, RCA. A self-penned UK no. 2 and a global hit. Vindication?

"Bye Bye Baby," Bay City Rollers (March 1975), Single, Bell. As Rollermania peaks in the UK, spends six weeks at no. 1.

Young Americans, David Bowie (March 1975), Album, RCA. UK no. 2; Billboard Top 10.

Welcome to My Nightmare, Alice Cooper (March 1975), Album, Warner Bros. Top 20 in the UK and a Top 10 in the US.

"Oh Boy," Mud (April 1975), Single, RAK. Two weeks at UK no. 1, proving that the market for classic rock 'n' roll covers remains buoyant.

Futurama, Be Bop Deluxe (May 1975), Album, Harvest. Follow-up to *Axe Victim*, featured the glam-sounding single "Maid in Heaven." Both single and album failed to chart, despite a band lineup refreshed by the addition of several ex–Cockney Rebels (who had been sacked by the autocratic Harley).

"Rock and Roll All Nite," KISS (May 1975), Single, Casablanca. Billboard no. 68.

"Thanks for the Memory," Slade (May 1975), Single, Polydor. Last UK Top 10 for six years.

"Three Steps to Heaven," Showaddywaddy (May 1975), Single, Bell. Rock 'n' roll revivalists take this Cochran cover to no. 2 in the UK.

"Once Bitten, Twice Shy," Ian Hunter (May 1975), Single, CBS. Instant solo success for ex–Mott the Hoople front man, featuring Mick Ronson on lead guitar. UK no. 14.

"Fame," David Bowie (July 1975), Single, RCA. Bowie's first Billboard no. 1; Top 10 in the UK. Featuring John Lennon on BVs.

"New York City," T. Rex (July 1975), Single, EMI. Bolan engineers a modest comeback as the single reaches the UK Top 20.

"Action," Sweet (July 1975), Single, RCA. UK Top 20.

"Get in the Swing," Sparks (July 1975), Single, Island. Peaks just inside the UK Top 30.

"Love Is the Drug," Roxy Music (September 1975), Single, Island. No. 2 in the UK and Roxy's biggest US hit to date, reaching no. 30 in early 1976.

Siren, Roxy Music (October 1975), Album, Island. UK no. 3; US no. 50. The success of "Love Is the Drug" in the States cannot significantly help LP sales.

"Space Oddity," David Bowie (October 1975), Single, RCA. Rerelease spends two weeks at UK no. 1.

Alive! KISS (October 1975), Album, Casablanca. US Top 10.

Face the Music, Electric Light Orchestra (October 1975), Album, Jet.

"New York Groove," Hello (October 1975), Single, Bell. One of the more obvious glam/disco mash-ups. UK Top 10.

"Looks Looks Looks," Sparks (October 1975), Single, Island. Another Top 30 . . . just.

"Dreamy Lady," T. Rex (October 1975), Single, EMI. And Bolan is clinging on too. This single peaks at no. 30 in the UK.

"Bohemian Rhapsody," Queen (November 1975), Single, EMI. Would spend a record nine weeks at no. 1 in the UK. Top 10 in the US. An apposite curtain call for the golden age of glam?

"Golden Years," David Bowie (November 1975), Single, RCA. A transatlantic Top 10.

A Night at the Opera, Queen (December 1975), Album, EMI. No. 1 in UK; no. 4 in US.

"Both Ends Burning," Roxy Music (December 1975), Single, Island. UK no. 25; DNC in the US.

1976–Present, "Who Can I Be Now?"

"The Lies in Your Eyes," Sweet (January 1976), Single, RCA. Peaks at just no. 35 in the UK, as the game would appear to be almost up for Sweet, if not glam-pop . . .

"Forever and Ever," Slik (January 1976), Single, Bell. Originally recorded by Kenny, spends a single week at UK no. 1 in February.

Station to Station, David Bowie (January 1976), Album, RCA. UK no. 5; but even more successful in the US, where it reaches no. 3 on Billboard and so becomes Bowie's biggest seller thus far.

"Let's Call It Quits," Slade (February 1976), Single, Polydor. Limps to UK no. 11. Enough said. (Although, by now, Slade had decamped to the States in a concerted effort to crack the only market that had resisted the band's charms.)

The Runaways, the Runaways (June 1976), Album, Mercury. Single "Cherry Bomb" was a no. 1 hit in Japan.

"I Love to Boogie," T. Rex (July 1976), Single, EMI. Still game, Bolan hits the UK Top 10.

"Laser Love," T. Rex (September 1976), Single, EMI . . . but cannot sustain any chart momentum, as this single misses the Top 40.

"Under the Moon of Love," Showaddywaddy (October 1976), Single, Bell. UK no. 1 for the rock 'n' roll pastichers.

A New World Record, Electric Light Orchestra (November 1976), Album, Jet.

Low, David Bowie (January 1977), Album, RCA. A UK no. 2; Top 20 in the US.

"Sound and Vision," David Bowie (February 1977), Single, RCA. A UK no. 3; but only reaches no. 69 on Billboard.

"Tie Your Mother Down," Queen (March 1977), Single, EMI. Still glamming it up, the opening track from *A Day at the Races* was a minor hit on both sides of the Atlantic.

The Idiot, Iggy Pop (March 1977), Album, RCA.

Lust for Life, Iggy Pop (September 1977), Album, RCA.

Heroes, David Bowie (October 1977), Album, RCA.

"Heroes," David Bowie (October 1977), Single, RCA. "Challenging" single still manages to reach the UK Top 30. Features King Crimson's Robert Fripp on lead guitar.

Out of the Blue, Electric Light Orchestra (November 1977), Album, Jet.

News of the World, Queen (November 1977), Album, EMI.

Never Mind the Bollocks, Here's the Sex Pistols, the Sex Pistols (November 1977), Album, Virgin. UK no. 1.

"White Punks on Dope," the Tubes (November 1977), Single, A&M. Vertiginous stacked heels, wigs, makeup, and outrageous theatrics made KISS look positively staid.

"Love Is Like Oxygen," Sweet (January 1978), Single, RCA. Sweet are back in the UK Top 10.

Van Halen, Van Halen (February 1978), Album, Warner Bros. And lo! Glam-metal is born.

Plastic Letters, Blondie (February 1978), Album, Chrysalis.

"Ready Steady Go," Generation X (March 1978), Single, Chrysalis. As this track demonstrates, the Billy Idol–fronted glam-punk outfit was always more playful and so less committed to UK punk's rather humorless "year zero" agenda.

Adolescent Sex, Japan (April 1978), Album, Arista. Japan managed to "telescope" a glam journey into just four short years, as the band morphed from the New York Dolls wannabes they appear to be—and often sound—on this album into cool, electro-pop stylists under the heavy influence of Bowie and Roxy in the early '80s.

Some Girls, the Rolling Stones (June 1978), Album, Rolling Stones. Real curate's egg of an LP—mixes glam, punk, and disco—sometimes on the same track in the case of "Shattered."

C'est Chic, Chic (August 1978), Album. UK no. 2; US no. 4. Nile Rodgers cites Roxy Music as a major influence. And of course, disco and glam have much in common.

Parallel Lines, Blondie (September 1978), Album, Chrysalis. Global, multiplatinum breakthrough LP is produced by UK glam-pop auteur Mike Chapman.

"Trash," Roxy Music (February 1979), Single, Polydor. Roxy Mark II return with UK no. 40 "hit."

Manifesto, Roxy Music (March 1979), Album, Polydor. UK no. 7; Billboard no. 21. Most successful US LP to this point.

"Boys Keep Swinging," David Bowie (April 1979), Single, RCA. UK Top 10; DNC in the US. Stateside failure is unsurprising, given the track's ubercampness. That glam was still in his dressing-up box can be literally seen in the promo video featuring a cross-dressing Bowie.

"Dance Away," Roxy Music (April 1979), Single, Polydor. UK no. 2; US no. 44. From the "US" side of the LP.

"Life in Tokyo," Japan (May 1979), Single, Arista. A Giorgio Moroder remix would see the track chart a few years later.

Lodger, David Bowie (May 1979), Album, RCA. UK no. 4. US no. 20.

Replicas, Tubeway Army (June 1979), Album, Beggars Banquet. Features the UK no. 1 single "Are Friends Electric?" Gary Numan's biggest influence—and idol—was David Bowie. It showed.

Risque, Chic (July 1979), Album. UK Top 30; US Top Five.

"DJ," David Bowie (July 1979), Single, RCA. Sneaks inside the UK Top 30.

"Angel Eyes," Roxy Music (August 1979), Single, Polydor. Remixed in New York by Bob Clearmountain and boosted by a "disco" twelve-inch version, reaches no. 4 in the UK.

The Pleasure Principle, Gary Numan (September 1979), Album, Beggars Banquet.

No. 1 in Heaven, Sparks (September 1979), Album, Virgin. A Moroder makeover for glam duo's "second coming," which spawned two big UK hit singles—"Beat the Clock" and "No. 1 Song in Heaven."

Quiet Life, Japan (January 1980), Album, Arista.

"Games without Frontiers," Peter Gabriel (February 1980), Single, Charisma. UK no. 4; US no. 48. Visuals + electronica = glam for the '80s.

"Holiday '80," Human League (April 1980), Single, Virgin. This EP featured covers of Gary Glitter's "Rock and Roll" and Iggy Pop's "Nightclubbing."

Flesh + Blood, Roxy Music (May 1980), Album, Polydor. UK no. 1; US no. 35.

"Over You," Roxy Music (May 1980), Single, Polydor. UK Top Five; but only no. 80 in America.

"Oh Yeah," Roxy Music (July 1980), Single, Polydor. Another UK Top Five.

"Ashes to Ashes," David Bowie (August 1980), Single, RCA. UK no. 1. Bowie's reinvention as a New Romantic? Nope. It's evolution. Ch-ch-ch-changes.

Scary Monsters, David Bowie (September1980), Album, RCA. UK no. 1; US no. 12.

Empires and Dance, Simple Minds (September 1980), Album, Arista.

Gentleman Take Polaroids, Japan (October 1980), Album, Virgin. UK no. 45.

"Telegram Sam," Bauhaus (October 1980), Single, Beggars Banquet. Early single from goth band is a reverential, if swagger-free, cover of classic T. Rex track. DNC.

Kings of the Wild Frontier, Adam and the Ants (November 1980), Album, CBS. UK no. 1; US no. 41. Stuart Goddard's raiding of the dressing-up box—pirate, highwayman, Native American, etc.—had been encouraged by ex-Pistols manager Malcolm McLaren and would meet with little resistance from a self-confessed glam fan.

"To Cut a Long Story Short," Spandau Ballet (November 1980), Single, Reformation. UK no. 5.

"Same Old Scene," Roxy Music (November 1980), Single, Polydor. A UK no. 12 and the sonic template for New Romantics like Duran Duran.

"We'll Bring the House Down," Slade (January 1981), Single, Polydor. The comeback is on with this UK Top 10.

Journey to Glory, Spandau Ballet (March 1981), Album, Reformation. UK Top Five.

Duran Duran, Duran Duran (June 1981), Album, EMI. UK no. 3; US no. 10 in '82. "Some New Romantic looking for the TV sound"—echoes of "All the Young Dudes."

Sons and Fascination. Simple Minds (September 1981), Album, Virgin.

Speak and Spell, Depeche Mode (October 1981), Album, Mute. Bowie and Roxy kids on the rise.

Dare, Human League (October 1981), Album, Virgin. UK no. 1; US no. 3 in spring 1982. Witness the high-glam campery of "Don't You Want Me."

Tin Drum, Japan (November 1981), Album, Virgin. UK no. 12.

"Under Pressure," Queen and David Bowie (November 1981), Single, EMI. UK no. 1.

Prince Charming, Adam and the Ants (November 1981), Album, CBS. UK no. 2; US no. 94. Could the promo video for the title track featuring faded '50s Brit starlet Diana Dors as a panto Fairy Godmother be any more glam?

Non-Stop Erotic Cabaret, Soft Cell (December 1981), Album, Some Bizarre.

"The Model," Kraftwerk (December 1981), Single, EMI. On its rerelease, a UK no. 1 in February 1982.

"Go Wild in the Country," Bow Wow Wow (January 1982), Single, RCA. UK no. 7, cowritten by former Sex Pistols and New York Dolls manager Malcolm McLaren.

"I Love Rock 'n' Roll," Joan Jett and the Blackhearts (April 1982), Single, Epic. UK no. 4; US no. 1. Ex-Runaway Jett also covered Gary Glitter's "Do You Want to Touch Me?," which became a Top 30 US hit in the same year.

"More Than This," Roxy Music (April 1982), Single, Polydor. UK no. 6.

Avalon, Roxy Music (May 1982), Album, Polydor. UK no. 1; US no. 51.

Rio, Duran Duran (May 1982), Album, EMI. UK no. 2; US no. 6.

Sulk, the Associates (May 1982), Album, Associates. UK no. 10, and three big hit singles.

"Avalon," Roxy Music (June 1982), Single, Polydor. UK Top 20; DNC in the US.

The Lexicon of Love, ABC (July 1982), Album, Neutron. UK no. 1. Peerless New (Glam) Pop.

A Broken Frame, Depeche Mode (September 1982), Album, Mute.

A New Gold Dream (81-82-83-84), Simple Minds (September 1982), Album, Virgin. UK no. 3; US no. 61.

"Ziggy Stardust," Bauhaus (September 1982), Single, Beggars Banquet. Yet another glam cover. This time a reverential reworking of a Bowie track that reaches no. 15 and so gives the goth rockers their biggest hit.

"White Wedding," Billy Idol (October 1982), Single, Chrysalis. A US Top 40 hit in 1983 and a UK Top 10 in 1985. As noted earlier, not so much as a reinvention for Idol as glam refresh.

Pyromania, Def Leppard (March 1983), Album, Vertigo. UK no. 18; US no. 2. Pioneers of the New Wave of British heavy metal, Def Leppard is drenched in glam—particularly its rockier variant (Queen, Mott the Hoople, Slade, Ronson, even late Sweet). Here exhibit A would be the single "Photograph."

"Cum On Feel the Noize," Quiet Riot (March 1983), Single, Columbia. US no. 5 that helps make the album *Metal Health* Billboard's first heavy metal no. 1.

"Let's Dance," David Bowie (March 1983), Single, EMI. Nile Rodgers–produced UK no. 1.

"She's in Parties," Bauhaus (April 1983), Single, Beggar's Banquet. Goth rockers' original material supplies a glam narrative that ticks all the topic boxes.

Construction Time Again, Depeche Mode (August 1983), Album, Mute.

Beauty Stab, ABC (November 1983), Album, Neutron. Commercial misstep for purveyors of blue-eyed New Pop, who try their hand at glammy rock. UK no. 12.

"My Oh My," Slade (November 1983), Single, Polydor. An anthemic sing-along that gives Slade its biggest UK hit since late '74. UK no. 2.

1984, Van Halen (January 1984), Album, Warner Bros. UK no. 15; US no. 2. Glam-metal perfection.

Sparkle in the Rain, Simple Minds (February 1984), Album, Virgin. UK no. 1; US no. 64.

"Run Run Away," Slade (February 1984), Single, Polydor. More UK Top 10 success.

Purple Rain, Prince and the Revolution (July 1984), Album, Warner Bros. That epic title track! Elsewhere, eclectic but undeniably glam fueled.

"Up around the Bend," Hanoi Rocks (July 1984), Single, CBS. Finnish glam-metal. Minor UK hit cover of CCR classic.

Some Great Reward, Depeche Mode (September 1984), Album, Mute.

"Get It On," Power Station (March 1985), Single, EMI. Glam fans Duran Duran's Andy and John Taylor combine forces with Robert Palmer and ex-Chic drummer Tony Thompson. Top 10 in the US; Top 30 in the UK.

Around the World in a Day, Prince and the Revolution (April 1985), Album, Warner Bros.

Theatre of Pain, Mötley Crüe (July 1985), Album, Elektra. UK no. 35; US no. 6.

"Love Missile F1-11," Sigue Sigue Sputnik (March 1986), Single, Parlophone. Much-hyped electro-glam debut from band led by ex–Generation X guitarist Tony James. UK no. 3.

Look What the Cat Dragged In, Poison (July 1986), Album, Capitol. DNC in UK; US no. 3. Glam-metal is now surely peaking?

Music for the Masses, Depeche Mode (September 1987), Album, Mute.

Open Up and Say . . . Ahh!, Poison (May 1988), Album, Capitol. UK no. 23; US no. 2.

Violator, Depeche Mode (March 1990), Album, Mute. Features the glam-stomp of "Personal Jesus."

"Motorcycle Emptiness," Manic Street Preachers (May 1992), Single, Columbia. UK no. 17. Channel glam staples like cross-dressing and androgyny.

Songs of Faith and Devotion, Depeche Mode (March 1993), Album, Mute.

Suede, Suede (April 1993), Album, Sony. UK no. 1; DNC in US. Bowie and Ronson flavors and flourishes make this debut arguably more old-school glam than new-school Brit-pop.

Definitely Maybe, Oasis (August 1994), Album, Creation. UK no. 1; US no. 58.

MTV Unplugged in New York, Nirvana (November 1994), Album, Geffen. Includes a cover of Bowie's "The Man Who Sold the World."

I Should Co Co, Supergrass (May 1995), Album, Parlophone.

Different Class, Pulp (October 1995), Album, Island.

(What's the Story) Morning Glory?, Oasis (October 1995), Album, Creation. UK no. 1; US no. 4.

"In the Meantime," Spacehog (May 1996), Single, Sire. UK no. 29. Bowie circa '73. US hit too.

Three EP, Mansun (September 1996), Extended Play, Parlophone. UK no. 19. Glam-prog in the mid-'70s bebop deluxe vein.

"Tainted Love," Marilyn Manson (March 2002), Single, Interscope. UK no. 5.

Permission to Land, Darkness (July 2003), Album, Atlantic. Queen tribute act? Ironic? Whatever. Everyone's having fun and being entertained. Undeniably glam. UK no. 1.

"Personal Jesus," Marilyn Manson (October 2004), Single, Interscope.

"Poker Face," Lady Gaga (late 2008/early 2009), Single, Interscope. UK and US no. 1.

INDEX

ABC, 161

Adam and the Ants songs: "Dog Eat Dog", 157; "Prince Charming", 157; "Stand and Deliver", 157; "Young Parisians", 155–156

Aerosmith, 129

Alice Cooper songs: "Eighteen", 24; "School's Out", 66

Almond, Marc (musician), xxx

Anderson, Brett (musician), 164

Ant, Adam, 143, 155–158. *See also* Adam and the Ants songs

Arrows (musicians), 112

the Associates (musicians), 161–162

Bad Company (musicians), 141

Barrett, Syd (musician), 20

Bauhaus (musicians), 162

Bay City Rollers, 124

Bell (record company), 83, 84

Bernstein, George (historian), 103–104

Bolan, June, 41

Bolan, Marc (musician): on being a mod, 30–31; on dandyism, 20, 30; death of, 150; on derivation of name, 31; on energy and excitement, 28; on glam, 78, 80–81; "Observations" (song), 32; and punk rock, 149; on rivals, 72; on rock 'n' roll, 40; on stardom, 30, 37; on teenage fans, 37, 44–45; on transition to T. Rex, 34; and the "underground",

35; "The Wizard" (song), 31–32. *See also* T. Rex; Tyrannosaurus Rex

Bono (musician), 67

Bowie, Angie, 55

Bowie, David: and the Arnold Corns project, 52; and the "Berlin Trilogy", 145–146; on Bolan, 30, 49; "comes out", 53–56; death of, xxvii, xxx, xxxviii; *Diamond Dogs* tour, 115–116; influence of Andy Warhol, 41–51; on glam, 78; and the Hype project, 24–25; "retires" Ziggy Stardust, 91; on Roxy Music, 87; on Sweet, 81; on teen audience, 52; and the USA, 50–51, 74, 87; *Ziggy* tour, 73–74

Bowie albums: *Aladdin Sane*, 87–91; *David Live*, 116; *Diamond Dogs*, xxxi, 112–115, 131; *Heroes*, 146; *Hunky Dory*, 49–50; *Lodger*, 146, 152; *Low*, 145; *The Man Who Sold the World*, 24–25, 49; *Pin Ups*, 1–6, 18, 19–20, 96; *The Rise and Fall of Ziggy Stardust and the Spiders from Mars*, 51–52, 57–61; *Station to Station*, 145; *Young Americans*, 135, 137–138

Bowie songs: "1984", 114; "Aladdin Sane", 87, 89; "All the Young Dudes", 68–69, 149; "Andy Warhol", 49; "Ashes to Ashes", 153–154; "Be My Wife", 146; "Bewlay Brothers", 19; "Boys Keep Swinging", 152–153, 162; "Changes",

ABOUT THE AUTHOR

Simon Philo teaches American studies and popular music in society at the University of Derby. He is the author of *British Invasion: The Crosscurrents of Musical Influence* and has written extensively on transatlantic popular culture. In twenty-five years at Derby, he has been instrumental in working pop and rock into the very heart of the curriculum. A true "child of the revolution," the first single he bought was Sweet's "Teenage Rampage."